Industry 4.0 - Perspectives and Applications

Edited by Meisam Gordan, Khaled Ghaedi and Vala Saleh

Published in London, United Kingdom

Industry 4.0 - Perspectives and Applications
http://dx.doi.org/10.5772/intechopen.100660
Edited by Meisam Gordan, Khaled Ghaedi and Vala Saleh

Contributors
Benjamin Appiah Osei, Emmanuela Kwao-Boateng, Olasupo Opeyemi Ajayi, Antoine Bagula, Hloniphani Maluleke, Lluís Echeverria, Francesc Bonada, Marta Camps, Maddi Etxegarai, Xavier Domingo, Marc Ribalta, Meng Joo Er, Jie Chen, Yani Zhang, Khalid Rasheed Memon, Say Keat Ooi, Juan Jose Saucedo-Dorantes, David Alejandro Elvira-Ortiz, Carlos Gustavo Manriquez-Padilla, Angel Perez-Cruz, Arturo Yosimar Jaen-Cuellar, Md. Mijanur Rahman, Fatema Khatun

First published in London, United Kingdom, 2023 by IntechOpen
IntechOpen is the global imprint of INTECHOPEN LIMITED, registered in England and Wales, registration number: 11086078, 5 Princes Gate Court, London, SW7 2QJ, United Kingdom

British Library Cataloguing-in-Publication Data
A catalogue record for this book is available from the British Library

Additional hard and PDF copies can be obtained from orders@intechopen.com

Industry 4.0 - Perspectives and Applications
Edited by Meisam Gordan, Khaled Ghaedi and Vala Saleh
p. cm.

This title is part of the Artificial Intelligence Book Series, Volume 16
Topic: Applied Intelligence
Series Editor: Andries Engelbrecht
Topic Editor: Carlos M. Travieso-Gonzalez

Print ISBN 978-1-80356-539-2
Online ISBN 978-1-80356-540-8
eBook (PDF) ISBN 978-1-80356-541-5
ISSN 2633-1403

IntechOpen Book Series
Artificial Intelligence
Volume 16

Aims and Scope of the Series

Artificial Intelligence (AI) is a rapidly developing multidisciplinary research area that aims to solve increasingly complex problems. In today's highly integrated world, AI promises to become a robust and powerful means for obtaining solutions to previously unsolvable problems. This Series is intended for researchers and students alike interested in this fascinating field and its many applications.

Meet the Series Editor

Andries Engelbrecht received the Masters and Ph.D. degrees in Computer Science from the University of Stellenbosch, South Africa, in 1994 and 1999 respectively. He is currently appointed as the Voigt Chair in Data Science in the Department of Industrial Engineering, with a joint appointment as Professor in the Computer Science Division, Stellenbosch University. Prior to his appointment at Stellenbosch University, he has been at the University of Pretoria, Department of Computer Science (1998-2018), where he was appointed as South Africa Research Chair in Artifical Intelligence (2007-2018), the head of the Department of Computer Science (2008-2017), and Director of the Institute for Big Data and Data Science (2017-2018). In addition to a number of research articles, he has written two books, Computational Intelligence: An Introduction and Fundamentals of Computational Swarm Intelligence.

Meet the Volume Editors

Dr. Meisam Gordan is a researcher in Structural Engineering with a focus on Industry 4.0 technologies and structural health monitoring systems. He has been recognized as a reliable referee and editor of different peer-reviewed journals. He is a member of renowned institutes such as the American Society of Civil Engineers, Board of Engineers Malaysia, and Institution of Engineers Malaysia. He has published various articles in high-quality journals in different fields such as structural health monitoring, data mining, artificial intelligence, vibration control systems, the Internet of Things (IoT), big data, blockchain, smart cities, finite element analysis, and materials. He is currently working on a European Union's Horizon 2020-funded ongoing project named PRECINCT as a postdoctoral research fellow at University College Dublin (UCD), Ireland. The PRECINCT project is developing serious games using digital twins and data mining to assess critical infrastructure protection against combined cyber and physical threats.

Dr. Khaled Ghaedi has experience in both academia and industry. He has published articles in prestigious journals that have produced novel patented damping devices, guidelines for structural retrofitting, and versatile models to predict structural damages. He has contributed to the process of knowledge sharing through his roles as editor, reviewer, speaker, and committee member for journals, conferences, and different organizations. Dr. Ghaedi is also a committee member of the well-known international design code ASCE 7-22. He is currently supporting the engineering industry in Southeast Asia as a structural technical director. He is the founder of PASOFAL Engineering group, a talented team recognized for solving complex engineering challenges. He is highly skilled in research funding acquisition, software training, and design consultation through finite element methods, computational fluid dynamics, structural health monitoring, building information modeling, performance-based design, and other organizations.

Dr. Vala Saleh received his MSc in Electrical and Communication Engineering from Tenaga Nasional University (UNITEN), Malaysia, and his Ph.D. from Shiraz University of Technology (SUTECH), Iran. His research interests include Industry 4.0, green Internet of Things, control systems design, signal processing, network coding, information and coding theory, and multi-objective optimization algorithms. He is currently a lecturer at the University of Sistan and Baluchestan, Iran. He is also a reviewer for several journals, including *Internet of Things and Cloud Computing*, and *Advances in Science, Technology and Engineering Systems Journal*.

Contents

Preface

Industry 4.0 involves a high level of digitization, which has been increasing the efficiency and flexibility of various manufacturing and non-manufacturing industries in civil, environmental, mechanical, electrical, petroleum, and medical engineering. The world is changing quickly and the Internet and digitalization are the driving forces of today's trades. In addition, new technologies deliver human-like accuracy and reliability in highly complex tasks. Nowadays, computer-based technologies such as the Internet of Things (IoT), artificial intelligence (AI), machine learning, deep learning, big data, and data mining approaches along with their applications are ubiquitous in automation, intelligence, and sustainability. DigiTech platforms facilitate intelligent tasks and diagnostics in the research and analysis of industries and organizations in predictive policing.

This book presents the key technological developments in Industry 4.0 and explores the potential benefits of using real-world applications. As a roadmap for decision-makers, it covers several evolutionary advances in Industry 4.0. I hope that readers will find this book useful, and I warmly welcome comments, suggestions, and criticisms.

Meisam Gordan, Ph.D.
University College Dublin,
Dublin, Ireland

Dr. Khaled Ghaedi
PASOFAL Engineering Group,
Kuala Lumpur, Malaysia

Dr. Vala Saleh
Shiraz University of Technology,
Shiraz, Iran

Chapter 1

The Fourth Industrial Revolution: A Technological Wave of Change

Olasupo Ajayi, Antoine Bagula and Hloniphani Maluleke

Abstract

This chapter focuses on the technological wave of change called the fourth industrial revolution (4IR), which is also known as the information age or industry 4.0. It starts off with a brief history of the concept, describing the evolution through the ages, from the age of industrialization to the current technological age. The chapter then presents industry 4.0 through three lenses, which are i) the key enabling technologies that serve as its foundational pillars, such as the Internet and Cloud Computing; ii) technologies and concepts that emanate from 4IR, as well as their applications, which are discussed using use-cases; iii) the impacts of industry 4.0 on the wider society (both positive and negative). Finally, the chapter closes with a discussion on some open challenges that need to be considered in future research works to enhance the widespread adaptation and/or implementation of industry 4.0.

Keywords: big data, cloud computing, cyber-physical systems, information and communication technology, industry 4.0, industrial revolution, internet of things

1. Introduction

The phrase "industrial revolution" (IR) is often associated with progressive transitions in the way things are done, specifically as a result of technological enhancement or enlightenment. Within any given society, IR reshapes the processes therein through several waves of changes that directly impact the people's general way of life. Manual and laborious processes are replaced with automated and mechanized systems, while antique processes are replaced with contemporary solutions.

Till date there have been four (4) industrial revolutions. Though historians refer to the "industrial revolution" as the first industrial revolution (1IR), this chapter makes a distinction between both, by referring to "industrial revolution" as the wave of technological advancements that bring about changes to societies, while 1IR is the first of such revolutions. The four IRs, their respective timelines and impacts are well documented in literature, hence not elaborately repeated in this work, but concisely highlighted on **Table 1**.

The third and fourth industrial revolutions are interwoven, with many of the offerings of the third industrial revolution (3IR), including pervasive computing and

Revolution	Timeline	Major influencers	Key innovations	Impacts
First or Industrial Revolution [1, 2]	1750–1850	Britain, France, Belgium, Germany, Japan, USA.	• Energy from fossil fuel • Development of the steam engines, railways. • Mechanized Textile industry. • Development of basic machineries.	• Improved agricultural processes and crop yields. • Emergence of cities. • Transition from manual labourers (craftsmen) to machine operators.
Second or Technological Revolution [3, 4]	1850–1914	Europe (Spain. Portugal, Italy, Turkey)	• Communication (Telegraph, radio, TV) • Electricity • Internal combustion engine • Synthetic materials (Plastics, metal alloys).	• Rail and road networks. • Mass & personal affordable transportation (via trains, automobiles, and bicycles). • Electrified factories & homes
Third or Digital Revolution [5]	1947–2000s	Asia, South America, Africa	• Transistors & integrated circuits. • Digitization & Computers • Internet & World Wide Web • Mobile phones. • Proliferation of Personal Computers and smartphones. • Move from Analog to digital. • Mass media replaced with contemporary and social media	
Fourth or Information Age [6]	21st Century	Global	• Cognitive computing • Big Data, Cloud Computing, and Internet of Things • Machine-to Machine/Human Communication • Cyber physical systems (CPS)	• Data & information explosion. • Advent of smart, virtual, and augmented systems (devices, homes, environment, cities). • Sustainable living, solutions & societies.

Table 1.
Summary of the four industrial revolutions.

digitization, still on-going today [7]. The fourth industrial revolution (4IR) can thus be considered a logical extension or continuation of the 3IR, as it builds on many of the same concepts and technologies that enabled the 3IR.

This chapter focuses on the 4IR, which is also known as the information age or industry 4.0. It discusses the 4IR through three lenses, viz., the key enabling technologies that form the foundational pillars of the 4IR, technologies and concepts that emanate from 4IR, and the impacts of 4IR on society, both positive and negative.

2. Enabling technologies of 4IR

This section would discuss five foundational technologies that enable the 4IR. These are: ICT & Networking, Internet of Things & Sensor Networks, Big Data & Data Analytics, Cloud, Fog & Edge Computing, and Artificial Intelligence & Machine Learning.

2.1 ICT and networking

2.1.1 Information and communication technology (ICT)

The phrase Information and Communication Technology (ICT) consists of two (2) parts: Information that refers to processed data and Communication or Telecommunication (Telecoms) and that can be defined as the transmission of information over wired or wireless media, and often over a considerable distance. Communication in itself often connotes the exchange of information between two or more parties; hence, the above definition is apt. Advancements in technology, particularly during the 3IR, led to the rapid growth of ICT. The key enablers of this unprecedented growth were transistor chips and the Internet (and its associated world wide web or www), as shown on **Table 1**. Transistors revolutionized computers, while the Internet "shrunk" the world and made it a global village.

The 4IR is characterized by rapid digitization, growth of pervasive & ubiquitous devices, and prevalence of connected devices – both personal and industrial. A relatable example is the "smartphone". **Figure 1** shows the growth of smartphone usage in the closing 5 years of the 3IR versus the last 5 years of the 4IR. The figure shows a steady rise in smartphone sales between 2007 and 2010, with the numbers escalating from around year 2011. Coincidentally, 2011 is arguably often regarded as the beginning of the fourth industrial revolution (4IR) by some authors. Another example is the Internet, with its increased penetration especially in the global south countries of the world. **Figure 2** shows the global percentage of users with access to the Internet in various regions of the world grouped based on level of development. In the figure, "developed" includes countries of the western world, "developing" includes countries in Africa, Asia, and South America, and "Least developed countries" (LDC) include rural remote regions of the world. Internet accessibility in LDC and developing countries is shown to have more than doubled in 2019 compared to 2009.

2.1.2 Next generation networks

Over the years communication networks have evolved through five generations. The first generation was mostly analogue based fixed telephone lines supporting voice calls

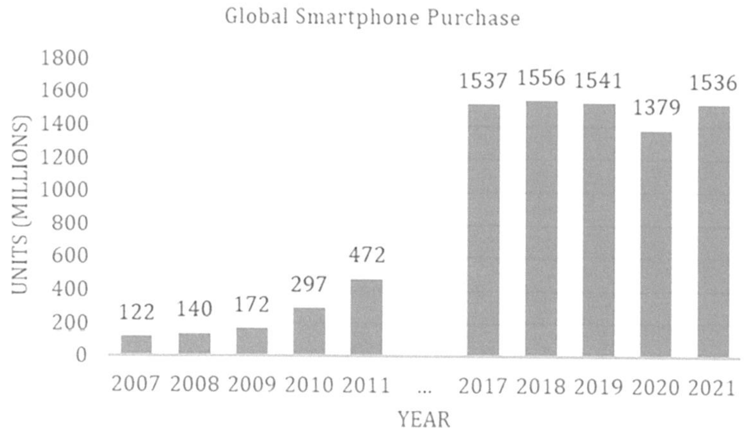

Figure 1.
Comparison of Smartphone sales between 2007 and 2011 and 2017–2021. Adapted from reference [8].

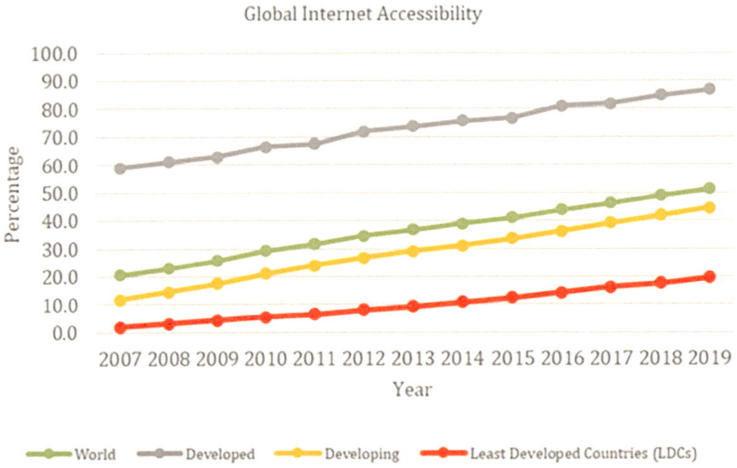

Figure 2.
Global Internet Usage. Adapted from [9].

only. The second generation introduced digitisation and mobile networks, as well as support for SMS and MMS through GPRS. The third generation introduced better support for multimedia including video streaming and social media, while the fourth brought improved download speeds and reduced latency. The 5th Generation (5G), which is the latest communication standard is still in its deployment stages. It promises several features including up to 10 Gb/s connection speed, lower energy utilization (up to 90% conservation), better availability and coverage, support for a significantly higher number of simultaneous connections, lower network latency (in the order of milliseconds), as well as support for multi-tenancy and modular programmability.

Figure 3 reveals some key application areas that will be significantly enhanced by the 5G mobile network such as i) residential use, ii) Internet-of-things, iii) infrastructure connection, iv) inter-vehicle connection, and v) augmented and virtual reality. These enhancements would leverage on the increased coverage, high bandwidth, low latency of 5G, coupled with cross-integration of multiple networks including terrestrial networks and aerial networks [10].

2.2 Internet of things and sensor networks

Internet of Things (IoT) can simply be described as fitting everyday objects with Internet connectivity feature. These objects or things might include TVs, air

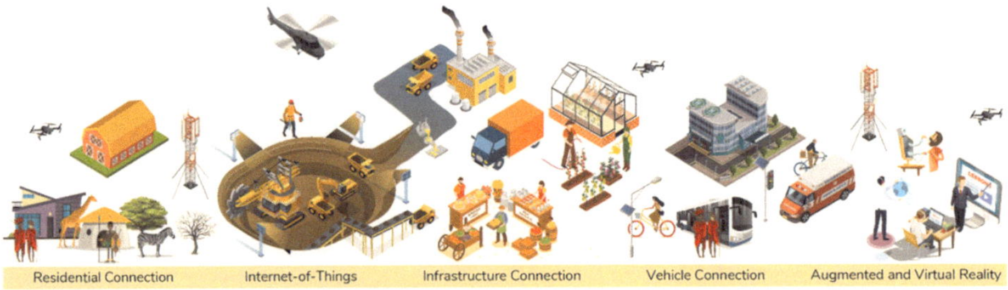

Figure 3.
5G use cases.

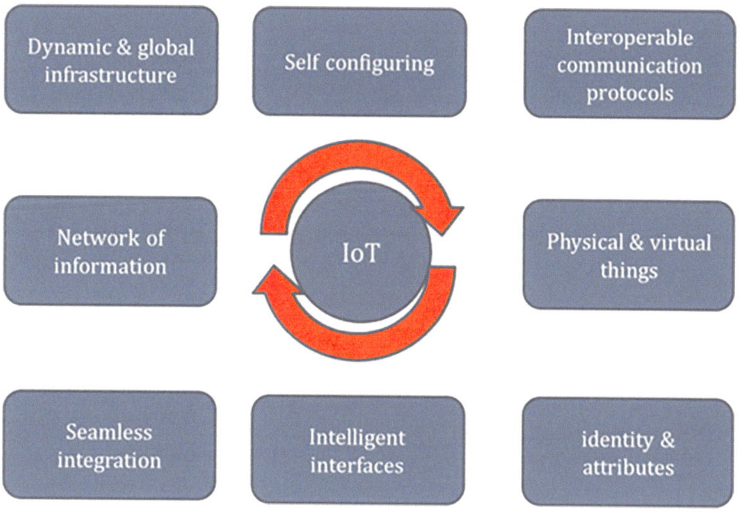

Figure 4.
Building blocks of IoT.

conditioners, doors/windows, vehicles, and heavy machinery etc. and are embedded with uniquely identifiable computing nodes. Key components of this IoT definition are "connectivity", which refers to networking; "embedded", which refers to the infusion of miniaturized devices with built-in sensing and actuation capabilities; and "uniquely identifiable", which implies distinct addresses either via IPv6 or Media Access Control address (MAC). **Figure 4** shows a depiction of the constituent features of IoT.

The simplicity, openness, and the fact that IoT builds upon existing network infrastructure and protocols, accelerates its growth and widespread adoption. It is widely estimated that the number of connected devices would grow exponential to close to 50 billion in the next few years [11]. Though several unique (closed) communication protocols exist for interconnecting IoT "things", recent years have seen a push for openness or interoperability between these protocols. **Table 2** shows the IoT stack (loosely based on [14]) compared to the classic network stack, as well as several IoT specific protocols and their respective operating layer.

2.3 Big data and analytics

Big data is a term used to describe large volume of data in different formats (variety), generated at a fast pace (velocity), are of good quality (veracity) and holds significant value. Big data emanates from different sources, including social media, streamed media (videos, images and audio), web pages, and IoT telemetry data; and can be structured, semi-structured, quasi-structured, or unstructured. Storage and processing can be challenging, because big data does not conform to the traditional notions of data structure, and often exceeds the storage and processing capacities of conventional computer systems. Federated CPS that relies on a federation of physical systems (such as those proposed in [15, 16]), and/or federation of virtual entities techniques (such as proposed in [17]) could be potential solutions to these issues.

Ref. layer	OSI model [12]	TCP/IP model [13]	IoT model [14]	IoT specific protocols & technologies
[6]	Application Layer	Application Layer	Collaboration & Processes	Smart applications (homes, cities, health),
[5]	Presentation Layer	Application Layer	Application (Analytics & Reporting)	Cyber-Physical Systems, Visualization, AI & Machine Learning.
[4]	Session Layer	Application Layer	Data Abstraction (Aggregation & Access)	AMQP, MQTT, CoAP, XMPP, Cloud Computing
[3]	Transport 3Layer	Transport Layer	Data Accumulation & Storage	NoSQL/SQL, Fog Computing
[2]	Network Layer	Internet Layer	Edge Computing	RPL, CARP, data filtration, SBCs/ Microcontrollers
[9]	Data Link Layer	Network Access Layer	Connectivity (Communication & Processing Units)	RFID, WiFi, BLE, ZigBee, Z-Wave, LoRa, LiFi, 3G/4G, LIBP
[1]	Physical Layer	Network Access Layer	Devices – Actuators, Sensors, and Machines	Fibre Optics, Ethernet, PoE

Table 2.
Comparison of models.

Typical big data processing pipeline include i) Data sourcing; ii) Data collection and ingestion; iii) Data storage & warehousing; iv) data preparation, including pre-processing, de-duplication, filtration etc.; v) Data processing and mining, which are the process of discovering patterns, trends, and/or valuable information from large data using statistical and/or machine learning models [18]; vi) Data analytics, vii) Data visualization; viii) result evaluation and application. These processes are summarized in **Figure 5**. By combining qualitative & quantitative analyses, visualization

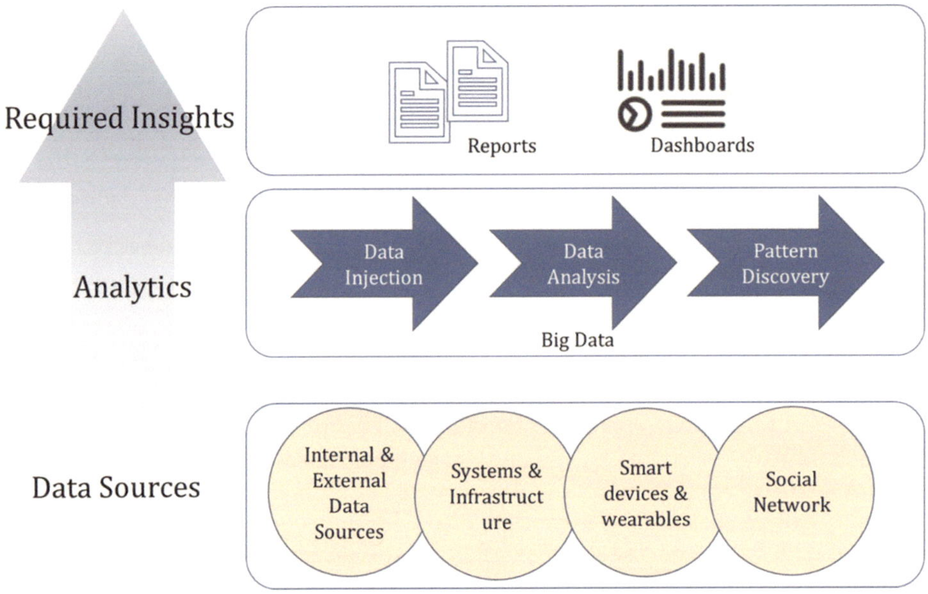

Figure 5.
Big data analysis overview.

& dash-boarding, with data mining performed on big data, big data analytics can improve processes in diverse domains including agriculture [19], education [20], health [21], etc.

2.4 Cloud, fog and edge computing

In simple terms and from the end-user's perspective, Cloud computing (CC) is a model that shifts computing from physical devices to a service [22]. It allows users transfer the "headaches" of managing computing infrastructure to a third party (Cloud service provider (CSP)), and instead focus on their core business or goal. On the other hand, the CSPs (with expertise in computing) ensure satisfactory service delivery at agreed price points, using virtual machines [23, 24]. Services offered by CC include but are not limited to storage, high performance computing (HPC), and software/hardware on demand, making CC a key backbone of many of today's disruptive industries.

Cloud computing offers several services, common amongst which are infrastructure as a service (IAAS), wherein HPC are dynamically provisioned for data warehousing, analytics, or machine learning tasks. When developing web, mobile or desktop applications, the platform as a service (PAAS) Cloud service model provides bespoke application development toolkits, which can significantly reduce application development time. Finally, the Software as a service (SAAS), avails Cloud users with ready-made software solutions, thus eliminating the need to install software on personal computer systems. CC can arguably be considered as the foundational enabler of the 4IR. The true power of the Cloud as an enabler of the 4IR comes in form of everything-as-a-service (or XAAS). Where X can be cars, as is the case of on-demand car services provided by the likes of Bolt and Uber; or X = Multimedia or video on demand, such as Netflix and Apple TV; or X = houses - Airbnb; or X = storage - Google Drive and One Drive; or X = Data, which incorporates elements of data analytics, data warehousing, visualization and dash-boarding; or X = productivity/office, where products such as Office 365, Zoho, SAP, and Salesforce, offer remote work and productivity solutions to billions of users globally; and X = Education, with Massive Open Online Courses (MOOC) and Learning Management Systems, such as Sakai, Udemy and EdX which offer remote teaching/learning and education management [25].

2.4.1 Fog and edge computing

Certain Cloud application domains, such as dynamic traffic routing, e-Logistics, ambulance routing, self-driving cars, require fast, on-demand and real-time information from processed data. CC, though capable, is ill-suited for such application areas due of latency emanating from the distance between the Cloud data centre and the data source. Fog and Edge computing have been proposed as potential solutions to this challenge. Fog Computing is a form of distributed CC, where portions of the computational processing that would typically have been done in the Cloud are handled by smaller computing nodes. The Fog layer thus serves as a middle layer between the Cloud layer and the data source. The proximity of the Fog nodes to the data source helps reduce latency emanating from network congestion, bottlenecks, and bandwidth limitations [26]. Being a HPC node, the Fog can perform high intensity computations in real-time and only forwards data meant for long-term storage, batch processing and/or advanced computations to the remote Cloud.

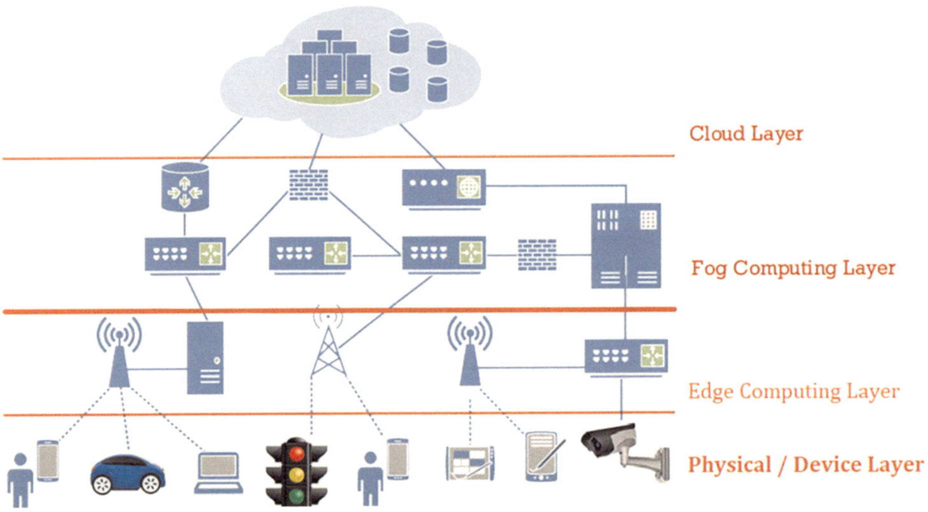

Figure 6.
The 4 Layers of a generic cyber-physical network based on ITU architecture [14].

On the other hand, Edge computing devices are low powered computing nodes placed next to the data source. These devices are responsible to routing, collecting, filtering, and aggregating data collected at the source. They might include network gateways, such as wireless access points, network switches, network routers, single board computers (such as the Raspberry Pi or Asus Tinker board), or micro-controllers (such as the Arduino or ESP32).

Figure 6 shows a depiction of the Cloud, Fog, and Edge computing layers in a generic Cyber-Physical network. The image shows the Fog and Edge layers being sandwiched in between the physical/device layer (data source) and the Cloud computing layer.

2.5 Artificial intelligence and machine learning

Artificial Intelligence (AI) is a technique for building systems that mimic human behaviour or decision-making. Machine Learning (ML) is a subset of AI that uses pre-existing data to learn and automatically classify or make predictions. There are four main types of ML methods, which are: Supervised ML, which learns by example and yields output based on provided data; Unsupervised ML, which seeks to identifies patterns in raw data without the need for examples; Reinforcement Learning, which learns using reward-based system, in which good decisions are rewarded, while incorrect decisions are penalised; Deep Learning, which is a special subset of ML that relies on multi-layered artificial neural networks to solve complex tasks. AI and ML have been used to identify faces and objects, detect tumours, navigate self-driving cars, and in language processing to analyse, understand, and generate human language, whether written or spoken.

Perhaps the most obvious/real life examples of AI are the ever so popular digital assistants – Amazon's Alexa, Apple's Siri, and Google's Assistant. These assistants are now seemingly commonplace and integrated into numerous "smart" products, including speakers, TVs, watches, and phones. With these assistants, users can order items from stores, control home appliances, pay bills or book flights by simple starting their voice command with "Alexa ... " or "Siri ... ".

3. Emergent technologies, concepts and applications

This section discusses several derivative solutions or systems of industry 4.0. The systems are presented as use-cases which showcase the various applications of technologies of the 4IR. For each system, a high-level description of the use-case is presented, followed by a brief discuss of the underlying 4IR technology. Building on **Figures 6** and 7 shows a CPS orchestration framework which encompasses both the physical and cyber worlds, through the integration of various 4IR technologies, particularly IoT, Cloud Computing, data analysis, storage, machine learning, and insights.

Many concepts emerging from industry 4.0 are largely deployed using the orchestration framework shown in **Figure** 7. The physical consists of appliances, machines, or human entities that need to be monitored or tracked. This is achieved using sensors which measure environmental and/or physiological variables such as temperature, humidity, oil level, running time, heart rate, oxygen level etc. These parameters are then collected at the edge, where pre-processing (aggregated and/or filtration) takes place, before being forwarded to the Fog or Cloud for advanced processing, storage, and analysis. The final output is inference, which can be used to make informed decisions and/or make necessary adjustments at the physical level. The entire process can be described as a data pipeline flowing from the physical space to the cyber-space and back to the physical, as described in [27]. **Figure** 7 would be used as a guide to discuss the selected use-cases, while **Table 3** summaries the various components of each level.

3.1 Use-case 1: health monitoring system

This is an application of 4IR wherein wearable devices fitted with sensors are used to actively monitor physiological parameters. These devices collect relevant data and are connected to software applications, through which the wearer or professional, such as healthcare officers (doctors) or fitness coaches, can monitor relevant information. Applications include sports and fitness trackers, cardio and respiratory

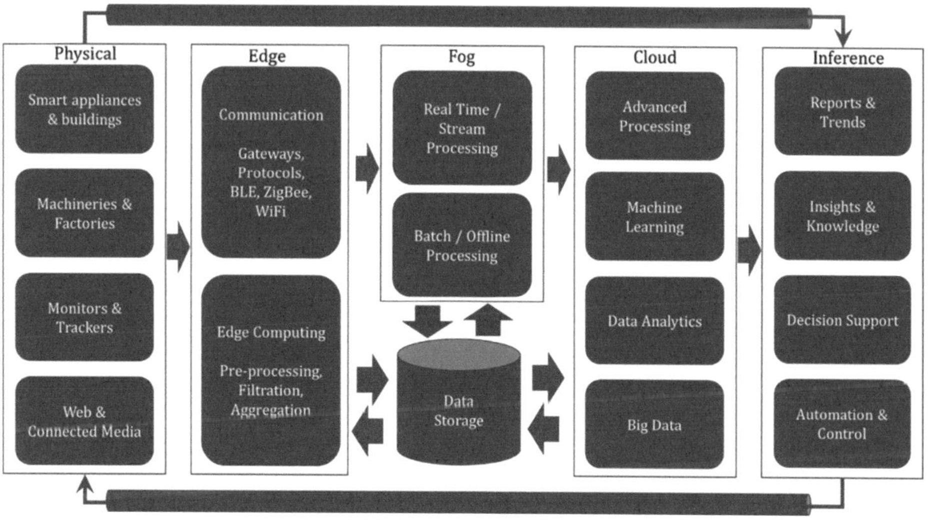

Figure 7.
CPS orchestration framework.

Use-case	Physical	Edge	Fog	Cloud	Inference	Actuation
Healthcare monitoring system	Fitness trackers, Blood pressure, ECG, Oxygen monitors	Protocols: BLE, IPv6, Wi-Fi. Communication: Wireless Access Points.	HL7 servers	SAAS (Hospital information system)	Health habits, lifestyle, fitness levels, medical aids/ plans.	Emergencies & ambulances, first aids and medical prescriptions.
Smart Traffic and Road Systems	Proximity sensors, light sensor, smart switches, and cameras	Protocols: LoRa, LPWAN, MQTT. Communication: Cellular & LPWAN network	Autonomous control systems, decision systems, short term storage.	HPC, data analysis & storage, machine learning.	Traffic flow patterns, road infrastructure planning & development.	Traffic light control, driver notification, vehicle tracking
e-Logistics	GPS, temperature sensors, tyre pressure sensors.	Protocols: LPWAN, Cellular network, Satellite.	Parcel management systems, data analysis & storage.		Route optimization, fuel management.	Parcel tracking, alternate paths / routing networks.
Smart Factories & Manufacturing.	Temperature, Oil & Fuel level, Gas, vibration sensors.	Protocols: M2M, M2H, BLE, ZigBee, Z-Wave. Communication: Ethernet switches.	Autonomous control systems, decision systems, short term storage	Data analytics and warehousing, management support solutions.	Failure metrics, repair, and replacement planning, fuelling schedule.	Autonomous power on/off.
Smart energy & grid systems.	Meters, solar panels, smart switches.	Protocols: BLE, ZigBee, Wi-Fi. Communication: Wireless Access Points.	HPC, data analysis & storage, machine learning, billing, and metering solutions.		Energy consumption reports, infrastructure upgrade & replacement planning.	Remote appliance control, smart billing.

Table 3.
CPS orchestration framework components for each use-case.

monitors, child minders and infant trackers etc. Several health and fitness monitoring systems were discussed in [15, 21, 28].

In context of the CPS orchestration framework, relevant sensors are used at the physical levels. Protocols, such as the Health Level 7 (HL7) and servers are considered at the Edge and Fog levels respectively, while hospital management systems can be deployed as SAAS solutions in the Cloud. Inference might include health conditions, sleep patterns, emergencies, etc. for which relevant actions, such as doctor's appointments, medical prescriptions, or ambulance could be dispatched. One such system is described in [29], where cyber-healthcare kiosks were proposed to support healthcare systems in developing countries.

3.2 Use-case 2: smart traffic and road systems

Smart traffic and road systems (STRS) include smart roads, driver assistant, traffic congestion monitoring, smart traffic and streetlights, smart parking, smart transportation etc., some of which are briefly described as follows.

Smart roads and intelligent highways are classic road networks which have sensors installed to monitor various road conditions and report same to commuters. Smart traffic and streetlights are improved versions of their traditional counterparts. Smart traffic lights are fitted with sensors to measure traffic intensity at road intersections and dynamically control traffic flow accordingly [30, 31], while Smart streetlights measure ambient light to autonomously switch themselves on or off. Driver assistant systems provide real time information on traffic situation to drivers and can also include drowsiness detection. Smart parking systems allow communities make optimal use of parking spaces while enabling drivers reserve or locate parking spots [32]. Other road-based solutions that have emerged from 4IR, including driver monitoring, smart mobility & carpooling, Bus Rapid Transport (BRT)), traffic surveillance & license plate detection, electric vehicles, etc. as reviewed in [33]. **Table 3** summaries the technologies at play at each level of the CPS orchestration framework w.r.t. STRS.

3.3 Use-case 3: e-Logistics

e-Logistics is multi-faceted and incorporates several complementary solutions, including transportation, real-time tracking, geo-location, courier, and cargo delivery services. Delivery services, encompasses the entire process flow required to transport cargo from pickup to delivery points. The technical requirements for each delivery differ and depend on the size, weight, type, and content of the cargo being transported. To instance, high valued items might require real-time tracking using GPS receivers, while sensitive and/or delicate cargo might require maintaining certain ambient conditions such as temperature and humidity.

For the CPS orchestration, the physical layer might require RFID or NFC modules for cargo tagging and identification, as well as sensors to gather data on the cargo and its surrounding environment. The Edge would include data aggregators and network gateways, through which telemetry data are sent to the Cloud, while the Cloud layer could house software for visualization, mapping, and customer engagement.

3.4 Use-case 4: smart factories and manufacturing

Perhaps the most direct impact of industry 4.0 is the automation of manufacturing processes. Gartner describes smart factories as new forms of efficient and flexible manufacturing, powered by the interconnection of processes, diverse real-time data sources, and individuals (operators, maintenance officers, etc.) who interact with these systems [34].

Smart factories connect the physical and cyber world together in a bid to monitor (and control) end-to-end manufacturing processes. These processes begin with the procurement of raw materials, tracking their shipment, monitoring parameters from various machines, packaging of finished produce, and the delivery of finished goods. Parameters of interest within the smart manufacturing process might include fuel levels and usage estimation, ambient temperatures, air quality, levels of CO_2 and other gases, oil levels etc. These data parameters are then fed into CPS, where ML and data analytics are used to obtain relevant inferences, such as failure metrics (Mean Time Between Failures - MTBF, Mean Time To Repair - MTTR, and Mean Time To Failure - MTTF). With this information, preventive and corrective maintenance can be scheduled, avoiding the need to shut down the factory (stopping production and revenue generation) due to faulty equipment.

3.5 Use-case 5: smart energy and grids

Traditional electric grids are based on a closed system of production, transmission, distribution, and consumption, with no provision for the exchange, visualization and security of information and energy flows between operators and customers [35, 36]. These classic grids adopted a top-down architecture, with a centralized producer supplying the necessary energy to consumers. Smart grids (SG) in contrast, are made up of decentralized power sources, mostly renewable or "green" energy, which rely on ICT to control the flow of energy and information in real-time to customers. Being made up of several decentralized power sources, SGs employ bi-directional architectures consisting of both the top-down and bottom-up architectures. The bottom-up architecture is one in which the consumers can also produce energy which is fed into the grid, thus, becoming "prosumers". Beyond the grid, sustainable energy usage is an ever-present concern in today's energy market. Several solutions have been proposed including energy efficient appliances and smart appliances, which learn usage patterns through machine learning, and automatically switch themselves on or off [37, 38].

Regarding the CPS orchestration framework, the physical layer might include solar panels, smart meters, adaptive lighting, and motion sensors. Gateway appliances running protocols such as Bluetooth Low Energy (BLE) and ZigBee might be found at the Edge layer, while the Fog and Cloud are merged to provide solutions for remote appliance control and monitoring, as well as billing and metering solutions. Finally, drawn inferences might include energy consumption patterns, while actuations involve remote appliance control.

3.6 Other emergent technologies

Digital Twin: A Digital Twin (DT) is a digital replica of a physical object or concept in the real world. The replica which receives data from the real world is able to mimic and "act" in a manner similar to its real world instance. This ability makes DT technology ideal for prototyping and simulating world events and settings to develop appropriate responses to external stimuli. It is a technology that infuses IoT, AI and Data analytics, as data received from IoT sensors in the real world are fed into AI, mathematical, and/or statistical models from which decisions and useful inferences are obtained.

Blockchain: A blockchain is a sequence of "blocks", each containing a list of transaction records, stored cryptographically in linked distributed databases (chain) [39]. In essence, Blockchain is an immutable way of storing information. It is characterized by high security, as it uses unique digital signatures and cryptography; and decentralized control, through a peer-to-peer network of consenting users, who control and authorize transactions. It has been applied in numerous fields including finance (cryptocurrency) [40], trading [41], health [42], logistics, construction engineering [43], and in almost any area where secure and accurate record keeping is required.

4. Impacts of the 4IR

This section discusses some of the direct impacts of Industry 4.0 on the lives of people and societies in general.

4.1 E-commerce

E-Commerce or electronic commerce is a system of trading carried out via the Internet. The growth of the Internet during the 3IR could be considered one of the catalysts for the wide adoption of e-commerce. This adoption has since risen astronomically, particularly in the 4IR era, with the proliferation of smartphones, tablets, and other mobile devices. Amazon, Alibaba, Best Buy, and eBay are some well-known global online retain stores, most of which accept payment through various means including physical cash, credit/debit cards and NFC-based payment [44] such as Apple Pay, Samsung pay and Google Pay.

The impact of e-Commerce became more apparent during the recent Covid-19 global pandemic, which called for isolation and physical distancing to reduce its spread. People relied heavily on technology to shop for necessities, contact-less deliveries, and payments. **Figure 8** shows the monthly year-on-year growth of

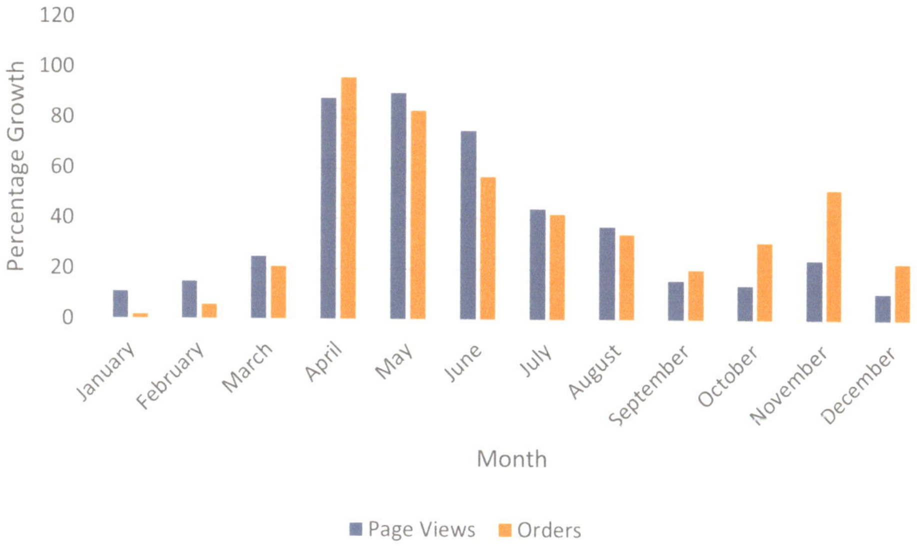

Figure 8.
Global growth of e-Commerce in 2020 (based on statistics from www.Bazaarvoice.com).

e-Commerce in 2019 vs. 2020. As of April 2020, the number of orders placed on e-Commerce platforms had almost doubled the number from the year before at 96% increase.

Hybrid stores or "Just Walk Out" or "till-free" stores are becoming increasingly popular. As the name implies, a "just walk out" store is one wherein a buyer, after picking any item of interest, simply walks out of the shop without visiting the counter/till to pay. These stores use artificial intelligence, weight sensors on shelves, and cameras to monitor buyers, automatically determine which items were selected and bill the customer. Examples of these stores are Amazon Go and Telesco GetGo stores.

4.2 Remote workers

An indirect impact of technologies of the 4IR is remote working or tele-working. This is a system wherein employees carry out their tasks or jobs from locations different from the physical building of the employer. Industry 4.0 technologies including high speed Internet (5G), tele-conferencing solutions (such as Zoom, Microsoft Teams), augmented/virtual realities, and collaboration tools (Github, SharePoint), have greatly enabled remote work. The Covid-19 pandemic also popularized remote work as "working from home" became a norm between late 2019 and 2021. These years saw tele-conferencing solutions including Google Meeting, Zoom Microsoft Teams etc. replace in-contact meetings.

4.3 Education

The education sector has also been greatly impacted by the 4IR. Like with remote workers, the education sector has also seen a surge in the number of remote teaching and learning especially through Massive Open Online Classes (MOOC). In the era of Industry 4.0 the traditional brick and mortar classrooms are either being complemented by or replaced by online alternatives. MOOC, such as Udemy and Coursera, offer teaching and learning solutions that are completely independent of physical classroom environments. In cases where traditional classrooms are being augmented, 4IR offerings, particularly virtual and mixed reality, allow students immerse themselves in a virtual world, giving them first-hand experiences of the concepts being taught. Immersive technologies are commonly used in specialized industries where training equipment are either too expensive or delicate to leave in the hands of trainees. These include the aviation industry, where augmented reality is used to teach pilots and astronauts [45], in medicine to train medical students [46], in agriculture to teach farmers the concept of crop rotations and use of tractors [47], etc.

Though the Internet has been the major catalysts of change, other factors have also played their roles in reshaping the education sector. For instance, smart television and touch screens now enable interactive learning for kids and toddlers, while Podcasts, Webinars and MOOC allow a single lesson to reach billions of globally disperse learners in an on-demand fashion. The authors in [25] discussed several considerations for remote teaching and learning especially from the perspective of developing countries.

4.4 Media and entertainment

The impact of 4IR has also been felt in media and entertainment. The penetration of smartphones, smart-TVs, and reliable internet has increased the consumption of

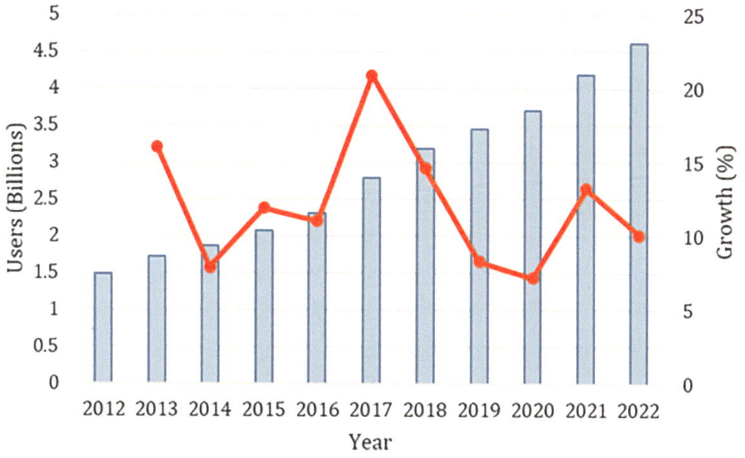

Figure 9.
Year-on-Year growth in Number of Social Media Users [48].

high-quality, and often bandwidth heavy contents, such as 4 K videos and game streaming. Industry 4.0 has brought about a major yearning for on-demand and ubiquitously accessible media contents. Classic videos on tapes, DVD and Blu rays have been replaced with on-demand streaming from online platforms such as Netflix, YouTube, Apple TV etc. Hard copies of photo albums have been replaced with Instagram and Snapchats, while classic hardware music players have been replaced with streaming services such as Spotify, Deezer and Apple Music. Recent statistics reveal that streamed contents accounted for over 83% of all consumed media, with Spotify accounting for about 33% (180 million subscribers), Apple music with 17.5% (or 90 million subscribers), Amazon music accounting for 14% (77 million), YouTube Premium with 50 million subscribers, and YouTube (free) with over 2 billion users monthly.

Furthermore, 4IR has also changed the way people socialize, with the shift from physical to online socialization. There are now a plethora of social media platforms including Facebook, Twitter, Instagram, Snapchat, WhatsApp etc., with built-in support for direct messages (chats), group messages, and voice & video calls. Using these solutions, friends and families can stay in touch with one another despite being globally disperse. Recent 2022 reports suggest that more than 58% of the world's population (4.6 billion people) use social media, with most users spending an average of about 2.5 hours daily on these platforms [48]. **Figure 9** shows that within the last decade, the number of social media users has tripled from about 1.5 billion in 2012 to over 4.6 in 2022.

4.5 Transportation

Smart transportation and mobility are another significant impact of the 4IR. Smart transportation encompasses a broad range of concepts including but not limited to vehicle-as-a-service (ride sharing/carpooling, riding hailing), bus rapid transit (BRT), smart roads, autonomous vehicles, electric cars and bicycles, transport monitoring and tracking, and car park management, most of which are accessible through a mobile device [33, 49]. Similarly, several 4IR technologies including IoT, Big data analytics, ML, Fog and Cloud computing are being fused together to achieve autonomous vehicles navigation. Likewise, IoT, GPS, RFID and NFC are highly influential 4IR technologies in Logistics services and delivery services globally.

Several smart transportation solutions, specifically variants of riding sharing, ride hailing, and courier/logistics services, have been deployed globally. These are mostly due to the increase in Internet and smartphone penetration rate in the last few years. For instance, online ordering and delivery of food, a form of logistics services, has become a norm in recent times [50, 51], while ride sharing services and ride hailing have continued to grow globally, even in developing countries [52, 53]. Leveraging on 4IR offering, insurance firms are able to monitoring driving behaviour [54, 55], while haulage companies can measuring fuel consumption in trucks [56].

5. Open challenges

The advantages and applications of industry 4.0 are numerous, some of which have been discussed above, however, there are several challenges hampering the widespread deployment of some of these applications. This section briefly discusses some of these open challenges.

5.1 Bandwidth and infrastructure requirement

With the plethora of social media applications, tele-conferencing solutions (Zoom, Teams), media streaming platforms (Netflix, Hulu), connected devices (smart appliances, connected homes), wearable technologies (smart watches, health monitors), the demand for reliable data access, greater network coverage, and bandwidth has sky-rocketed. Internet service providers (ISP) must be prepared to upgrade or perish. ISPs of today need to be flexible, dynamic, and agile enough to changes their mode of operations to suit dynamic customer demands, as well as, be ready to upgrade or replace ageing infrastructure with modern alternatives. For instance, classic active devices such as routers and switches might need to be replaced with those that support software defined networks, wherein the control and data planes are decoupled, and traffic flows are customised [57]. 5G and 6G are also on the horizon, hence, ISPs must make extensive plans and invest in capacity building. There is also the concern of seamless integration with existing solutions that must be considered, as the transition to 5G/6G would most likely be in phases. Adequately maintaining existing solutions while gradually adopting emerging ones is pivotal for the success of 4IR solutions providers. It is also important to note that Internet penetration in rural and less developed areas is on the rise and must be catered for. The utilization of Unmanned Aerial Vehicles (UAVs) to provide 5G network support in these locations might be viable solutions to consider [10].

5.2 Big data

By definition, "Big data" should implicitly spell trouble for data centres and ISPs, as they must process enormous volume of data (in petabytes) with minimal delays. Managing, processing, storing, and backing up these enormous amounts of data in batches or in real-time (streaming) can be a major challenge. Building data warehouses and HPC solutions to manage & process petabytes of data can be prohibitively expensive for most organizations. One solution could be cooperative Fog/Cloud federation, whereby small Cloud infrastructures are collaboratively operated, networked, and managed by a group of organizations with common interest [16, 58]. Another alternative could be through partnership with third party solution providers such as Google (Google Cloud Services), Amazon (Amazon Web Services) and Microsoft (Azure).

5.3 Security and privacy concerns

Preservation of security and privacy is a major concern in today's data-centric world. The IoT, despite its bells and whistles still has several privacy concerns. There is the ever-present threat of unauthorized access to smart systems (homes, buildings, cars) or hackers tapping into feeds from security cameras to spy on people. Moreover, in wearable technology where BLE is prevalent, performance degradation due to electromagnetic and inter-channel inference, specifically for medical devices, is also a major concern [59].

Beyond IoT, issues such as transboundary data ownership and jurisdictions are also major concerns. In many countries, legal, privacy and ethical issues relating to the use and access to sensitive data, such as those on health, judicial, and intellectual properties, remain open challenges, especially in instances where such data are stored on remote Cloud servers located in a different country [60]. Though policies are now in place to address some of these challenges, such as the Protection of Personal Information Act (POPIA) [61], and the General Data Protection Regulation (GDPR) [62], implementation and/or compliance remain a big challenge.

5.4 Interoperability

There are several protocols upon which 4IR technologies operate. These protocols enable the collection, storage, and exchange of data between various components. They include but are not limited to Li-Fi, Wi-Fi, 3G/4G/5G, ZigBee, Z-Wave, BLE, SigFox, NB-IoT, LTE-M etc. Unfortunately, many of these protocols are developed by different manufacturers and are used on their own appliances, hence, closed off to solutions from different manufacturers. This closed-source ecosystem limits the interplay between equipment and often forces users to be locked into using solutions from specific vendors. Currently, no single vendor can provide equipment to cater for all the phases of an integrated industry 4.0 system, and by operating in closed-source silos, manufacturers increase overall cost of ownership, limit vertical and horizontal scalability, and stifle innovation. Collaboration is thus paramount for scalability and growth. However, multiple studies have shown that proprietary technology, poor coordination, and lack of standards are primary factors limiting inter-operability and collaboration. To combat this, open industrial standards are required which allows for cross-vendor support and global interoperability. By providing APIs, standardized open-source messaging protocols (such as MQTT, HTTP) and RESTful solutions can be deployed to expand the application use-cases.

6. Conclusion

The fourth industrial revolution (4IR) or Industry 4.0 has indeed brought about a disruption to societal lives and the world in general. The world is now driven by data and the Internet, with some describing data as the new oil of the 21st century. Globally, data intensive activities, such as remote learning, gaming, video streaming, and video conferencing, have grown dramatically in recent times and would probably keep growing.

This chapter has discussed the technological wave of change called the 4IR. It started off by defining the concept of Industry 4.0, and then its evolution, from the industrial age in the seventeenth century till date, was discussed. The foundational enabling technologies of the 4IR, including ICT, IoT & Big data, Cloud computing, etc. were presented; followed by a discussion on various application use cases using an orchestration framework. Finally, some societal impacts of industry 4.0 were given, including its impact on education and transportation. The chapter then concluded by discussing some open challenges facing the full-scale adoption and/or implementation of industry 4.0, and proposed plausible solutions to them, including cooperative collaborations and the need to embrace open standards.

Author details

Olasupo Ajayi*†, Antoine Bagula† and Hloniphani Maluleke†
Department of Computer Science, University of the Western Cape, Cape Town, South Africa

*Address all correspondence to: ooajayi@uwc.ac.za; olasupoajayi@gmail.com

† These authors contributed equally.

References

[1] Wrigley E. Reconsidering the industrial revolution: England and wales. Journal of Interdisciplinary History. 2018;**49**(01):9-42

[2] Pat H. The Industrial Revolution. New York: Routledge, Chapman, and Hall, Inc; 1992. p. 3. ISBN 978-0-7131-6531-9

[3] Hull J. The second industrial revolution: The history of a concept. Storia Della Storiografia. 1999;**36**:81-90

[4] Bairoch P. International industrialization levels from 1750 to 1980. Journal of European Economic History. 1982;**11**(2):269

[5] Shannon CE. A mathematical theory of communication. The Bell System Technical Journal. 1948;**27**(3):379-423

[6] Colombo A, Karnouskos S, Bangemann T. Towards the next generation of industrial cyber-physical systems. Industrial Cloud-based Cyber-physical Systems. Springer, Champions; 2014. pp. 1-22

[7] Schoenherr SE. The Digital Revolution. 2004. Available from: www.ermarketer.com. [Accessed: April 7, 2022]

[8] O'Dea S. Number of Smartphones Sold to End Users Worldwide from 2007 to 2021. 2022. Available from: https://www.statista.com/statistics/263437/global-smartphone-sales-to-end-users-since-2007/ [Accessed: March 22, 2022]

[9] Johnson J. Global Internet Access Rate 2005-2021. 2022. Available from: www.statista.com/statistics/209096/share-of-internet-users-in-the-total-world-population-since-2006/ [Accessed: June 6, 2022]

[10] Maluleke H, Bagula A, Ajayi O. Efficient airborne network clustering for 5G backhauling and fronthauling. In: Proc 16th Int. Conf. on Wireless and Mobile Computing, Networking and Communications (WiMob). IEEE; 2020. pp. 99-104

[11] Evans D. The Internet of Things: How the Next Evolution of the Internet is Changing Everything. Vol. 1. CISCO White Paper; 2011. pp. 1-11

[12] Zimmermann H. OSI reference model-the ISO model of architecture for open systems interconnection. IEEE Transactions on Communications. 1980; **28**(4):425-432

[13] Braden R. Requirements for Internet Hosts - Communication Layers. STD 3, RFC 11221989. DOI: 10.17487/RFC1122

[14] ITU TS. Overview of the Internet of Things. Recommendation ITU-T Y. Vol. 20602012. p. 22 https://www.itu.int/rec/dologin_pub.asp?lang=eid=T-REC-Y.2060-201206-I!!PDF-E type=items [Accessed: April 18, 2022]

[15] Celesti A, Fazio M, Galán Márquez F, Glikson A, Mauwa H, Bagula A, et al. How to develop IoT cloud e-health systems based on FIWARE: a lesson learnt. Journal of Sensor and Actuator Networks. 2019;**8**(1):7

[16] Ajayi O, Bagula A, Ma K. Fourth industrial revolution for development: The relevance of cloud federation in healthcare support. IEEE Access. 2019;7: 185322-185337

[17] Yang Q, Liu Y, Chen T, Tong Y. Federated machine learning: Concept and applications. ACM Transaction on Intelligent Systems and Technology (TIST). 2019;**10**(2):1-9

[18] IBM Cloud Education. Data Mining. 2021. Available from: https://www.ibm.com/cloud/learn/data-mining [Accessed: June 25, 2022]

[19] Ogrezeanu AE. Data mining in smart agriculture. Education, Research and Business Technologies. Singapore: Springer; 2022. pp. 249-257

[20] Okewu E, Adewole P, Misra S, Maskeliunas R, Damasevicius R. Artificial neural networks for educational data mining in higher education: A systematic literature review. Applied Artificial Intelligence. 2021;**35**(13):983-1021

[21] Gordan M, Sabbagh-Yazdi S, Ismail Z, Ghaedi K, et al. State-of-the-art review on advancements of data mining in structural health monitoring. Measurement. 2022:110939

[22] Odun-Ayo I, Goddy-Worlu R, Ajayi O, Grant E. A systematic mapping study of High Performance Computing and the Cloud. ARPN Journal of Engineering and Applied Sciences. 2018;**13**(24): 9886-9700

[23] Odun-Ayo I, Ajayi O, Omoregbe N. Cloud service level agreements–issues and development. In: Proc. Int. Conf. on Next Generation Computing and Information Systems (ICNGCIS). IEEE; 2017. pp. 1-6

[24] Odun-Ayo I, Ajayi O, Okereke C. Virtualization in cloud computing: Developments and trends. In: Proc. int. Conf. on Next Generation Computing and Information Systems (ICNGCIS). IEEE; 2017. pp. 24-28

[25] Ajayi O, Maluleke H, Bagula A. Least cost remote learning for under-served communities. In: Proc. int. Conf. on e-Infrastructure & e-Services for Developing Countries. Cham: Springer; 2020. pp. 219-233

[26] Ma K, Bagula A, Nyirenda C, Ajayi O. An IoT-based Fog computing model. Sensors. 2019;**19**(12):2783

[27] Talebkhah M, Sali A, Marjani M, Gordan M, et al. IoT and big data applications in smart cities: Recent advances, challenges, and critical issues. IEEE Access. 2021;**9**:55465-55484

[28] Huifeng W, Kadry SN, Raj E. Continuous health monitoring of sportsperson using IoT devices based wearable technology. Computer Communications. 2020;**160**:588-595

[29] Bagula M, Bagula H, Mandava M, Kakoko L, Bagula A. Cyber-healthcare kiosks for healthcare support in developing countries. In: Int. Conf. on e-Infrastructure and e-Services for Developing Countries. Cham: Springer; 2018. pp. 185-198

[30] Ajayi O, Bagula A, Isafiade O, Noutouglo A. Effective management of delays at road intersections using smart traffic light system. In: Int Conf. on e-Infrastructure & e-Services for Developing Countries. Cham: Springer; 2019. pp. 84-103

[31] Ajayi O, Bagula A, Chukwubueze I, Maluleke H. Priority based traffic pre-emption system for medical emergency vehicles in smart cities. In: IEEE Symp. on Computers and Communications (ISCC). IEEE; 2020. pp. 1-7

[32] Bagula A, Castelli L, Zennaro M. On the design of smart parking networks in the smart cities: An optimal sensor placement model. Sensors. 2015;**15**: 15443-15467

[33] Ajayi O, Bagula A, Maluleke H, Odun-Ayo I. Transport inequalities and

the adoption of intelligent transportation systems in Africa: A research landscape. Sustainability. 2021;**13**(22):12891

[34] Gartner. Smart Factory. Information Technology Gartner Glossary. Available from: https://www.gartner.com/en/information-technology/glossary/smart-factory; [Accessed: April 8, 2022]

[35] Ayele G. Semantic description of IoT security for smart grid [Master's thesis]; Universitetet i Agder; University of Agder

[36] Rifkin J. The Third Industrial Revolution: How Lateral Power is Transforming Energy, The Economy, and The World. 4th ed. London, UK: Palgrave Macmillian; 2011

[37] Reyes-Campos J, Alor-Hernández G, Machorro-Cano I, Olmedo-Aguirre JO, Sánchez-Cervantes J, Rodríguez-Mazahua L. Discovery of resident behavior patterns using machine learning techniques and IoT paradigm. Mathematics. 2021;**9**(3):219

[38] Chen Y, Ko Y, Peng W, Lee W. Mining appliance usage patterns in smart home environment. In: Pacific-Asia Conf. on Knowledge Discovery and Data Mining. Berlin, Heidelberg: Springer; 2013. pp. 99-110

[39] Zheng Z, Xie S, Dai H, Chen X, Wang H. An overview of blockchain technology: Architecture, consensus, and future trends. In: IEEE Int. Congress on big data (BigData congress). IEEE; 2017. pp. 557-564

[40] DeVries PD. An analysis of cryptocurrency, bitcoin, and the future. International Journal of Business Management and Commerce. 2016;**1**(2): 1-9

[41] Malakani C, Bagula A, Ajayi O, Maluleke H. Trading 4.0: An online peer-to-peer money lending platform. In: Int. Conf. on e-Infrastructure and e-Services for Developing Countries. Champions: Springer; 2022. pp. 149-169

[42] Xu L, Bagula A, Isafiade O, Ma K, Chiwewe T. Design of a credible blockchain-based E-Health Records (CB-EHRS) platform. In: ITU Kaleidoscope: ICT for Health: Networks, Standards and Innovation (ITU K). IEEE; 2019. pp. 1-8

[43] Gordan M, Ismail Z, Mohd Rahim FA, Chao OZ, Ibrahim Z, Hashim H, et al. Defining a conceptual framework for vibration-based damage detection platforms using blockchain. Journal of Civil Engineering and Materials Application. 2021;**5**(1):25-33

[44] Bond C. Apple Pay, Samsung Pay and Google Pay: How They Stack Up Mobile Payments Could Completely Replace Your Wallet. USNews; 2019 Available from: https://money.usnews.com/credit-cards/articles/apple-pay-samsung-pay-and-google-pay-how-they-stack-up [Accessed: April 9, 2022]

[45] Labedan P, Darodes-De-Tailly N, Dehais F, Peysakhovich V. Virtual reality for pilot training: Study of cardiac activity. In: VISIGRAPP (2: HUCAPP). 2021. pp. 81-88

[46] Ruthenbeck GS, Reynolds KJ. Virtual reality for medical training: The state-of-the-art. Journal of Simulation. 2015;**9**(1):16-26

[47] Mabiletsa O, Viljoen S, Farrell J, Ngqwemla L, Isafiade O. An immersive tractor application for sustainability: A south African land reform and learners' perspective. International Journal of Virtual and Augmented Reality (IJVAR). 2020;**4**(1):35-54

[48] Datareportal. Digital 2022 Global Overview Report (January 2022) v05.

2022. Available from: https://www.slideshare.net/DataReportal/digital-2022-global-overview-report-january-2022-v05 [Accessed: April 10, 2022]

[49] Adamu A, Wang D, Salau A, Ajayi O. An integrated IoT system pathway for smart cities. International Journal of on Emerging Technologies. 2020;**11**(1):1-9

[50] Azman NIB, Mashuri NABA, Ibrahim SOA-EBW. The online food delivery service and their impact on customer satisfaction among university students in Malaysia. International Journal of Academic Research in Business and Social Sciences. 2021;**11**(6):1665-1674

[51] Banerjee SP, Jain D, Nayyar R. Measuring service quality of food delivery services: a study of generation Z. African Journal of Hospitality, Tourism and Leisure. 2019;**8**(1):1-2

[52] Nagare DB, More KL, Tanwar NS, Kulkarni SS, Gunda KC. Dynamic carpooling application development on android platform. International Journal of Innovative Technology and Exploring Engineering. 2013;**2**(3):136-139

[53] Ghoseiri K, Haghani A, Hamed M. Real-Time Rideshare Matching Problem. Final Report of UMD-2009-05 U.S. Department of Transportation. 2010. pp. 1-74. Available from: https://rosap.ntl.bts.gov/view/dot/25988 [Accessed: August 12, 2022]

[54] Joubert JW, De Beer D, De Koker N. Combining accelerometer data and contextual variables to evaluate the risk of driver behaviour. Transportation Research Part F: Traffic Psychology and Behaviour. 2016;**41**:80-96

[55] Thakur A, Malekian R, Bogatinoska DC. Internet of things based solutions for road safety and traffic management in intelligent transportation systems. In: Int. Conf. on ICT Innovations, Skopje, Macedonia. Cham, Switzerland: Springer; 2017. pp. 47-56

[56] Hoffman AJ, van der Westhuizen M. An empirical model for the assessment of truck driver fuel economy. In: Proc. of the 2019 IEEE Intelligent Transp. Systems Conf. Auckland, New Zealand: ITSC; 2019. pp. 637-642

[57] Kurose J, Ross KW. Computer Networking: A Top-Down Approach. 4th ed. Boston, Massachusetts, USA: Addison Wesley Longman Publishing Co. Inc.; 2007

[58] Ajayi O, Bagula A, Maluleke H. Africa 3: A continental network model to enable the african fourth industrial revolution. IEEE Access. 2020;**8**:196847-196864

[59] Hasan M, Shahjalal M, Chowdhury MZ, Jang YM. Real-time healthcare data transmission for remote patient monitoring in patch-based hybrid OCC/BLE networks. Sensors. 2019;**19**(5):1208

[60] Sello P, Bagula A, Ajayi O. Laws and regulations on big data management: The case of South Africa. Int. Conf. on e-Infrastructure and e-Services for Developing Countries. Cham: Springer; 2019. pp. 169-179

[61] Protection of Personal Information Act (POPI Act). Available from: https://popia.co.za/ [Accessed: April 17, 2022]

[62] Voigt P, Von dem Bussche A. The eu General Data Protection Regulation (gdpr). A Practical Guide, 1st Ed. Vol. 10, No. 3152676. Cham: Springer Int. Publishing. 2017. pp. 10-5555

Chapter 2

Challenges and Prospective of AI and 5G-Enabled Technologies in Emerging Applications during the Pandemic

Md. Mijanur Rahman and Fatema Khatun

Abstract

5G is being implemented in the Internet of things (IoT) era. This book chapter focuses on 5G technology and the integration of other digital technologies, such as artificial intelligence (AI) and machine learning, IoT, big data analytics, cloud computing, robotics, and other digital platforms into new healthcare applications. Now, the healthcare industry is implementing 5G-enabled technology to improve health services, medical research, quality of life, and medical professionals' and patients' experiences everywhere, at any time. Technology can facilitate faster medical research progress and better clinical and social services management. Furthermore, AI approaches with 5G connectivity may be able to combat the epidemic challenges with minimal resources. This book chapter underlines how 5G technology is growing to address epidemic concerns. The study highlights many technical issues and future developments for creating 5G-powered healthcare solutions. This chapter also addresses the key challenges AI and 5G technology face in emerging healthcare solutions. In addition, this book chapter highlights perspective, policy recommendations, and future research directions of AI and 5G-enabled technologies in confronting future pandemics. More research will be incorporated into future projects, including studies on developing a digital society based on 5G technology in healthcare emergencies.

Keywords: 5G technology, artificial intelligence, COVID-19 pandemic, deep learning, healthcare, internet of things, machine learning

1. Introduction

The healthcare industry benefited from the development of a number of digital technologies in 2020. These technologies are used to address issues in conventional healthcare systems and the pandemic, including the "Internet of things (IoT)" with high-speed wireless networks [1], big data [2], "artificial intelligence (AI)" including machine learning and deep learning [3], and blockchain technology [4]. 2019 was the year that witnessed the broad deployment of the latest wireless mobile phone technology, known as "Fifth Generation (5G)." Even though the 5G network is still in its infancy, some nations have already implemented 5G networks. These nations include China, South Korea, Japan, the United Kingdom, and the United States [5]. 5G home services and some large applications are currently being developed in many cities of the United States [6]. At the "Winter Olympics" in February of 2018, South Korea demonstrated the 5G technology. They have been expanding their 5G networks and anticipate having 5G deployment throughout the nation by 2023. China is extending 5G communication as part of its "Made in China 2025" goal in research and development initiatives. Commercial 5G networks were introduced in China in 2019, and the country is currently expanding 5G communication. In 2020, Japan launched a 5G network for commercial use. Several European countries, like Austria, Spain, and Switzerland, have already launched 5G services and are planning to extend their network capacities. Many other countries have plans to deploy 5G networks by 2025 [7]. By 2025, it is expected that the 5G cloud will support around 1.8 billion connections and cover nearly one-third of the world's population [8, 9].

Compared to current wireless networks, 5G offers fast data rates, reduced latency, and high-volume device connectivity with excellent energy efficiency, high reliability, and support for mobility [10]. In 2019, 204 billion applications were downloaded over the Internet, and 67% of people worldwide had mobile device subscriptions, of which 65% had smartphones [11]. It was anticipated that there would be 3.8 billion people utilizing social media regularly by January 2020 [12]. Despite the constantly increasing number of digital devices connected to 5G, further research is currently being conducted to determine the level of variety in RF exposure.

Meanwhile, the world is facing a public health calamity due to the unique "2019 Coronavirus Disease (COVID-19)" [13]. Many experts researched the genetic code of COVID-19 and attempted to tackle the coronavirus pandemic health emergency when China initially identified the virus in December 2019 [14]. However, the World Health Organization (WHO) identified COVID-19, which was caused by a novel coronavirus named "severe acute respiratory syndrome coronavirus-2 (SARS-CoV-2)" in December 2019 in China [15]. On January 30, 2020, the WHO labeled the Chinese COVID-19 outbreak a public health emergency and proclaimed a global pandemic on March 11, 2020, posing a severe threat to public health systems. The COVID-19 pandemic has swept through 228 countries and territories, resulting in almost 6.6 million deaths and 637 million infected cases worldwide, reported by the" Worldometers" on November 4, 2022 (see **Figure 1**) [16]. As of October 2019, 50 cities in China had commercially

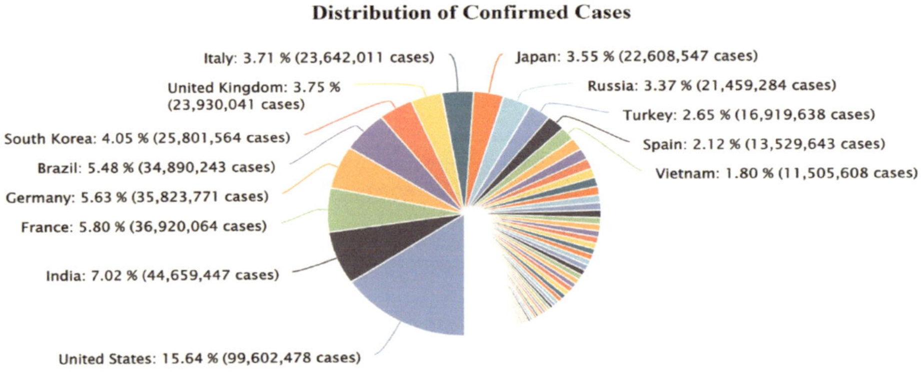

Figure 1.
Country-wise coronavirus confirmed cases distribution on November 4, 2022, adapted from Worldometers [16].

provided 5G wireless networks, and several people claimed ownership of the idea of 5G connectivity with the coronavirus. In December 2018, South Korea was the first to market 5G technology using a mobile hotspot successfully. However, South Korea was not the source of just one coronavirus, which has devastated many countries that do not yet have access to 5G networks. These countries include Malaysia, India, Bangladesh, Iran, France, Singapore, and Nigeria. Thus, the 5G-coronavirus theory makes a misleading claim, and the novel coronavirus has nothing to do with 5G, and there is no scientific evidence [17, 18]. Furthermore, according to several studies, 5G-related telecommunications technologies do not affect the human immune system [19].

Nevertheless, the pandemic has negatively influenced economic, medical, and political situations. Initial identification, isolation, quick management, spread prediction, and contact tracing technologies are all approaches to combat the spread of the coronavirus. The key challenges are virus tests, prescription or pharmaceutical delays, and providing services to critical zones. Modern digital technologies, such as artificial intelligence and 5G-based solutions [20], are essential for health, social, and economic outcomes to combat the coronavirus effectively. The worldwide health catastrophe brought on by this pandemic can be mitigated using these technologies, which can give improved digital solutions. With its potential effects in many industries, the use of 5G-enabled technology is overgrowing, offering more real-time services than anticipated. This study intends to highlight the perspective of AI and 5G-based solutions that can address COVID-19 difficulties in various contexts by concentrating on digital technology and existing socioeconomic issues. The chapter also examines numerous technological challenges and policies in implementing AI and 5G-powered emerging applications for handling post-pandemic issues.

2. Related works

Individuals and different industries are using multiple types of AI and 5G-powered solutions. The main application categories include diagnosis, patient treatment, administrative tasks, and services. During the global epidemic, numerous studies on AI and 5G-enabled technologies have been conducted, and they suggested many solutions in different sectors. M.M. Rahman et al. [21] aimed to describe the current technical aspects of artificial intelligence and other relevant technologies and their implications for combating COVID-19 and preventing the devastating effects of the pandemic. This study highlighted and categorized AI approaches in tackling the COVID-19 pandemic, including disease detection and diagnosis, data analysis and treatment procedures, research and drug development, social control and services, and predicting outbreaks. An early review paper [22] also discussed the role of AI in the fight against COVID-19 and its current limitations. They identified six critical areas in which AI contributed significantly during the pandemic: (i) early warnings and alerts; (ii) tracking and prediction; (iii) pandemic data dashboards; (iv) diagnosis and prognosis; (v) treatments and medication; and (vi) social control. Fei Jiang et al. [23] looked at how AI is currently being used in healthcare. This survey showed that AI could be used with different kinds of health data (structured and unstructured).

Modern AI techniques like "support vector machine" and "artificial neural network" can be used to learn from structured data. In contrast, advanced deep learning models and natural language processing are used to learn from and understand unstructured data. They talked about how AI could be used in three areas: early detection and diagnosis, treatment, predicting the outcome, and figuring out the prognosis. In a survey report [4], the authors looked at how blockchain and AI could be used to stop coronavirus outbreaks. First, they introduced a new conceptual architecture that integrates blockchain and AI for COVID-19 fighting. Then, they talked about how blockchain and AI could help fight the COVID-19 outbreak in fundamental ways. They also looked at the most recent research on how blockchain and AI can be used in different ways to fight COVID-19.

Using the geolocation of the patients and massive amounts of data, researchers developed a system capable of detecting and predicting the early spread of an epidemic [24]. A framework [25] enabled by an AI approach was proposed to detect COVID-19 using smartphone sensors. The designed AI-enabled framework can interpret the smartphone sensor's signal readings to predict pneumonia and the disease's outcome. Due to the rapid global spread of coronavirus disease, it is desirable to develop an automatic and accurate detection method for COVID-19 using chest CT. Numerous researchers developed a model based on deep learning to identify COVID-19 on a chest CT scan [26]. Using radiology and chest radiography to screen COVID-19-infected patients effectively is a crucial task [27]. The COVID-Net is a deep neural network-based model designed to detect COVID-19 cases in chest X-ray (CXR) images. In a screening approach [28], the authors sought to develop a deep learning-based early screening model to differentiate COVID-19 pneumonia from Influenza-A viral pneumonia and healthy cases using pulmonary CT images. Deep learning-based methods, like the "Deeper-Feature Convolutional Neural Network (DFCNN)" model [29], can effectively find and rank the interactions between proteins and ligands. The DFCNN can screen people quickly through virtual means. It can discover possible drugs for 2019-nCoV protease by screening drugs against four databases of chemical compounds. Other research used three different convolutional neural network (CNN)-based models (like ResNet50, InceptionV3, and Inception-ResNetV2) to look for patients with coronavirus pneumonia in chest X-rays. In addition, models built on AI were created to enhance the critical care provided to COVID-19 patients [30]. Clinical, paraclinical, personalized medicine, and epidemiological data were included in this model. The healthcare system can use an AI-based decision-making system to defeat COVID-19 and assist in better patient management in the ICU. Seven significant applications of AI for the COVID-19 pandemic were identified by R. Vaishya et al. [31]. By gathering and analyzing historical data, this AI-based solution is crucial in determining the cluster of cases and forecasting virus infection in the future.

Additionally, it is crucial to comprehend and recommend creating a COVID-19 vaccine. Result-driven technology is employed to screen, analyze, predict, and track current and future patients. This technology has already tracked data from confirmed, recovered, and deceased cases. Furthermore, Industry 4.0 can meet the demand for personalized face masks and gloves and gather data for healthcare systems to effectively manage and treat COVID-19 patients [32]. With the proper surveillance systems, it helps to resolve pandemic-related issues and provide a daily update on an infected patient, area, age, and state-wise. The use of various AI-based automated techniques and tools, including "Brain-Computer Interface (BCI)," "Arterial Spin Labeling—Magnetic Resonance Imaging (ASL-MRI)," biomarkers, iT bra, and different machine learning algorithms, aids in reducing errors and controlling disease progression [33]. AI software, expert systems, decision support systems, and computerized diagnosis can help doctors by minimizing intra- and interobserver variability. Deep learning and machine learning methods like artificial neural network (ANN) models can uncover hidden correlations and patterns in medical data, which can be used to create efficient clinical support systems. The IoT era is ushering in the most recent 5G technology. MM Rahman et al. [20] concentrated on 5G-based solutions that could address COVID-19 problems in various contexts. This study also offered a thorough analysis of 5G technology, incorporating other digital technologies in emerging healthcare applications to address epidemiological challenges. The adoption of 5G-based technologies in healthcare is currently taking place to support better health services, more productive medical research, improved quality of life, and better interactions between medical staff and patients worldwide.

3. AI and 5G-enabled technologies in real world

COVID-19 has introduced the capability of digital transformation. Industry 4.0 has the prospects to reshape and restore economic systems in a post-pandemic world via 5G smart infrastructure with IoT and AI, integrated automation, and cloud innovation (see **Figure 2**). All of the available technologies for Industry 4.0 are linked together with the help of 5G connectivity. Medical stakeholders can talk to each other for many different reasons, such as finding and diagnosing COVID-19, supporting healthcare equipment and logistics, remote health monitoring, improving treatment processes and care, controlling and managing COVID-19 patients, lowering the high risk of death, speeding up drug manufacturing and vaccine production, fighting local and global medical emergencies, etc., with less human physical involvement [34]. Using these technologies correctly would help to improve public health education and communication. While the school is on lockdown, these technologies assist in teaching and learning in remote places [35]. These give digital and many different places to find free educational resources. People are working from home and understanding a new office culture, work hours, virtual offices, virtual meetings, and a lot of written communication thanks to Industry 4.0 technologies. Industry 4.0 uses innovative production methods to make essential disposable items in short supply because of the COVID-19 pandemic. Industry 4.0 technologies can help people find better digital solutions during this crisis. Here are some of the ways that Industry 4.0 can help lessen the effects of the COVID-19 pandemic:

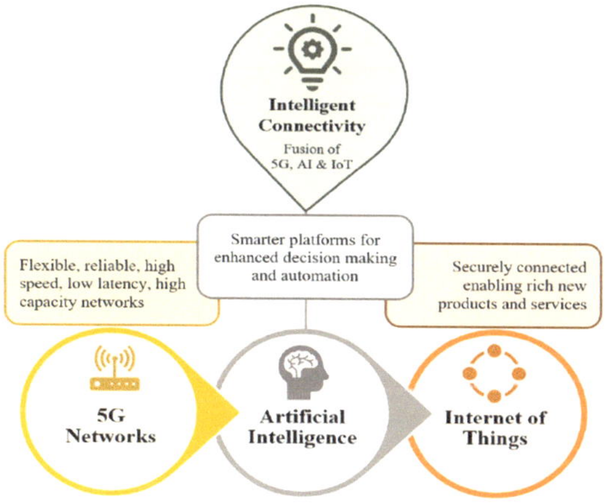

Figure 2.
The intelligent wireless edge innovation, integrating 5G connectivity with IoT and AI, that brings new and enhanced services.

- Planning activities related to COVID-19; giving patients and healthcare professionals better services;
- Making medical items that have to do with the pandemic;
- Creating an intelligent healthcare system;
- Using robots to treat patients to reduce risks and make the work environment more flexible;
- Putting virtual reality and augmented reality to the test for training;
- Helping people do the work they need to do to live during the lockdown;
- Using advanced digital technologies to come up with many new ideas;
- During the pandemic, taking care of local and global public health emergencies;
- Helping students and researchers find strange information.

Artificial intelligence (AI), including machine learning and deep learning, the Internet of things, big data and e-health, virtual reality (VR) and augmented reality (AR), holography, cloud computing, robots and robotics, 3D scanning and printing, biosensor, blockchain, smart devices/sensors, online digital platforms, are some of Industry 4.0's powerful technologies that could be useful during this pandemic. Digital technology has significantly altered almost every aspect of human life in the last few years, including how we communicate, work, enjoy, travel, bank, and shop. Nowadays, advanced digital technologies allow for the explosive expansion of the potential of diverse diagnostic and therapeutic instruments and systems [36]. Implementing digital medical technologies can improve the general public's healthcare accessibility and adaptability. Digital technology is currently a great way to support teaching and learning processes in institutions like schools and colleges. Therefore, rather than being driven by a particular technology, the effective use of digital technology is determined by learning and teaching goals. It enhances interactions between teachers and students. The COVID-19 pandemic clearly illustrates online education's importance for teaching and learning. Today's communication is entirely dependent on digital technology. Many digital tools facilitate communication between two or more parties. These include email, phone calls, video conferencing, social media, blogs, news portals, forums, and chat and instant messaging via smart devices. It is the most convenient method of communication, as anyone can have a real-time conversation with people from around the world without leaving their desks. The phenomenon of the digital revolution is gaining increasing attention in tourism management. This industry is undergoing digital transformations, including Tourism 4.0 and Smart Tourism [37]. Consequently, the physical structure is labeled "smart" to describe the integration of the physical and digital worlds, such as smartphones, smartcards, smartTV, and smart cities.

Using cutting-edge technologies, media companies can create an efficient end-to-end strategy for developing digital platforms for users. With the development of computer-mediated digital technologies, significant portions of the media and entertainment industries can become a reality. Over the past few years, the entertainment sector has undergone significant digital innovations. Future banking will be transformed by digital technology. The rise in AI, blockchain, and IoT demand has promoted the development of modernizing the banking industry. Banking is undergoing technological disruption due to increased competition from fin-tech startups and growing concern about cybersecurity. The digital revolution is a big chance for the agricultural sector to become more productive and advanced. Farmers can use digital technologies to make their farms more productive and develop long-term solutions to climate change. A smart city is a model for urban development that uses digital technologies to make city operations and services more efficient. It improves life for the people who live there and helps the environment [38]. Almost every part of our daily lives is affected by digital technology. In the last few decades, it has given us new devices like smartwatches, tablets, and voice assistants that have changed our world and daily lives. Also, digital technology improves the safety and security of our homes and lifestyles.

3.1 AI approaches

AI can contribute to the coronavirus pandemic in various ways, including early detection, tracing, forecasting, diagnosis, projection, treatments and pharmaceuticals, and social management and services [22]. In healthcare applications, AI methods can be divided into two primary categories: (i) machine learning and deep learning approaches and (ii) natural language processing approaches. AI approaches, particularly machine learning models, have the potential to benefit human civilizations and healthcare systems in the fight against the worldwide pandemic. In healthcare, machine learning techniques provide enormous prospects. These technologies can be used to develop effective strategies and aid scientists and medical professionals in addressing and resolving the difficulties presented by the coronavirus pandemic crisis. Many companies have recently introduced a range of AI skills, including those for outbreak estimation, coronavirus detection, diagnosis, analysis of data and treatment methods, drug development, research, and future outbreak prediction. Moreover, the term “AI” refers to a collection of technologies [39] that have the potential to significantly advance the field of healthcare (see **Figure 3**).

The three terms “artificial intelligence,” “machine learning,” and “deep learning” can occasionally be used interchangeably, which frequently causes misunderstanding among nontechnologists [40]. The phrase “artificial intelligence” refers to a vast, established, and highly developed area of computer science study that addresses issues relating to machine intelligence, such as simulating cognitive functions, detecting the environment, and acting independently. Robotics, vision, natural languages, learning, planning, reasoning, and other areas of study are now being studied. Deep learning, or neural network, is a machine learning model used in clinical data analysis and disease identification [41]. Moreover, data mining and statistics are involved in machine learning, where a decision model is learned rather than explicitly programmed by a person. Traditional machine learning methods can handle issues with hundreds or thousands of features, such as decision trees and support vector machines. **Figure 4** illustrates how a machine learning model works in data analysis and prediction. Problems related to computer vision, natural language processing, speech and image recognition, time series analysis, etc. have succeeded when deep learning techniques have been used. With their ability to interpret data effectively, deep learning model can improve their capacity to identify correlations and connections as they analyze additional data, basically learning from prior findings in the healthcare industry [42].

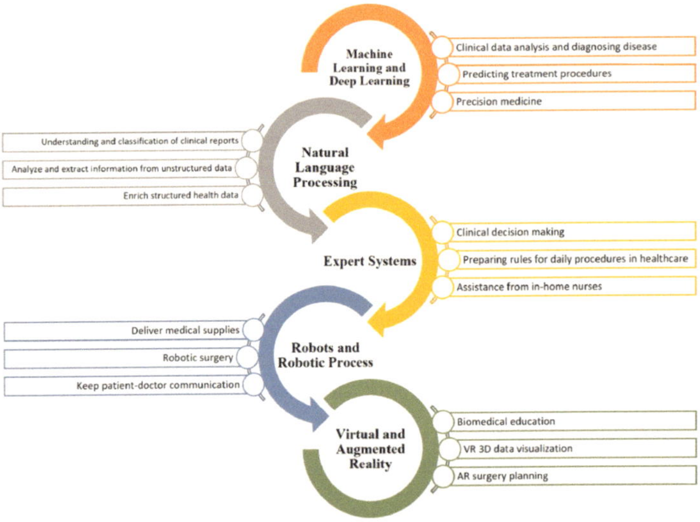

Figure 3.
Major AI-related technologies in healthcare applications.

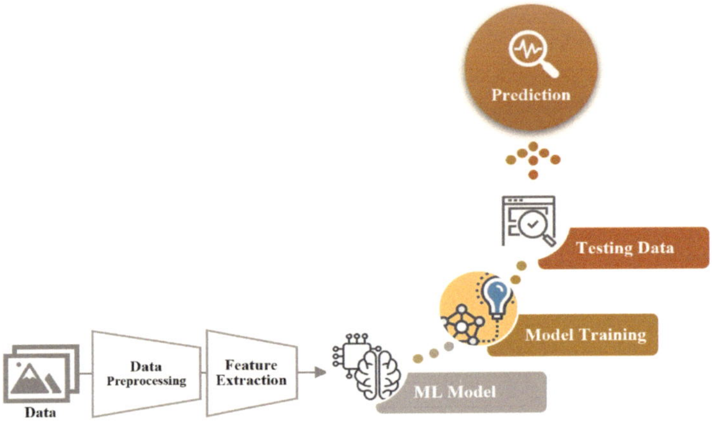

Figure 4.
How does a typical machine learning model work?

A convolutional neural network (CNN) is one sort of deep learning (see **Figure 5**) that is particularly well suited to interpreting images, such as MRI data and X-rays. This CNN model can assist medical personnel in detecting health issues in their patients more quickly, accurately, and reliably. Furthermore, deep learning models can assess structured and unstructured data in electronic health records, such as clinical notes, laboratory test results, diagnoses, and prescriptions, at high speeds and with high accuracy. During the global outbreak, deep learning models were used by researchers in a variety of applications, including early COVID-19 detection and prediction, assessing chest X-ray or CT images, managing intensive care, risk analysis for COVID-19, and providing essential services.

Figure 6 illustrates the volume of text data (unstructured and structured) produced by healthcare organizations. Some of it is arranged or organized into particular

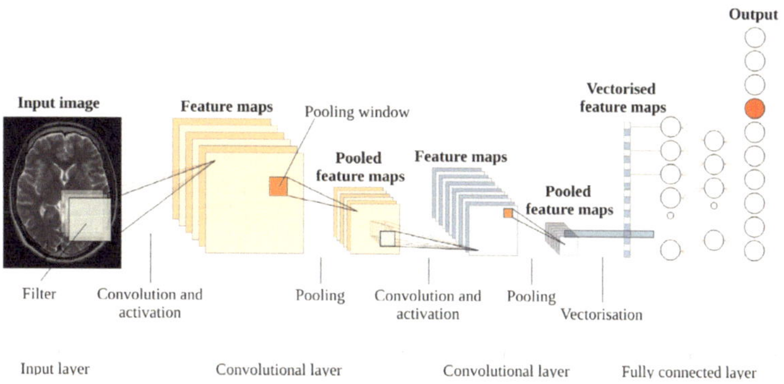

Figure 5.
Basic building blocks of a typical CNN model for interpreting medical image data, adapted from [43].

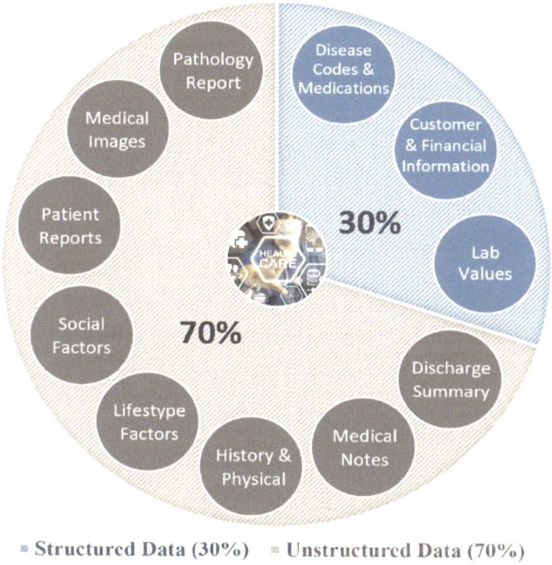

Figure 6.
Unstructured and structured data generated by healthcare organizations, adapted from [44].

EHR (electronic health record) fields [45]. With the help of this structure, medical professionals and other software programs may easily find, exchange, analyze, and utilize the data they need. However, a sizable portion of clinical data (about 70–80%) is still retained in narrative reports, patient records, observations, and other textual forms. To find the information they need from textual documents, clinicians must manually go through mountains of paperwork. It causes obstacles in administrative processes and emergencies, resulting in hiccups and delays in medical care. Additionally, EHRs receive a lot of unstructured patient data, making it challenging for a system to assist doctors in gathering this crucial information.

Another AI model, known as "natural language processing (NLP)," helps computers understand and make sense of what people say and write or what it means. NLP can help us do many things, such as extracting information, turning unstructured data into structured data, putting documents into groups, and summarizing documents [46]. Two main types of algorithms used in NLP: (i) rule-based systems analyze text using pre-established grammatical rules, and (ii) machine learning models employ statistical techniques and acquire knowledge over time by being fed training data. NLP uses free-text medical information to figure out the best ways to treat medical conditions. The use of NLP tools in healthcare offers the ability to accurately give voice to the healthcare industry's unstructured data, yielding considerable insight into comprehending quality, refining methodologies, and improving patient outcomes. Most modern NLP techniques can understand and analyze data with little or no preprocessing [47]. The following are the critical usage cases:

A. Text Classification: An NLP technique can assist in categorizing vast amounts of unstructured health data, such as organizing patient application forms by urgency or detecting fraudulent claims.

B. Information Extraction: NLP tools can extract useful information from unstructured health data. The technology, for example, can tag data from patient histories, discharge summaries, or call center reports and then organize them in an EHR according to a schema.

C. Improving Clinical Documentation: At the level of care, NLP uses speech-to-text dictation and structured data entry to extract crucial data from EHR. As a result, physicians can concentrate on treating patients with the necessary care while ensuring that clinical data is accurate and up to date.

D. Accelerating Clinical Trial Matching: Using NLP, healthcare providers may search through massive volumes of unstructured clinical and patient data to locate qualified persons for clinical trials.

E. Supporting Clinical Decisions: NLP enables physicians to access health-related information quickly, easily, and efficiently, allowing them to make more informed decisions at the point of treatment.

F. Language Modeling: Using NLP techniques, one may comprehend spoken text and generate natural sounding writing. The software can transcribe medical notes accurately, summarize them, or classify and extract data.

3.2 5G-powered emerging technologies

The latest 5G mobile networks have excellent technical characteristics, including faster transfer speeds of up to 20 Gbps, ultrareliable low latency (less than a millisecond), enhanced network security, massive machine-to-machine communications, and improved device energy efficiency. The deployment of 5G networks will expand wireless broadband services far beyond mobile Internet to more sophisticated Internet of things systems. These systems have the low latency and high-reliability level required to handle critical applications in all significant industries. The advent of 5G mobile networks will facilitate the development of novel applications in the medical industry [9]. The provision of a platform for inventive uses that enable segmented degrees of latency will be made possible by enhanced broadband experiences, large-scale Internet of things networks, and mission-critical services. Even while edge computing can be employed in a 4G context, coupling this with 5G networks and AI is likely to open up new possibilities in accelerating the adoption of Industry 4.0. The deployment of 5G networks makes it feasible to construct "smart factories" and reap the benefits of technologies such as automation and robotics, artificial intelligence, computer vision, augmented reality, and the Internet of things in various disciplines and applications.

In addition, it is projected that the 5G technology would connect billions of devices while improving their functionality. Applications that are supported by 5G have the potential to deliver transformative impacts in a variety of industries, including healthcare, education, resource management, transportation, agriculture, and other sectors, to address the challenges brought about by the current pandemic [48]. **Figure 7** depicts the industries that make the most use of 5G-powered emerging technologies and provides an estimate for the amount of income that digital markets will generate in the year 2026 [49]. Since the year 2020, the entire world has been experiencing a health disaster. The use of 5G in conjunction with other sophisticated digital technologies is an assistance in the fight against the issues posed by the coronavirus in many countries [50]. This cutting-edge 5G technology will revolutionize fast connection, storage in the cloud, billions of intelligent gadgets, and improved medical services in the healthcare field. As a result, 5G will revolutionize the healthcare industry and add more than 1.1 trillion USD to the global economy by 2035 [51].

5G technology has the potential to assist in medical research, diagnosis, and treatment, and improving healthcare services for both medical professionals and patients remotely [52]. **Figure 8** depicts a straightforward 5G-based health platform that can be useful to patients and medical practitioners. Since 5G promises superspeed with large data bandwidth and low latency (around 100 Mbs), AI technologies deployed in 5G networks can enable intelligent and autonomous functionality to control the coronavirus outbreak. According to a report by IHS Market Ltd. [53], 5G would make it possible for the global healthcare industry to sell more than one trillion dollars worth of goods and services by 2020. In addition, it is anticipated that the 5G network will accommodate approximately 212 billion sensors and about 50 billion smart devices [54]. These health gadgets, medical wearables, and remote sensors in 5G networks all efficiently contribute to healthcare to assist the health emergency difficulties that the

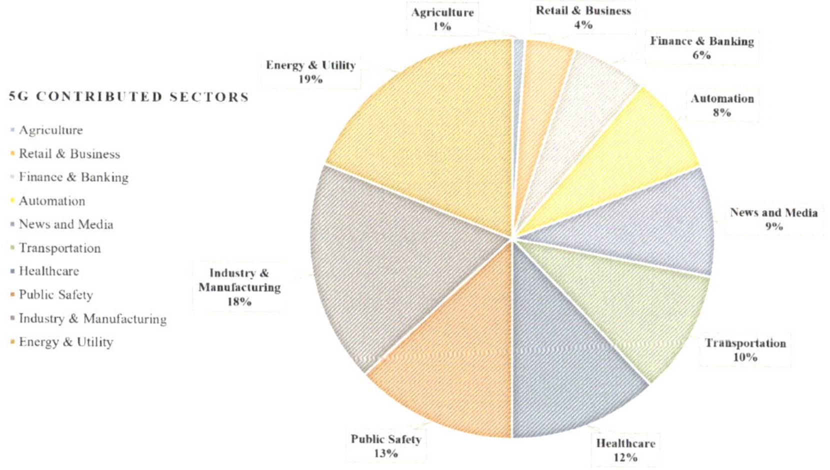

Figure 7.
Industries that make the most use of 5G-powered emerging technologies, adapted from [49].

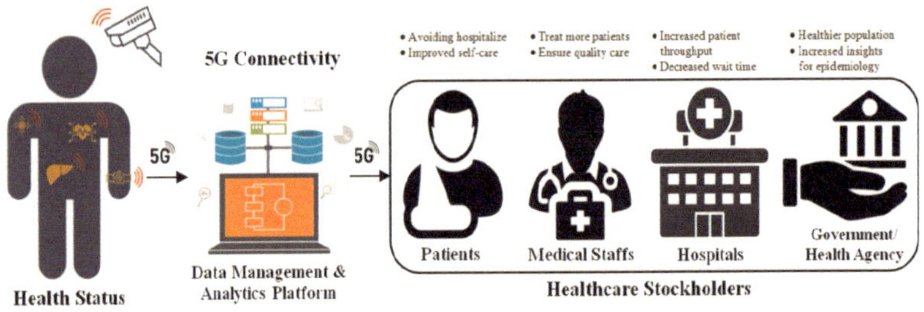

Figure 8.
A typical 5G-powered health framework for distant treatment and services, adapted from [20].

COVID-19 outbreak has produced. Now, the healthcare industry is implementing digital technologies with 5G connectivity that can provide health services and improve the quality of life and the experiences of medical personnel and patients. It is anticipated that the expansion of this technology will achieve a compound annual growth rate of 16.5% from 2019 until 2023 [55].

5G connectivity is improving healthcare services in various ways [56], including facilitating home healthcare, digitizing pathological analysis, managing patient information files, robotic surgery and medications, training, and therapeutics, securing staff-patient communication and management, etc. The favorable characteristics of 5G also significantly impact future healthcare research and the advancement of treatment. In today's world, cutting-edge digital technologies are transforming the healthcare industry. The promising digital technologies powered by the 5G standard have aided the public health schemes to fix the shortcomings in healthcare services and to confront the coronavirus epidemic [57]. **Figure 9** illustrates some of the characteristics of the 5G technology that can bring about significant breakthroughs in the medical field [58]. The following paragraphs provide further explanations of these aspects.

A. Telemedicine: It demands a network connection that is dependable as well as speedier, and it must be able to provide high-quality video and real-time conversation. 5G standards make it possible to create a suitable telemedicine environment, enhancing online health consultancy [59]. The market for telemedicine in the healthcare sector is anticipated to expand at a rate of 16.5% each year from 2017 to 2023 [55].

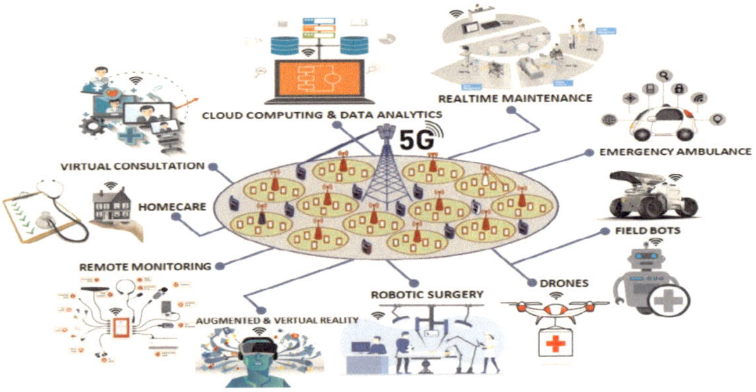

Figure 9.
Few aspects of 5G interconnected technologies in healthcare to tackle the pandemic, adapted from [20].

B. Telesurgery: Telesurgery and other forms of remote medical care are made possible by 5G's extremely low latency and lightning-fast speeds. A health surgeon in China was the first to undertake a 5G-assisted remote surgery utilizing "da Vinci surgical robots" [60] in January 2019 that was performed on an animal. In China in March of 2019, telesurgery was conducted remotely on a human brain utilizing a 5G mobile network.

C. Internet of Medical Things: The infrastructure of 5G networks can connect one billion digital devices and wearable medical equipment, also known as the "Internet of medical things (IoMT)" objects, which creates a bridge between the digital and physical worlds and enables real-time analytics to improve patient's health. It can collect important health data, store it in the cloud, and make it available online for users, medical professionals, and researchers [61].

D. Remote Diagnosis and Treatment: 5G connectivity assists healthcare professionals in continuously monitoring contagion and a remote diagnosis from any location throughout the pandemic [62]. In January 2020, China was the first country to develop a 5G-powered remote diagnosis and treatment system. During the pandemic, this device can assist with the diagnosis and treatment of patients remotely.

E. 5G-Powered Digitized Platforms: Numerous technologically established nations, including the United States, China, Japan, and South Korea, are rapidly launching their own specific 5G wireless networks for digitalized, data-driven, and cloud-based emergency platforms [63]. These digital platforms aid healthcare in various ways, including accelerated reaction times, remote monitoring, data analysis and diagnosis, resource allocation, and many others.

4. Challenges and prospective

AI technologies are growing as emerging digital innovations in the healthcare industry. In addition, the 5G network's real-time superspeed and extremely low latency offer a variety of new prospects to serve developing healthcare applications. In the context of healthcare services during the current pandemic, the following subsections discuss the principal difficulties and opportunities presented by AI and 5G-enabled technologies.

4.1 Key challenges faced by AI

Though AI, including machine learning, has fantastic capabilities in healthcare in fighting against the epidemic, this field also has a few limitations or challenges in improving the current healthcare systems. Therefore, this study also addresses some challenges faced by AI in healthcare that are listed below:

A. Require a high volume of relevant data for AI: Finding rich health data is one of the biggest challenges of using AI in healthcare. AI algorithms cannot be fully trusted until they are built and trained on a large amount of relevant data in healthcare applications. Thus, AI depends on various data gathered from millions of people who have suffered from similar conditions. It must require sufficient data on a particular group of such patients in AI databases to make the correct comparison. But enough data on patients is often challenging to find from a specific background. Moreover, medical data has a sensitive nature and ethical constraints that make it challenging to collect. In this case, AI will make an inaccurate diagnosis with insufficient data, and doctors might make a mistake in taking proper treatment.

B. Need a better understanding of applying AI: AI models are becoming increasingly complex to achieve better results. Because of its intricacy, AI sometimes operates in a "black box," which makes it more challenging to comprehend how the model functions. Therefore, healthcare professionals must frequently understand how and why AI produces specific results to behave appropriately. The absence of explanation raises concerns about reliability for individuals and the healthcare companies they use. Methods of "Explainable Artificial Intelligence (XAI)" [64] can tackle this issue and develop trust between humans and computers by clarifying the processes through which they arrive at particular solutions.

C. Need more testing and verification of AI: Though AI can offer more accurate diagnostics, there is a chance of making mistakes. So, it causes individuals and companies to falter about implementing AI approaches in diagnosis. For example, hundreds of AI systems and tools have been built during the pandemic to diagnose COVID-19 cases. But many of them failed to provide accurate diagnosis results or caused errors [65]. Moreover, if the AI models are not adequately trained or trained on poor-quality data, these do not accurately represent its underlying real-world process to prevent diagnostic errors. Thus, proper testing and verification with the right and representative data must be ensured without underfitting or overfitting against the training data [66].

D. Invest in data privacy mechanisms for AI: Patient data includes sensitive data, such as medical history, identity, and payment information. So, people who use AI systems need to keep in mind that they are dealing with machines. AI systems have enabled the tracking of a patient's personal information and health/test reports. A person can promise privacy between a doctor and a patient, but machines cannot do that, and machines can break down. This problem can cause the system to fail or cause data to be lost. It can also hand over control of the system to the wrong people, who can easily use the information against the people involved. It often happens when the AI system is not safe enough from hackers. The healthcare industry needs to use technologies that improve privacy to get the most out of AI while minimizing the risks [67].

E. Require training or education for AI: Though the rise of AI technology replaces routine tasks and opens up new job opportunities, it causes a slowdown in the industry's adoption of AI. Even though AI tools can make many technical and nontechnical jobs more efficient, they still require human expertise. Some diagnostic procedures, for example, are hard to understand and require a lot of work. So, healthcare organizations should give their workers the training they need to learn more about machine learning and how it can be used. On the other hand, when people see new technologies and tools, it can make them think twice. Another big problem with using AI in healthcare is that patients do not always want to use it. For example, in the early stages of the pandemic, patients did not feel comfortable with online checkups. So, it needs to teach patients about the benefits of AI in healthcare to help them feel more comfortable with it.

4.2 Key challenges faced by 5G technology

As we move toward a 5G world, we'll have to deal with many problems. Compared to older wireless technologies, 5G needs a new standard to provide customers with high-speed, low latency, reliable, and safe services. Because of this, the design, development, and implementation of 5G networks are full of big problems. Here are some other issues that have been found in the literature:

A. Health Risks: Concerns have been raised regarding possible adverse effects on human health caused by radiofrequency from 5G networks [68]. Rural residents are raising esthetic concerns and anxieties about the superfast network's effects on their communities. However, a large number of institutions, such as the US "National Institutes of Health" and "Food and Drug Administration," as well as the "World Health Organization" and the "Federal Communications Commission," concluded that the concerns were unfounded.

B. 5G's Range and Coverage: The range of the 5G network is reduced when there are obstructions in the network. Therefore, to obtain a better 5G signal, 5G networks need a more significant number of smaller devices or antennae spaced closely together. It is tough to set up 5G connectivity in rural areas because of this, which are the places with the least developed healthcare systems.

C. Deployment Costs: For 5G-enabled health solutions to work well, there needs to be a good setup for patients, doctors, and clinics. So, the costs of setting up 5G, buying related devices, developing the infrastructure, and paying more for maintenance are big problems in 5G-powered applications. As a result, it makes sense that the patient will have to pay more for their treatment.

D. Training and Adapting New Technology: 5G-powered health solutions are gradually being implemented using intelligent devices and tools. However, healthcare personnel and patients require knowledge and skills to implement new technology and practices. As a result, sufficient training is required for patients and medical personnel to understand how to use these new platforms. Moreover, many developing countries cannot ultimately adopt an innovative healthcare solution based on the 5G standard, particularly in rural locations where building 5G networks is challenging.

E. Security and Privacy Threats: Because 5G is gifted with the quickest data transmission and provides other healthcare services remotely, there is a continuous rise in the variety of potential security and privacy threats. As a result, it is necessary to pay additional attention to the concerns regarding the security of 5G networks, such as the protection of data, devices, and infrastructure; the filtering of data and the management of digital rights; the confidentiality of patient data; national security, network security, cybersecurity, and the protection of cybercrime [69, 70].

4.3 Prospective of AI and 5G-enabled technologies

AI and 5G-enabled technologies are concurrently expanding and enhancing efforts to improve global healthcare. Patients throughout the world benefit from more advanced healthcare systems that include intelligence and 5G standard in their practices. Thus, the fundamental aspects of healthcare could be entirely reimagined by the capabilities of 5G. 5G-powered technologies may prove helpful in many facets of today's healthcare, such as telehealth, remote surgery, the transfer of substantial medical records, tracking patient activities and real-time monitoring, and providing patients with proper treatment and support. This technology can provide vital services on a massive scale that are precise, efficient, convenient, and cost-effective. The following are many significant prospects that explain why technology enabled by 5G ought to be a component of every healthcare system across the globe.

A. Fastest and Precise Health Services: The fastest 5G network is equipped to provide the speedy and dependable delivery of significant amounts of medical data. The reduced latency feature of 5G technology can allow surgeons to do remote robotic surgery and give patients quicker and more dependable treatment that can be delivered remotely. In addition, AI can forecast potential health issues that a person may have in the future.

B. Real-Time Advancements in Healthcare: The advent of 5G technology has the potential to provide individualized and preventative medical care. Telemedicine enabled by AI and 5G networks make it possible to receive immediate medical advice and treatment for medical emergencies. Therefore, with the 5G network, AI approaches can give surgeons real-time information about patients who are now undergoing treatment. In addition, a completely operational 5G network will improve medical processes and management and deliver a high-quality treatment experience to patients and doctors.

C. Integration of Innovative Technologies: The use of AI models, with the "Internet of medical things," "augmented reality," and "virtual reality," is now permitted in healthcare apps that run on 5G networks. They can improve real-time treatment and diagnosis operations, as well as provide healthcare facilities that are novel and transformative. Besides, robot-assisted or robotic surgery powered by 5G is becoming an emerging thing of the future in the medical field.

D. Meet Service Quality and Cost-Effectiveness: 5G-powered technologies like "mHealth technology," "telemedicine," "Internet of medical things," "wearable devices," and "digital health platforms" can help patients in both cities and rural areas get medical help from afar. It will save money by preventing costly trips to the hospital without lowering the quality of care. It will also let doctors help with the diagnosis from a distance and meet the service standards needed for a complete medical exam. AI and machine learning can also help doctors diagnose by finding biomarkers [71]. If practitioners use AI to make an accurate diagnosis, it will be less cost-effective, and individuals will not have to undergo expensive lab tests anymore.

E. Advancements in Intervention Management and Administrative Operations: 5G-enabled healthcare systems will bring new insights to the healthcare industry, allowing for uninterrupted data entry and querying. As a result, it is an annoying procedure while documenting medical data. Making available critical healthcare facilities and equipment, like operating rooms and electrocardiogram (ECG) monitors, improves intervention management. These invaluable resources aid in the administration of government operations and guarantee their security and efficacy.

F. Improving Accessibility of Healthcare Worldwide: The World Bank and the WHO have released reports indicating that at least half of the world population does not have access to elementary healthcare services. In addition, people living in rural areas of countries that lack a developed healthcare infrastructure do not have access to healthcare facilities. Many organizations utilize cutting-edge technology powered by 5G to provide medical treatment to underserved communities. These solutions are both cost-free and applicable even in rural areas for serving medical treatment.

5. Policy recommendations to the states

Universal accessibility of 5G-enabled technologies depends on the state's positive measures and various factors (such as socioeconomic, geographic location, and digital ecosystem). Currently, a number of organizations are creating digital frameworks and other ideas to bridge the digital gap. For considering the post-pandemic, we are suggested a few recommendations to the states, listed below.

A. Enhancing digital literacy programs: From a human rights point of view, the states need to speed up the process of making short-term and long-term public policies to improve digital literacy programs. During the pandemic, it will also support digital health-education-works measures that make it possible for everyone to be self-sufficient, independent, and responsible when using AI and 5G-enabled technologies. But digital technologies could limit the right to privacy and other fundamental freedoms. So, states must ensure that laws set up a guideline for the digital environment.

B. Diminishing risks of increased digital devices and activities: During the pandemic, one's spending time with digital devices (like smartphones, computers, television, or video game console) is increasing. In case of problematic usages of digital technologies, it needs practical recommendations to help reduce the risks of increased use of digital devices and online activities. Professionals and policymakers must convey these recommendations to their clients and the general population.

C. Improving safety and security: The coronavirus pandemic has demonstrated the transformative power of the Internet, and digital technology has saved millions of lives by allowing them to work, study, and interact online in safety. Unfortunately, the epidemic has also exacerbated the digital divide and the negative aspects of technology, such as the rapid dissemination of misinformation, cybercrime, cyberbullying, and digital violence. It requires maintaining a high emphasis on security in government policies and regulations. Authorities and network operators should protect online data flows and maintain Internet users' and organizations' trust. Therefore, states and policymakers must guarantee a secure digital environment for the public.

D. Ensuring permanent and sustainable accessibility: Since 2019, the pandemic has highlighted the significance of digital technologies during a crisis. The internet platform has enabled millions of individuals to work and study remotely. We may emerge from this crisis with the knowledge that appropriate digital policies can promote global economic recovery and ensure that no one is left behind. States and officials must ensure that access is permanent and enduring, eliminate obstacles to community-driven connectivity, and make it easy for all groups to access resources.

6. Conclusion

In healthcare, using 5G networks to integrate other digital technologies (such as AI and machine learning, IoT, big data analytics, and cloud computing) is now a reality. The results of this study are summed up, and a deep connection with 5G-enabled technologies, especially artificial intelligence and machine learning. This study aims to find out the existing technological facets of AI strategies that can be used in healthcare to deal with the pandemic. This book chapter addresses several challenges faced by implementing AI and 5G-enabled technologies in medical services and highlights the prospects of emerging technologies. AI has played a significant role in combating the coronavirus pandemic and assisting researchers in developing systems to limit human interaction in afflicted areas, provide services, and manage health emergencies. In addition, they can help with the legal and ethical difficulties associated with producing medications in response to public health emergencies.

Future pandemic concerns and public health issues will necessitate the most effective and convincing AI methods, AI-based searching strategies, probabilistic models, and supervised learning. Thus, professionals must thoroughly understand the system they are utilizing and be aware of its security measures. Even if artificial intelligence and 5G-enabled technologies have many benefits for healthcare, AI will not replace doctors or other professionals; instead, it will improve their performance. Additionally, 5G-enabled digital technologies have been utilized to control the COVID-19 outbreak and enhance public health plans in 2020. Some advanced technology leaders are studying 5G-related applications to tackle the health hazards associated with undesired diseases. The 5G network will give a comprehensive road to a smart society with numerous potentially beneficial applications in the field of healthcare when combined with the latest technology advancements.

When deploying the 5G network in healthcare, some issues need to be considered since it is a new field of research. These issues include the development of infrastructure, the establishment of technical standards, the implementation of efficient regulations and policies, the safeguarding of personal information, and the accessibility of research data. More studies need to be done on how to expand a digital society based on 5G while addressing some challenges such as safety, security, privacy, availability, accessibility, and integrity, and improving resilience to future health crises, which lead to the following research directions in fighting against future pandemics:

- To develop the specialized AI and 5G-based architectures, along with the Internet of things and big data that will solve issues related to epidemics and build a comprehensive system to respond to crises similar to the COVID-19 pandemic.

- To modernize the medical industry that will be aided by applying AI and 5G-enabled technologies to support decision-making, drug development and therapy, administrative automation, and storing patient information in private clouds.

- To digitize the patients-doctors communication by implementing natural language processing, speech recognition, and text recognition that could be used to assist patients and physicians in communicating with one another and analyzing clinical records during remote treatment.

- To build centralized and comprehensive databases that will be helpful for the investigation of technical issues and for constructing intelligent systems for predicting, diagnosing, forecasting, transmissibility, pathogenicity, and treating the disease.

Acknowledgements

The authors wish to acknowledge the research and extension cell of Jatiya Kabi Kazi Nazrul Islam University, Bangladesh, for their support and cooperation in conducting the research.

Conflict of interest

The authors declare no conflict of interest.

Author details

Md. Mijanur Rahman[1*†] and Fatema Khatun[2†]

1 Department of Computer Science and Engineering, Jatiya Kabi Kazi Nazrul Islam University, Trishal, Mymensingh, Bangladesh

2 Department of Electrical and Electronic Engineering, Bangabandhu Sheikh Mujibur Rahman Science and Technology University, Gopalganj, Bangladesh

*Address all correspondence to: mijan@jkkniu.edu.bd

† These authors contributed equally.

References

[1] Ting DS, Lin H, Ruamviboonsuk P, et al. Artificial intelligence, the internet of things, and virtual clinics: Ophthalmology at the digital translation forefront. The Lancet Digital Health. 2020;**2**(1):e8-e9

[2] Shilo S, Rossman H, Segal E. Axes of a revolution: Challenges and promises of big data in healthcare. Nature Medicine. 2020;**26**(1):29-38

[3] LeCun Y, Bengio Y, Hinton G. Deep learning. Nature. 2015;**521**(7553):436-444

[4] Nguyen DC, Ding M, Pathirana PN, Seneviratne A. Blockchain and AI-based solutions to combat coronavirus (COVID-19)-like epidemics: A survey. IEEE Access. 2021;**9**:95730-95753

[5] Christie L. 5G technology. UK Parliament POST. 2019. Available from: https://post.parliament.uk/research-briefings/post-pb-0032/

[6] Segan S. What is 5G? PCMag Asia. 2020. Available from: https://www.pcmag.com/news/what-is-5g

[7] Bass B. GSMA: Asia Set to Become World's Largest 5G Region by 2025. London, UK: GSM Association. 2018

[8] Ghosh I. Visualizing the state of 5G networks worldwide. In: Visual Capitalist, Technology. 2020. Available from: https://www.visualcapitalist.com/visualizing-the-state-of-5g-networks-worldwide/

[9] West DM. How 5G technology enables the health internet of things. Brookings Center for Technology Innovation. 2016;**3**:1-20

[10] Agiwal M, Roy A, Saxena N. Next generation 5G wireless networks: A comprehensive survey. IEEE Communications Surveys Tutorials. 2016;**18**(3):1617-1655

[11] Perez S. App stores saw record 204 billion app downloads in 2019, consumer spend of $120 billion. TechCrunch. 2020. Available from: https://techcrunch.com/2020/01/15/app-stores-saw-record-204-billion-app-downloads-in-2019-consumer-spend-of-120-billion/

[12] Kemp S. Digital 2020: Global Digital Overview. Available from: https://datareportal.com/reports/digital–global-digital-overview

[13] Wang C, Horby PW, Hayden FG, et al. A novel coronavirus outbreak of global health concern. The Lancet. 2020; **395**:470-473

[14] Zhou P et al. A pneumonia outbreak associated with a new coronavirus of probable bat origin. Nature. 2020;**579** (7798):270-273

[15] Sohrabi C et al. World Health Organization declares global emergency: A review of the 2019 novel coronavirus (COVID-19). International Journal of Surgery. 2020;**76**:71-76

[16] Worldometers. COVID-19 Coronavirus Pandemic. 2022. Available from: https://www.worldometers.info/coronavirus/

[17] Ahmed W, Vidal-Alaball J, Downing J, et al. COVID-19 and the 5G conspiracy theory: Social network analysis of twitter data. Journal of Medical Internet Research. 2020;**22**(5):e19458

[18] Amgain K, Neupane S, Panthi L, et al. Myths versus truths regarding the novel coronavirus disease (COVID-2019)

outbreak. Journal of Karnali Academy of Health Sciences. 2020;**3**(1):1-6

[19] Kostoff RN, Heroux P, Aschner M, et al. Adverse health effects of 5G mobile networking technology under real-life conditions. Toxicology Letters. 2020; **323**:35-40

[20] Rahman MM, Khatun F, Sami SI, Uzzaman A. The evolving roles and impacts of 5G enabled technologies in healthcare: The world epidemic COVID-19 issues. Array. 2022;**14**:100178

[21] Rahman MM, Khatun F, Uzzaman A, Sami SI, Bhuiyan MA-A, Kiong TS. A comprehensive study of artificial intelligence and machine learning approaches in confronting the coronavirus (COVID-19) pandemic. International Journal of Health Services. 2021;**51**(4):446-461

[22] Naudé W. Artificial Intelligence against COVID-19: An Early Review. IZA Discussion Paper. 13110; 2020. https://covid-19.iza.org/publications/dp13110/

[23] Jiang F et al. Artificial intelligence in healthcare: Past, present and future. Stroke Vascular Neurology. 2017; **2**(4):230-243

[24] Soussi MB, Hadjila M, Merzougui R. A novel m-health system for epidemic tracking and prediction using big data and electronic health record. In: 2020 4th International Symposium on Informatics and its Applications (ISIA). M'sila, Algeria: IEEE; 2020. pp. 1-7

[25] Maghded HS, Ghafoor KZ, Sadiq AS, et al. A novel AI-enabled framework to diagnose coronavirus COVID-19 using smartphone embedded sensors: Design study. In: 2020 IEEE 21st International Conference on Information Reuse and Integration for Data Science (IRI). Las Vegas, NV, USA: IEEE; 2020. pp. 180-187

[26] Li L et al. Using artificial intelligence to detect COVID-19 and community-acquired pneumonia based on pulmonary CT: evaluation of the diagnostic accuracy. Radiology. 2020; **296**(2):E65-E71

[27] Wang L, Lin ZQ, Wong A. Covid-net: A tailored deep convolutional neural network design for detection of covid-19 cases from chest x-ray images. Scientific Reports. 2020;**10**(1):1-12

[28] Xu X et al. A deep learning system to screen novel coronavirus disease 2019 pneumonia. Engineering. 2020;**6**(10): 1122-1129

[29] Narin A, Kaya C, Pamuk Z. Automatic detection of coronavirus disease (covid-19) using x-ray images and deep convolutional neural networks. Pattern Analysis Applications. 2021;**24**(3):1207-1220

[30] Rahmatizadeh S, Valizadeh-Haghi S, Dabbagh A. The role of artificial intelligence in management of critical COVID-19 patients. Journal of Cellular Molecular Anesthesia. 2020;**5**(1):16-22

[31] Vaishya R, Javaid M, Khan IH, et al. Artificial intelligence (AI) applications for COVID-19 pandemic. Diabetes Metabolic Syndrome: Clinical Research Reviews. 2020;**14**(4):337-339

[32] Javaid M, Haleem A, Vaishya R, et al. Industry 4.0 technologies and their applications in fighting COVID-19 pandemic. Diabetes Metabolic Syndrome: Clinical Research Reviews. 2020;**14**(4):419-422

[33] Mishra S, Takke A, Auti S, et al. Role of artificial intelligence in health care.

BioChemistry: An Indian Journal. 2017; **11**(5):1-14

[34] Javaid M, Haleem A. Industry 4.0 applications in medical field: A brief review. Current Medicine Research Practice. 2019;**9**(3):102-109

[35] Fisher D, Wilder-Smith A. The global community needs to swiftly ramp up the response to contain COVID-19. Lancet. 2020;**395**(10230):1109

[36] Mitchell M, Kan L. Digital technology and the future of health systems. Health Systems Reform. 2019;**5** (2):113-120

[37] Bouronikos V. How digital Technology in Tourism is affecting the way we travel. Institute of Entrepreneurship Development. 2021. Available from: https://ied.eu/blog/how-digital-technology-in-tourism-is-affecting-the-way-we-travel/

[38] Momot T, Muraev Y. Model of organizational and information support of smart city strategy development in the conditions of digital economy. Innovative Technologies Scientific Solutions for Industries. 2021;**1**(15): 83-90

[39] Davenport T, Kalakota R. The potential for artificial intelligence in healthcare. Future Healthcare Journal. 2019;**6**(2):94

[40] Williams D, Hornung H, Nadimpalli A, Peery A. Deep learning and its application for healthcare delivery in low and middle income countries. Frontiers in Artificial Intelligence. 2021;**4**:30

[41] Vial A et al. The role of deep learning and radiomic feature extraction in cancer-specific predictive modelling: A review. Translational Cancer Research. 2018;**7**(3):803-816

[42] Bresnick J. What is deep learning and how will it change healthcare? Health IT Analytics. 2018. Available from: https://healthitanalytics.com/features/what-is-deep-learning-and-how-will-it-change-healthcare

[43] Lundervold AS, Lundervold A. An overview of deep learning in medical imaging focusing on MRI. Zeitschrift für Medizinische Physik. 2019;**29**(2):102-127

[44] Linguamatics. Easily extract social determinants of health with multimission NLP. 2022. Available from: https://www.linguamatics.com/solutions/social-determinants-health-sdoh

[45] Rinty MR, Prodhan UK, Rahman MM. A prospective interoperable distributed e-health system with loose coupling in improving healthcare services for developing countries. Array. 2021;**13**(2022):1-13

[46] Murff HJ et al. Automated identification of postoperative complications within an electronic medical record using natural language processing. JAMA. 2011;**306**(8):848-855

[47] Rangasamy S, Rosanne N, Mahi R, Alex S. Natural language processing in healthcare. MicKinsey Company Healthcare Systems Services. 2018. Available from: https://www.mckinsey.com/industries/healthcare-systems-and-services/our-insights/natural-language-processing-in-healthcare

[48] Abubakar AI, Omeke KG, Öztürk M, Hussain S, Imran MA. The role of artificial intelligence driven 5G networks in COVID-19 outbreak: Opportunities, challenges, and future outlook. Frontiers in Communications. 2020;**1**:1-22

[49] Martynova O. Top Uses of 5G in the Energy Sector. Intellias: Global Technology Partner; 2019

[50] Ting DSW, Carin L, Dzau V, Wong TY. Digital technology and COVID-19. Nature Medicine. 2020;**26**(4):459-461

[51] Valencia R. Previewing 5G's Effect on the Health Care Industry. San Diego, California: Qualcomm Technologies, Inc; 2017

[52] Angelucci A, Kuller D, Aliverti A. A home telemedicine system for continuous respiratory monitoring. IEEE Journal of Biomedical Health Informatics. 2020;**25**(4):1247-1256

[53] Baskaran A. How will 5G impact different industries? PreScouter Newsletter. 2018. Available from: https://www.prescouter.com/2018/01/5g-impact-different-industries/

[54] Chang LF. Journey to 5G. In: 2019 International Symposium on VLSI Technology, Systems and Application (VLSI-TSA). Taiwan, China: IEEE; 2019. pp. 1-1

[55] Bekaroo G, Santokhee A, Augusto JC. 5G smart and innovative healthcare services: Opportunities, challenges, and prospective solutions. 5G Multimedia Communication: Technology, Multiservices, Deployment. 2020:279-297

[56] Latif S, Qadir J, Farooq S, Imran MA. How 5g wireless (and concomitant technologies) will revolutionize healthcare? Future Internet. 2017;**9**(4):93

[57] Soldani D. Fighting pandemics by exploiting 5G, AI and Bigdata enabled technologies: How 5G can help contain the spread of COVID-19. Journal of Telecommunications the Digital Economy. 2020;**8**(2):146

[58] Dananjayan S, Raj GM. 5G in healthcare: How fast will be the transformation? Irish Journal of Medical Science. 2021;**190**(2):497-501

[59] Jnr BA. Use of telemedicine and virtual care for remote treatment in response to COVID-19 pandemic. Journal of Medical Systems. 2020;**44**(7):1-9

[60] Cuthbertson A. Surgeon performs World's first remote operation using '5G Surgery'on animal in China. The Independent. 2019. Available from: https://www.independent.co.uk/tech/5g-surgery-china-robotic-operation-a8732861.html

[61] Singh RP, Javaid M, Haleem A, et al. Internet of medical things (IoMT) for orthopaedic in COVID-19 pandemic: Roles, challenges, and applications. Journal of Clinical Orthopaedics Trauma. 2020;**11**(4):713-717

[62] Liu L et al. Application and preliminary outcomes of remote diagnosis and treatment during the COVID-19 outbreak: Retrospective cohort study. JMIR mHealth and uHealth. 2020;**8**(7):e19417

[63] Ho CW-L, Caals K, Zhang H. Heralding the digitalization of life in post-pandemic east Asian societies. Journal of Bioethical Inquiry. 2020;**17**(4):657-661

[64] Adadi A, Berrada M. Peeking inside the black-box: A survey on explainable artificial intelligence (XAI). IEEE Access. 2018;**6**:52138-52160

[65] Heaven WD. Hundreds of AI tools have been built to catch covid. None of them helped. MIT Technology Review. 2021. Available from: https://www.technologyreview.com/2021/07/30/1030329/machine-learning-ai-failed-covid-hospital-diagnosis-pandemic/

[66] Koehrsen W. Overfitting vs. underfitting: A complete example. Towards Data Science. 2018. Available from: https://towardsdatascience.com/overfitting-vs-underfitting-a-complete-example-d05dd7e19765

[67] Jordan S, Fontaine C, Hendricks-Sturrup R. Selecting privacy-enhancing Technologies for Managing Health Data use. Frontiers in Public Health. 2022;**10**: 1-13

[68] Melnick RL. Commentary on the utility of the National Toxicology Program study on cell phone radiofrequency radiation data for assessing human health risks despite unfounded criticisms aimed at minimizing the findings of adverse health effects. Environmental Research. 2019;**168**:1-6

[69] Ahmad I, Kumar T, Liyanage M, et al. Overview of 5G security challenges and solutions. IEEE Communications Standards Magazine. 2018;**2**(1):36-43

[70] Ji X et al. Overview of 5G security technology. Science China Information Sciences. 2018;**61**(8):081301

[71] Yadav AK, Verma D, Kumar A, et al. The perspectives of biomarker-based electrochemical immunosensors, artificial intelligence and the internet of medical things toward COVID-19 diagnosis and management. Materials Today Chemistry. 2021;**20**:100443

Chapter 3

Critical Review on Internet of Things (IoT): Evolution and Components Perspectives

Benjamin Appiah Osei and Emmanuela Kwao-Boateng

Abstract

Technological advancement in recent years has transformed the internet to a network where everything is linked, and everyday objects can be recognised and controlled. This interconnection is popularly termed as the Internet of Things (IoT). Although, IoT remains popular in academic literature, limited studies have focused on its evolution, components, and implications for industries. Hence, the focus of this book chapter is to explore these dimensions, and their implications for industries. The study adopted the critical review method, to address these gaps in the IoT literature for service and manufacturing industries. Furthermore, the relevance for IoT for service and manufacturing industries were also discussed. While the impact of IoT in the next five years is expected to be high by industry practitioners, experts consider the current degree of its implementation across industry to be on the average. This critical review contributes theoretically to the literature on IoT. In effect, the intense implementation of the IoT, IIoT and IoS will go a long way in ensuring improvements in various industries that would in the long run positively impact the general livelihood of people as well as the way of doing things. Practical implications and suggestions for future studies have been discussed.

Keywords: internet of things, evolution, components, internet of services, industrial internet of things, fourth industrial revolution

1. Introduction

In the words of Schwab [1], "Internet of Things (IoT) is one of the main bridges between the physical and digital applications enabled by the fourth industrial revolution". The concept of IoT is more focused on enabling and accelerating the adoption of Internet-connected technologies across industries, both manufacturing and non-manufacturing [2]. Also known as the Internet of all things; it is a promising direction in productions systems and expected to bring to bear the full potential of the fourth industrial revolution [3]. Likewise Cyber Physical Systems (CPS), most researchers and scholars have attributed IoT as the key enabler or initiator of the fourth industrial revolution [4–6].

In this sense, Lee et al. [7] opined that, "all the items that can be imagined in terms of the Fourth Industrial Revolution have their basis on all the technologies required for manufacturing and implementation of the IoT evolution". The researchers further explained that, unless all the IoT-related technologies are developed and implemented, all the possibilities mentioned and discussed regarding the fourth industrial revolution cannot be realised. IoT enables objects to be sensed and/or controlled remotely across existing network infrastructure, creating opportunities for more direct integration of the physical world into based systems [8].

Sharma, Shamkuwar and Singh [9] elucidated that, the technological advancement in recent years has transformed the internet to the network where everything is linked, and everyday objects can be recognised and controlled via Radio Frequency Identification (RFID) tags, sensors and smart phones. This interconnection is made possible with a combination of software, sensor, processor, and communication technologies. Kamble et al. [10] also explained the role and/or relationship between CPS and IoT in the fourth industrial revolution. They posited that, the IoT is connected alongside Cyber-Physical Systems in such a way that the system develops the potential to generate and feed information, adding value to the manufacturing and service process. This project the relevance of the IoT for manufacturing and service industries.

Nevertheless, limited studies have focused their argument on the evolution and components of this disruptive technology in our industries. Additionally, there exist non-consensual agreement among researchers on the evolution of the IoT scholars [9, 11]. Furthermore, there is non-consensual theorisation on the IoT technological concept among scholars [12–14]. Also, there is differing information on the components of IoT in the literature [2, 10]. Hence, there is the need to understand the etymology, evolution, and the components of this interesting technology. Therefore, the objective of this review is to explore the evolution, components, benefits as well as the implications of the IoT for manufacturing and service industries.

2. Literature review

2.1 Evolution of internet of things (IoT)

The term IoT was first coined by British entrepreneur, Kevin Ashton in 1999, to highlight the power of connecting Radio Frequency Identification tags globally to the internet, in the context or domain of supply chain management [12, 15]. According to Zhong et al. [11], the concept of IoT first came from RFID (Radio Frequency Identification) fields; stating that it is the information network constructed by the radio frequency identification technology and communication technology. **Figure 1** illustrates the chronology of IoT evolution from 1969 till date.

Although the term IoT have been attributed to the works of Ashton in 1999, Sharma et al. [9] also elucidated that that technologies behind IoT had already existed and were under development many years ago. The researchers highlighted the evolution of IoT and its supporting or associated technologies in chronological order from 1969 to the 2000s. In 1969, the Internet, which is the main technology behind IoT emerged as Advanced Research Project Agency Network (ARPANET). It was mainly used by academic and research fraternity to share research work, to develop new interconnection techniques and to link computers to many general-purpose computer centres of the United States Defence Department and in public and private sectors.

In 1973, another essential technology for IoT called Radio-Frequency Identification (RFID) resurfaced, although the roots of RFID can be traced back to the second world war. For instance, the developments associated with RFID continued through 1950s and

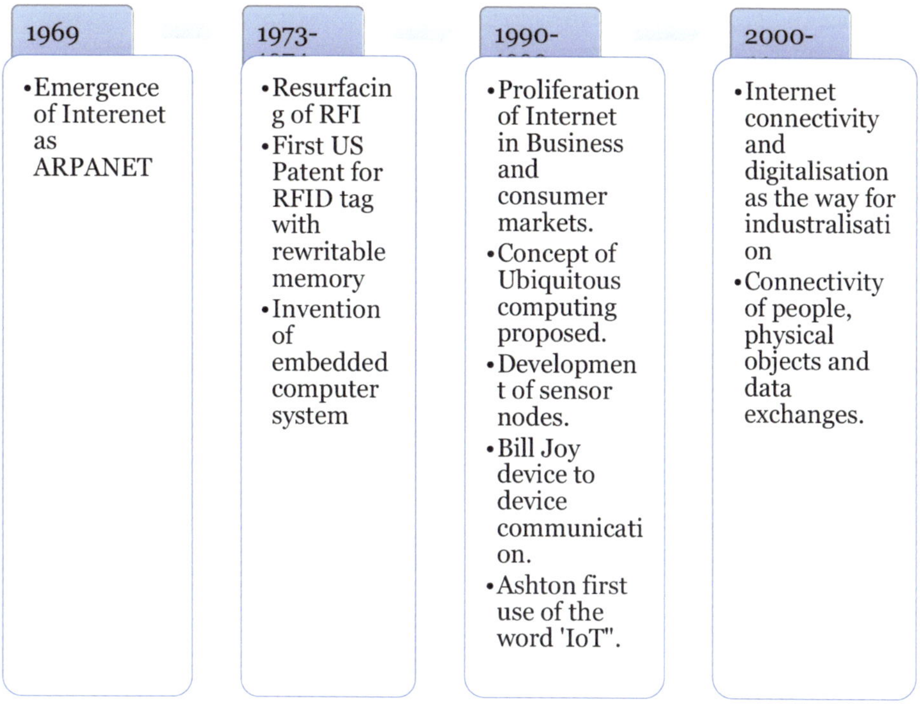

Figure 1.
Chronology of IoT evolution.

1960s, but the first U.S. patent for RFID tag with rewritable memory was received by Mario W. Cardullo in 1973. In the same year, Charles Walton, a California based entrepreneur, also received a patent for passive transponder to unlock the door remotely. In the year 1974, embedded computer system, which is also another important technology for IoT was invented. These systems are implemented using single board computers and microcontrollers and are embedded in the bigger system to form its integral part.

IoT was earlier used in 1984 without it being christened. Sharma et al. [9] explained that a coke machine was connected to internet to report the availability and temperature of the drink. During the year 1990, there was a proliferation of internet in business and consumer markets. Howbeit, its use was still limited due to low performance of network connectivity. In 1991, Mark Weiser proposed the concept of ubiquitous computing, another essential technological component for IoT. Weiser's ubiquitous computing made use of advanced embedded computing as a computer to be present in everything, yet invisible. It later became known as pervasive computing.

In the mid-90s, sensor nodes were developed to sense the data from uniquely identified embedded devices and seamlessly exchange the information to realise the basic idea of IoT [15]. Bill Joy in 1999 introduced device to device communication in his taxonomy of internet and the term 'IoT' was used for the first time [12]. During that same time, the RFID technology was boosted by an establishment of the Auto-ID Center at the Massachusetts Institute of Technology (MIT) to produce an inexpensive chip which can store information and can be used to link objects to the internet [9].

From the year 2000, because of digitalization, internet connectivity became the sine qua non for many applications because of digitalisation and automation. Most businesses and products were expected to have their presence on the internet and provide information and services online [16]. Since then, the true potential of IoT begun; with imperceptible technology being operated behind the scenes and dynamically responding to our expectations for the "things" to act and behave.

Following the pronouncement of the "IoT" in 1999, its connotation has been in continuous development and expansion. The connotation of IoT has been continuously enriched. The ideal goal of IoT is that any person, any physical object, any transaction, or any process can communicate with each other by using any network at any time in anywhere [11, 15]. In other words, making a computer sense information without the aid of human intervention.

Gubbi et al. [15] writes a beautiful explication of the fast-rising industry-changing technology (i.e. IoT). They write, "a radical evolution of the current Internet into a network of interconnected objects that not only harvests information from the environment (sensing) and interacts with the physical world (actuation/command/ control), but also uses existing Internet standards to provide services for information transfer, analytics, applications, and communications". Contemporarily, IoT has outgrown its infancy and is transforming the current state of the internet into the inclusive internet of the future, covering wide range of systems in industries like transport, healthcare, logistics, etc.

3. Methodology

Based on the literature gaps highlighted, and the relative novelty of the areas considered for this study, the researchers adopted the critical review method [13, 16]. With this, the study broadened its search strategies, to unearth seminal papers on IoT by different scholars from diverse academic fields. Particular interest and attention were also given to the evolution and the concept of the IoT, as well as the components and relevance of IoT for industries. Tables were prepared to summarise the areas the study captured and their supportive references.

Specifically, these include the evolution, components and further developments of the IoT (i.e. IIoT and IoS). After this, an exegesis was done on IoT implications for manufacturing and service industries. Additionally, a table was prepared and organised to show the major findings or references that were identified for the conceptualisation of IoT. Finally, practical implications of the IoT for the industry practitioners and suggestions for future research were also discussed.

4. Discussion

4.1 Conceptualising IoT

Since the introduction of the concept of IoT in academic literature, it has received various definitions from different scholars and researchers. Most definitions of IoT emerged in the past ten years based on the latest technology and applications in existence at that time. These definitions depended on the way the researchers conceived and perceived the potency of IoT. Nonetheless, there is yet no universally agreed definition of IoT in the academic literature. Sharma et al. [9] clarified that, "different researchers, scientists define the term in their own way; some focus more objects, devices, Internet Protocols and Internet, while others focus on the communication

No.	Definition	Author(s)
1.	IoT is defined as the "interconnection of sensing and actuating devices providing the ability to share information across platforms through a unified framework, developing a common operating picture for enabling innovative applications. This is achieved by seamless ubiquitous sensing, data analytics and information representation with Cloud computing as the unifying framework".	Gubbi et al. [15]
2.	IoT is "a network in which CPS cooperate with each other through unique addressing schemas. Use of the IoT can be, for example, the Smart factories, homes or networks.".	Hermann et al. [4]
3.	IoT is "a world where basically all (physical) things can turn into so-called "smart things" by featuring small computers that are connected to the internet".	Hofmann and Rüsch [5]
4.	"IoT represents a fundamental concept in the integration of all smart devices that are parts of major smart projects".	Roblek et al. [14]
5.	IoT in its simplest form is "as a relationship between things (products, services, places, etc.) and people that is made possible by connected technologies and various platforms".	Schwab [1]
6.	World Economic Forum in its publication, Impact of the Fourth Industrial Revolution on Supply Chains, defined the IoT as "the virtual interconnection of intelligent assets and devices to achieve improved user experience and/or usability".	World Economic Forum [17]
7.	World Economic Forum [18] in its publication, 'Harnessing the Fourth Industrial Revolution for the Earth', explained IoT as "a network of advanced sensors and actuators in land, air, oceans and space embedded with software, network connectivity and computer capability, which can collect and exchange data over the internet and enable automated solutions to multiple problem sets".	World Economic Forum [18]
8.	IoT is "an inter-networking world in which various objects are embedded with electronic sensors, actuators, or other digital devices so that they can be networked and connected for the purpose of collecting and exchanging data. In general, IoT is able to offer advanced connectivity of physical objects, systems, and services, enabling object-to object communication and data sharing".	Zhong et al. [11]
9.	IoT is "a new industrial ecosystem that combines intelligent and autonomous machines, advanced predictive analytics, and machine-human collaboration to improve productivity, efficiency, and reliability".	Kamble et al. [10]
10.	IoT is "enabling advanced services by interconnecting (physical and virtual) things based on existing and evolving interoperable information and communication technologies".	Turcu and Turcu [2]
11.	IoT is "an evolution of mobile, embedded application and everything that is connected to internet to integrate greater communication ability and use data analytics to extract meaningful information".	Sharma et al. [9]
12.	IoT is "as a global infrastructure for the information society, enabling advanced services by interconnecting (physical and virtual) things based on existing and evolving interoperable information and communication technologies".	Lee et al. [7]
13.	IoT is "the inter-networking of physical devices, vehicles, buildings, and other items embedded with electronics, software, sensors, actuators, and network connectivity that enable these objects to collect and exchange data".	Oztemel and Gursev [8]

Table 1.
Definitions of IoT by authors in their publications.

processes involved". **Table 1** summarises some notable definitions of IoT by scholars and researchers in their papers.

For the purpose of this study, IoT is conclusively theorised based on the varying cues of definitions as "*the network of physical and virtual objects (things) connected with sensors, RFID and actuators, for the purpose of collecting, sharing and/or exchanging information through a unified platform over the internet which enables automated solutions to multiple problem sets*".

4.2 Components of IoT

Gubbi et al. [15] presented a taxonomy that aided in defining the components required for the IoT from a high-level perspective. According to the researchers, there are three IoT components which enables seamless ubiquitous computing. These are Hardware, Middleware and Presentation. They classified hardware component of IoT as those objects made up of sensors, actuators, and embedded communication hardware. This level also includes central units. Leloglu [19] described the central unit as a source of centralised services in IoTs; and has a capability of storing, processing, and delivering data to users.

Middleware component of IoT comprises on-demand storage and computing tools for data analytics [9, 15]. An example of middleware is cloud computing. This style of computing relies on sharing of resources are provided as a service over the Internet to achieve coherence and economy of scale [20]. Also, Presentation component includes new and easy-to-understand visualisation and interpretation tools which can be widely accessed on different platforms, and which can be designed for different applications.

Some enabling technologies in these categories that make up the three components given above include RFID, wireless sensor networks, cloud computing, addressing schemes, data storage & analytics, visualisation [4, 19]. These technologies help in realising the fruitful operations of the entire IoT network. The development of IoT ecosystem or network enables the object to be uniquely identified and be able to connect and communicate with other objects anytime and anywhere. According to Sharma et al. [9], the two main components of an "IoT object" are its ability to capture data via sensors and transmit data via the Internet. This internet connectivity allows object to have their own identities as well as receive and send valuable communication making them smart.

Again, these objects are embedded with electronics (Microcontrollers and transceivers), software, sensors, actuators, and network connectivity that enables them to collect and exchange the data using various protocols. In other words, the IoT allows "'things' and 'objects', such as RFID, sensors, actuators, mobile phones, which, through unique addressing schemas, interact with each other and cooperate with their neighbouring 'smart' components, to reach common goals [4]. IoT technology is purposely utilised for collecting, analysing, controlling, and managing data in manufacturing systems [20]. Hence, IoT offers connectivity of devices, systems, and services; and caters to variety of application in different domains. Kamble et al. [10] elucidated that IoT products are allotted unique identifiers and are intricately linked to information about their provenance, use, and destination.

Leloglu [19] also proposed four layers of a secured IoT architecture to guide theoretical research. The scholar referenced that the architecture of IoT should be an open architecture, using open protocols to support a variety of existing network applications; additionally, incorporating security, adaptability, and semantic representation middleware to promote data world integration with Internet. The four layers proposed by the researcher are Perception, Network, Support and Application layers. Perception Layer consists of the sensor technology, intelligence embedded technology, nano technology and tagging technology. He explained that the main purpose of this layer is the identification of unique objects and the collection of information from the physical world with the help of its sensors.

Additionally, network layer contains Wireless Sensor Networks (WSN), optical fibre communication networks, broad television networks, 2G/3G communications networks, fixed telephone networks and closed IP data networks for each carrier. The researcher further added that the responsibility of this layer also includes the transfer of collected information from sensors, devices, etc., to an information processing system. Thirdly, the support layer involves information processing systems which takes information in one form and processes (transforms) it into another form. This processed data is stored in a database and will be available when there is a demand. According to Leloglu [19], this layer works very closely with applications. Last but not least, application layer harbours practical and useful applications which are developed based on user requirements or industry specifications such as smart traffic, precise agriculture, smart home, mining monitor, etc.

Another indispensable part of IoT worth noting is, smart connectivity with existing networks and context-aware computation using network resources. Gubbi et al. [15] highlighted three IoT demands that will allow technology to disappear from the consciousness of the user; and evolve into connecting everyday existing objects and embedding intelligence into our environment. First, a shared understanding of the situation of its users and their appliances. Secondly, software architectures and pervasive communication networks to process and convey the contextual information to where it is relevant. Thirdly, the analytics tools in the IoT that aim for autonomous and smart behaviour. With these three fundamental grounds in place, smart connectivity and context-aware computation can be accomplished.

No.	Components	Reference(s)
1.	Hardware, Middleware and Presentation	Gubbi et al. [15]
2.	Electronics (Microcontrollers and transceivers), software, sensors, actuators, and network connectivity	Hermann et al. [4]
3.	RFID, wireless sensor networks, cloud computing, addressing schemes, data storage & analytics, visualisation	Kamble et al. [10]; Mourtzis et al. [20]; Sharma et al. [9]
4.	Perception, Network, Support and Application layers of a secured IoT architecture	Leloglu [19]
5.	Industrial Internet of Things	Ardito et al. [21]; Chen [22]; Lampropoulos et al. [23]; Turcu & Turcu [2]
6.	Internet of Services	Contreras et al. [24]; Hofmann & Rüsch, [5]

Table 2.
Summary of the components of IoT.

Table 2 below summarises the various components of IoT that are discussed in this paper and their associated references.

4.3 Further developments of the IoT

4.3.1 Industrial internet of things (IIoT)

IoT serve as a foundation that allows objects to interact and communicate with each other in order to collect and share information among themselves. To this end, an industry-hardened IoT was needed to provide the reliability and security that were required by industry for manufacturing applications. An industry consortium initiated by General Electric (GE) is developing Internet technology for industry, resulting in a special IoT system for industrial application called the Industrial Internet of Things (IIoT) [22]. Lampropoulos et al. [23] opined that, "IoT is well aligned with the architecture of intelligent manufacturing industries, therefore IoT includes a specific category focusing on its applications and use cases in modern industries and manufacturing, named IIoT".

Just as IoT, the IIoT do not have a universally agreed definition in the academic literature. IIoT have been used along with other technological terms like IoT, CPS, Industry 4.0, Big Data, Machine Learning, Machine-to-Machine Communication [2, 22, 23]. However different researchers have given different definitions for IIoT. For instance, Chen [22] postulated that, "the IIoT refers to the integration and connectivity of complex physical machines and devices, humans, and resources through networked sensors and software for the purposes of industry production and operations".

Later, Ardito, Petruzzelli, Panniello and Garavelli [21] also defined Industrial IoT as the use of IoT technologies in demand-focussed and supply-focussed process; which favours the interoperability between devices and machines that use different protocols and have different architectures, thus allowing to have real-time data across the value-chain. Turcu and Turcu [2] also added their voice and defined the IIoT as, "a universe of intelligent industrial products, processes and services that communicate with each other and with people over a global network. It is a distributed network of smart sensors that enables precise control and monitoring of complex processes over arbitrary distances". IIoT is considered to be a complex system of many independent systems. It combines several contemporary key technologies to produce a system which functions more efficiently than the sum of its parts; and focuses on automation, services, cloud computing, big data, CPS and people [23].

The term IIoT was first introduced by Frost and Sullivan around the turn of the 21st century [21]. According to Chen [22], the Industrial Internet, which is the fundamental tool for the implementation of IIoT, was used as a collective toolset for a digital enterprise transformation at that time. Other than regular Internet applications, such as office automation, the Industrial Internet requires conditions such as a hardened environment on the factory floor and extreme dependence on its reliability. Furthermore, IIoT provides functions that help develop insight and improve the ability to monitor and control company processes and assets through the use of appropriate services, networking technologies, applications, sensors, software, middleware and storage systems [23].

IIoT is of great importance and has a lot of benefits for industries that attend to its use. Turcu and Turcu [2] gave some key benefits of IIoT in an industrial context. They highlighted, "monitoring production flow and inventory; enhancing automation, productivity, industrial safety, efficiency, security and quality control; enabling easy maintenance, inventory management, products tracking and tracing, development of new business models, services and/or products; optimisation of packaging, logistics and supply chain; reduction of human errors and manual labour, and of costs (both in terms of time and money)", as some key benefits of IIoT ([2]; p. 57). In addition, Lampropoulos et al. [23] elaborated that, IIoT offers enormous potential for unprecedented levels of economic growth and productivity efficiency in the years ahead. They further added that, IIoT will attract the interest both of businesses and governments as well as researchers and academics who will have to collaborate closely and feverishly in order to harness and exploit this huge opportunity.

4.3.2 Internet of services (IoS)

Another technological concept, Internet of Services (IoS), is emerging which is similar to IoT. This is as a result of the world being classified as a "service society" and the idea that services are made easily available through web technologies than physically. Internet of Services is allowing companies and private users to combine, create and offer new kind of value- added services via the internet [5]. Internet of Services can be simply defined as platforms that allows internet users to provide services via the internet [24]. Chen [22] also defined Internet of Services as the connection of non-physical systems (service or social elements) to the internet through embedded systems, sensors, software, and network devices.

Internet of Services are characterised by participants, infrastructure services, business models and the services themselves. The services are offered and merged into value-added services from different vendors, and communications via various communication channels. This approach allows different variants of distribution in the value chain. Hofmann and Rüsch [5] agreed with Barros and Oberle, with regards to their proposed definition of the term service, which reads "a commercial transaction where one party grants temporary access to the resources of another party in order to perform a prescribed function and a related benefit. Resources may be human workforce and skills, technical systems, information, consumables, land and others".

The main goal or destination of Internet of Services is to enable service providers to offer services via the Internet. Contreras et al. [24] elaborated that, the CPS, the hardware and software are represented as services. They further added that, this way of conceiving the elements as services, allows a new form of dynamic variation distribution in individual activities of the value chain [24]. Using the IoS during the fourth industrial revolution implies that, the elements of the value chain adopt a service-oriented architecture (SOA); which requires a platform for networking and a series of layers in each element than can be accessed from other elements as services [5, 24]. From a pure technological perspective, concepts such as Service-Oriented Architecture (SOA), Software as a Service (SaaS) or Business Process Outsourcing (BPO) are closely related to the IoS. It is quite promising and prospective that that internet-based market places of services are playing and will continue to play a key role in future industrial operations.

Penultimately, while the impact of IoT in the next five years is considered to be high by business leaders, experts consider the current degree of implementation of IoT applications across businesses and organisations to be on the average [17, 18]. Some developed countries such as France and developing countries such as China and India are working collaboratively to employ the IoT for specific projects. These collaborations not only enhance the development of IoT technologies, but also address global issues, since it is necessary for countries and districts to work collaboratively, especially when adopting a cutting-edge technology such as the IoT [11].

5. Conclusion

IoT technologies have been widely used in industrial fields such as smart cities, manufacturing, and healthcare. To achieve improvements, specific applications of IoT is employed. Sensors and numerous other means of connecting things in the physical world to virtual networks are proliferating at an astounding pace. Smaller, cheaper, and smarter sensors are being installed in homes, clothes and accessories, cities, transport and energy networks, as well as manufacturing processes. Today, there are billions of devices around the world such as smart phones, tablets and computers that are connected to the internet. Their numbers are expected to increase dramatically over the next few years, with wider application in Agriculture, healthcare, manufacturing as well as the tourism and services provision.

Penultimately, while the impact of IoT in the next five years is considered to be high by business leaders, experts consider the current degree of implementation of IoT applications across businesses and organisations to be on the average. Some developed countries such as France and developing countries such as China and India are working collaboratively to employ the IoT for specific projects. The IoT application even though not so advanced in Africa, a lot of effort are being made to ensure the very good use of IoT, IIoT and IoS to achieve massive developmental changes in the African continent. The intense implementation of the IoT, IIoT and IoS will go a long way in ensuring improvements in various industries that would in the long run positively impact the general livelihood of people as well as the way of doing things. Minimization of human errors and process down times due to human interventions and errors could be readily achieved.

5.1 Practical implications of IoT for industries

The IoT Technology, as identified in academic literature, is impacting every aspect of our daily lives as well as the way we work [11, 20]. This implies that a large number of traditional areas with regards to our daily lives and living, will be affected by IoT technology. The quality of life is undergoing fast transformation and will be improved drastically in future. The IoT is expected to open up numerous economic opportunities and is considered one of the most promising technologies with a huge disruptive potential [5]. Sharma et al. [9] opined that, governments are believed to be the second-largest adopter of such technological solutions; and will also take a keen interest in such technologies to improve the quality of life of their people. The prospects of IoT will dramatically improve security, energy efficiency, education, health, and many other aspects of daily life for consumers, through amazing solutions. The ecosystem or network of connected devices has great benefit in all industries and fields, including energy, safety and security, industry, manufacturing, retail, healthcare, independence of elderly persons, people with reduced mobility, environment, transport, smart cities, entertainment, etc. [10, 22].

Again, IoT offers a lot of prospects or benefits for business and enterprises that utilise its technology. The business intelligence sector will adopt IoT solutions at a bit faster rate than other sectors. These business sectors are expected to increase their productivity, have a higher growth of profit as well as lower their costs of operations, with the adoption of IoT technology. This will be possible as a result of IoT technology enhancing their operational efficiency, decreasing their product time-to-market by reducing unplanned downtime, and optimising their overall operational efficiency. IoT also improve decision-making and productivity of businesses in retail, supply chain management, manufacturing, agriculture, and other sectors by reinforcing solutions. Enterprises can further enhance overall availability and maintainability thanks to the vital solutions for more effective scheduling, planning, and controlling of manufacturing operations and systems that IoT provides [23].

Interestingly, the IoT Technology provides a unique and much-needed foundation that is capable of connecting all the elements of a manufacturing system together [22]. Smart-connected products offer exponentially expanding opportunities for new functionality, far greater reliability, much higher product utilisation, and capabilities that cut across and transcend traditional product boundaries [5]. In this way, not only can the efficiency of data collection be improved, but the quality of the data can also be significantly improved. The IoT also enables network control and the management of manufacturing equipment, assets, and information flow.

In this line of thought, Kamble et al. [10] explained the use of the IoT in helping the effective co-ordination and synchronisation of product, and information flows. The researchers postulated that, "the CPSs based on IoT technology find applications in smart manufacturing to achieve intelligent perception and access to various manufacturing resources, to connect multiple parties using social networks to facilitate open innovations, for process control using RFID to provide more flexibility to the manufacturing process, to improve the productivity of the microdevices assembly, and to manage dynamics in production logistics processes".

IoT is radically transforming the way supply chains are managed for businesses and customers as well. It is enabling businesses to monitor and optimise assets and activities to the very granular level. This transformative impact on supply chains will also cut across all industries in its process, from manufacturing to infrastructure to healthcare. Also, 1oT systems like the RFID allows a company to track its products as they move through the supply chain. A widespread application of the IoT that makes this possible is termed as remote monitoring [1]. With remote monitoring, any package, container or pallet can now be equipped with a sensor, transmitter or radio frequency identification (RFID) tag that allows it to be tracked, know how it is performing, and how it is being used. Similarly, IoT also allows customers to practically and continuously track the progress and location of their product or package they are expecting in real time.

Furthermore, IoT does not only ensure effective collection and gathering of data but also acquisition of real-time data for effective decision-making and data analytics. Connected devices ensure the availability of real-time data, enable the geographic distribution of operations and manufacturing, and result in improvements in operational efficiency, processing time and operating and management costs [17, 18]. Ardito et al. [21] highlighted three ways IoT benefit in the acquisition of real-time data for marketing and supply chain functions. They include real-time acquisition of market data (customer data and product-customer interactions); real-time acquisition of operational data (e.g. products life-cycle and material flow); and possibility to elaborate and integrate both market and operational data. The IoT provides real-time sensing/actuating ability and fast transmission capability of data/information, so that the remote operation of manufacturing activities and efficient collaboration among stakeholders are greatly facilitated.

For instance, the RFID technology provides one such example; and this influence most of industries, especially manufacturing sectors. Zhong et al. [11] explained that, "RFID technology has been used for identifying various objects in warehouses, production shop floors, logistics companies, distribution centres, retailers, and disposal/recycle stages. After identification, such objects have smart sensing abilities so that they can connect and interact with each other through specific forms of interconnectivity, which may create a huge amount of data from their movements or sensing behaviours. The interconnectivity between smart objects is predefined; such objects are given specific applications or logics, such as manufacturing procedures, that they follow after being equipped with RFID readers and tags. RFID facilities not only help end-users to fulfil their daily operations, but also capture data related to these operations so that production management is achieved on a real-time basis".

In addition, the application of IoT, especially in industry, results into the creation of vast amounts of heterogeneous information that needs special manipulation and analysis to perform meaningful reasoning and extract the actual value. The extraction of the knowledge from the data collected in all levels of manufacturing systems can create autonomous smart manufacturing system. Oztemel & Gursev [8] elucidated that, IoT manufacturing systems make decisions that are quick, more optimistic, and faster than those of others. However, this depends upon the architecture and related intelligence embedded into the system. Moreover, the information networks that are based on the IoT application also create new business models, improve business processes, and reduce costs and risks [20].

There are a lot of independent technologies that come together or involved in the IoT eco-system. They include RFID, cloud computing, communication technologies, sensor technologies, advanced analytics, Big Data, machine learning [2, 19]. However, they are also prone to cyber risk, which exerts pressure on both stakeholders (government and business) to implement appropriate security and privacy policies across organisations, manufacturing networks and supply chains [17, 18].

5.2 Limitations and suggestions for future research

Notably, this review serves as a theoretical foundation for further studies. Future studies should empirically evaluate the IoT components that are in use at manufacturing and service firms. Furthermore, studies can also explore the prospects of the use of the IoT systems for industries using pragmatic methods. Also, other studies can also focus on the extent to which IoT systems of the Fourth Industrial Revolution apply to industries. Again, the impact of IoT operations on employee productivity, organisational performance and customer satisfaction can also be investigated. Additionally, an empirical study could be done to understand the challenges associated with the implementation of IoT and solutions that could be used to address these challenges. Finally, factors that would enhance the adoption of IoT systems in the face of the incoming technology revolution, could be the focus of future studies.

Author details

Benjamin Appiah Osei[1]* and Emmanuela Kwao-Boateng[2]

1 Department of Human Resource and Organisational Development, Kwame Nkrumah University of Science and Technology, Ghana

2 Department of Chemical Engineering, Kwame Nkrumah University of Science and Technology, Ghana

*Address all correspondence to: oseibenjaminappiah@gmail.com

References

[1] Schwab K. The Fourth Industrial Revolution. United Kingdom: Penguin Random House; 2016

[2] Turcu CO, Turcu CE. Industrial internet of things as a challenge for higher education. International Journal of Advanced Computer Science and Applications. 2018;**9**(11):55-60

[3] Kumar A. Methods and materials for smart manufacturing: Additive manufacturing, internet of things, flexible sensors and soft robotics. Manufacturing Letters. 2018;**15**:122-125

[4] Hermann M, Pentek T, Otto B. Design principles for industrie 4.0 scenarios. 49th Hawaii International Conference on System Sciences (HICSS). 2016. pp. 3928-3927. DOI: 10.1109/hicss.2016.488

[5] Hofmann E, Rüsch M. Industry 4.0 and the current status as well as future prospects on logistics. Computers in Industry. 2017;**89**:23-34

[6] Kagermann H, Wahlster W, Helbig J. Recommendations for Implementing the Strategic Initiative Industrie 4.0. Berlin: Industrie 4.0 Working Group of Acatech; 2013

[7] Lee M, Yun JJ, Pyka A, Won D, Kodama F, Schiuma G, et al. How to respond to the fourth industrial revolution, or the second information technology revolution? Dynamic new combinations between technology, market, and society through open innovation. Journal of Open Innovation: Technology, Market, and Complexity. 2018;**4**(21):1-24

[8] Oztemel E, Gursev S. Literature review of industry 4.0 and related technologies. Journal of Intelligent Manufacturing. 2020;**31**(1):127-182. DOI: 10.1007/s10845-018-14338

[9] Sharma N, Shamkuwar M, Singh I. The history, present and future with IoT. In: Balas V, Solanki V, Kumar R, Khari M, editors. Internet of Things and Big Data Analytics for Smart Generation. Intelligent Systems Reference Library. Cham: Springer; 2019;**154**:27-51. DOI: 10.1007/978-3-030-04203-5_3

[10] Kamble SS, Gunasekaran A, Gawankar SA. Sustainable industry 4.0 framework: A systematic literature review identifying the current trends and future perspectives. Process Safety and Environmental Protection. 2018;**117**:408-425

[11] Zhong C, Zhu Z, Huang R-G. Study on the IoT architecture and access technology. In: 16th International Symposium on Distributed Computing and Applications to Business, Engineering and Science (DCABES), 13-16 Oct. 2017. Anyang, China; 2017. pp. 113-116

[12] Ashton K. That "internet of things" thing. RFID Journal. 2009;**22**:97-114

[13] Osei BA, Ragavan NA, Mensah HK, Kandappan B. "Hospitality revolution 4.0": A literature review on a unified typology of IR 4.0 technologies for the tourism and hospitality industry in the era of COVID-19. Asia-Pacific Journal of Innovation in Hospitality and Tourism. 2020;**9**(1):25-45

[14] Roblek V, Meško M, Krapež A. A complex view of industry 4.0. SAGE Open. 2016;**6**(2):1-11

[15] Gubbi J, Buyya R, Marusic S, Palaniswami M. Internet of things (IoT): A vision, architectural elements, and future directions. Future Generation Computer Systems. 2013;**29**(7):1645-1660

[16] Osei BA. Travel to emerging tourist destinations: Motivations and decision-making processes. In: Mensah I, Balasubramanian K, Jamaluddin M, Alcoriza G, Gaffar V, Rasoolimanesh SM, editors. "Marketing Tourist Destinations in Emerging Economies", Palgrave Studies of Marketing in Emerging Economies. Cham: Palgrave Macmillan; 2022. DOI: 10.1007/978-3-030-83711-2_5

[17] World Economic Forum. Harnessing the Fourth Industrial Revolution for the Earth. Fourth Industrial Revolution for the Earth Series. Geneva, Switzerland: World Economic Forum; 2017a

[18] World Economic Forum. Impact of the Fourth Industrial Revolution on Supply Chains. Geneva, Switzerland: World Economic Forum; 2017b

[19] Leloglu E. A review of security concerns in internet of things. Journal of Computer and Communications. 2017;**5**:121-136

[20] Mourtzis D, Milas N, Vlachou A. An internet of things-based monitoring system for shop-floor control. Journal of Computing and Information Science in Engineering. 2018;**18**(2):021005-1-021005-10

[21] Ardito L, Petruzzelli AM, Panniello U, Garavelli AC. Towards industry 4.0: Mapping digital technologies for supply chain management-marketing integration. Business Process Management Journal. 2018;**25**(2):323-346

[22] Chen Y. Integrated and intelligent manufacturing: Perspectives and enablers. Engineering. 2017;**3**(5):588-595

[23] Lampropoulos G, Siakas K, Anastasiadis T. Internet of things (IoT) in industry: Contemporary application domains, innovative technologies and intelligent manufacturing. International Journal of Advances in Scientific Research and Engineering. 2018;**4**(10):109-118

[24] Contreras JD, Garcia JI, Pastrana JD. Developing of industry 4.0 applications. International journal of online and biomedical. Engineering. 2017;**13**(10):30-47

Chapter 4

New Trends and Challenges in Condition Monitoring Strategies for Assessing the State-of-charge in Batteries

Juan Jose Saucedo-Dorantes, David Alejandro Elvira-Ortiz, Carlos Gustavo Manriquez-Padilla, Arturo Yosimar Jaen-Cuellar and Angel Perez-Cruz

Abstract

Condition monitoring strategies play an important key role to ensure the proper operation and/or working conditions in electrical, mechanical, and electronic systems; in this sense, condition monitoring methods are commonly implemented aiming to avoid undesired breakdowns and are also implemented to extend the useful life of the evaluated elements as much as possible. Therefore, the objective of this work is to report the new trends and challenges related to condition monitoring strategies for assessing the state-of-charge in batteries under the Industry 4.0 framework. Specifically, this work is focused on the analysis of those signal processing and artificial intelligence techniques that are implemented in experimental and model-based assessing approaches. With this work, important aspects may be highlighted as well as the conclusions and prospects may be included for the development trend of condition monitoring strategies to assess and ensure the state-of-charge in batteries.

Keywords: condition monitoring, state-of-charge, battery

1. Introduction

Condition monitoring strategies have been successfully implemented as a part of Condition-Based Maintenance (CMB) programs for several decades with the aim of preventing the occurrence of malfunction problems. Although CBM programs have been effectively implemented, in the last years, Industry 4.0 is changing the landscape in different sectors with the rise of the smart factory and the use of data, such changes have been possible through the digitization of value chains, where the aim is to improve the efficiency, sustainability, and flexibility of operations. These new trends present new tools to further maximize the value of the data that are collected during the equipment operation to coordinate tasks in a predictive environment (before a functional failure occurs). However, it is important to clearly define what information or data to collect will represent a meaningful value to the decision-making process. In this regard, it should be noted that the proper implementation/conversion to the Industry 4.0 may lead to numerous advantages to any process [1, 2]. Thus, **Figure 1** shows the most important benefits that may be reached by the implementation of Industry 4.0, the order of importance may differ according to the process and/or application where Industry 4.0 is implemented.

Thus, the most important profits that are taken into account focused on monitoring strategies applied to assess the condition of a specific system are described below:

- *Productivity improvement*: optimization of the processes carried out in organizations, which refers to the decrease in time and resources allocated to achieve them, as well as the reduction of failures and interruptions in production are eliminated.

- *More security:* it is possible, in some scenarios, to introduce machines or robots in dangerous environments, which increases the safety of the workers who work in these areas.

- *Data management (processing):* allows efficient data management since defined and authorized personnel can access and interact with them from anywhere.

- *Support in decision-making:* factories have large volumes of information, which, when properly treated and classified, improves the decision-making process.

- *Greater traceability:* the traceability of all day-to-day records generated as a result of the business management process is increased.

Under this framework, the term Industry 4.0 can be interpreted as the hyperconnection, where all systems are connected between them and can send,

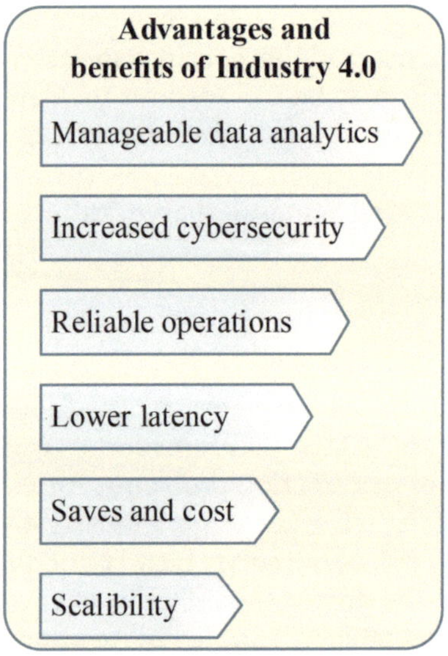

Figure 1.
Most important advantages and benefits reached through the implementation of the Industry 4.0, where such advantages may be found in several research papers focused on the Industry 4.0 [1, 2].

receive, and analyze data and are no longer a novelty. Thus, this new concept is currently used during the collection and monitoring of the control parameters of the equipment to optimize its operation. It is well known that the Industry 4.0 has profoundly changed industrial processes, in fact, in a constant optimization process, also, the Industry 4.0 would reduce energy and resource consumption while improving production. Accordingly, many problems that have been and are still faced by our planet are the product of industrialization, such as climate change, unsafe levels of air pollution, the depletion of resources, or the loss of biodiversity are some examples of the impact of our activity in the world [2, 3]. Also, the implementation of the Industry 4.0 has impacted different subject areas, and it should be noted that engineering and data science applications have been significantly benefited and other areas such as energy have not been widely studied, this statement is supported by the percentage of published papers related to Industry 4.0 for the different subjected areas as **Figure 2** depicts.

As stated, condition monitoring strategies have been extensively applied and its implementation as a CMB program has benefited the industry sector since major of the procedures are accomplished by electronic, electrical, and mechanical elements, where its combination leads to electromechanical systems [4–6]; moreover, it is worth noting that condition monitoring is also a very active area of research in aerospace and civil engineering where the objective also remains to ensure its functionality. In this regard, CBM programs may be implemented with different aims, for example, by analyzing the remaining useful life (RUL), it is possible to predict the occurrence of faults that may affect the functionality of the whole system in a near future, as well as the detection and isolation of faults that have been occurred and are present by analyzing the state-of-health (SOH), and the detection and identification of multiple and combined faults that may occur simultaneously. As stated, despite most of the condition monitoring strategies being developed under a particular framework, i.e., RUL and/or SOH, the principal aim remains to identify abnormal states and/or operations that tend to present deviations from an optimal condition or state of operation; therefore, the most appropriated way of implementing such condition monitoring practices will depend on the application or problem being addressed [7, 8].

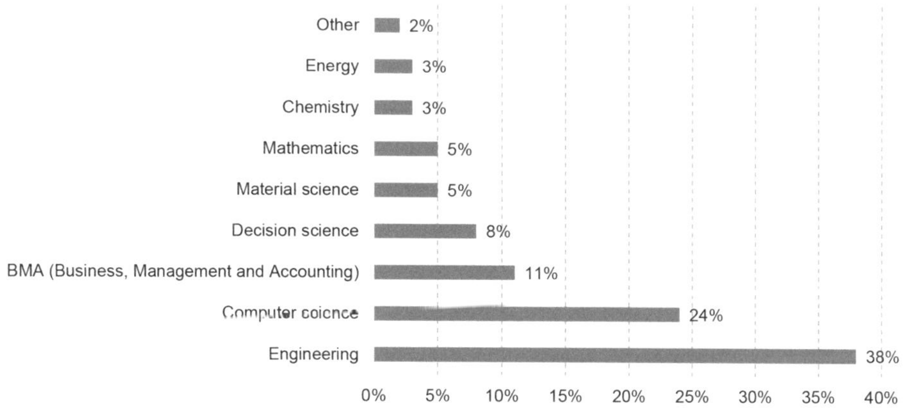

Figure 2.
Percentages of papers that have been published and focused on the Industry 4.0 for different subject areas.

On the other side, the Industry 4.0 framework also aims to face pollution problems through the proposal of green solutions and by the implementation of renewable energy systems. In this context, environmental pollution, which is one of the most critical global problems affecting today's world, has attacked the attention of many scientists aiming to provide successful solutions. Certainly, it is well known that the world's pollution (measured in terms of air quality) is in general produced due to the effects associated to the global greenhouse gas emissions, where carbon dioxide (CO_2) is the most dangerous gas produced by the use of fossil fuel and also produced in industrial processes, which has a concentration of about 65% only for the global greenhouse gas emissions; meanwhile, the remaining 35% of gases are composed by carbon dioxide, methane, nitrous oxide, among others. Therefore, cars, trucks, and/or industrial processes that are based on the use of fossil fuel are the main sources that contribute the environmental pollution, specifically, to the pollution of the air. In this sense, in the most recent decades, it has been noticed that electrification may be the key solution that can lead to the reduction of those high percentages of gas concentrations that increase the world's pollution and that endanger human health [9–11]. Accordingly, since electrification can be considered the most adequate solution to the reduction of environmental pollution, it may be understood as the reconversion of those traditional systems that are dependent on fossil fuel to new systems that only use electric drives. Hence, nowadays, new scientific and technological advances have made it possible to innovate as the readily technology is scalable; in this regard, the new trends are toward the manufacturing of electric vehicles if possible and/or hybrid vehicles to reduce the emission of polluting gases. Although the manufacturing of electric or hybrid vehicles has been promoted by technologically developed countries, some challenges must be faced; thereby, the energy storage and management are probably the most critical issues that are recently addressed. Certainly, the monitoring of the state-of-charge in batteries may be the key point that allows the characterization of the efficiency and/or autonomy in electric and hybrid vehicles [12–15].

In fact, the Industry 4.0 can be the solution to face actual problems and to overcome challenges that have not been addressed, thus, it should be highlighted that the Industry 4.0 is adaptable to a specific application. For example, for electromobility and electric vehicles, the most critical challenges are the range, charging time, and charging infrastructure. Consequently, most of the recent research has been focused on the condition assessment of the state-of-charge in batteries under the Industry 4.0 framework, which involves the general terms of automation, big data, cloud computing, autonomous Internet of Things (IoT), and data management. Moreover, the efficiency of electric vehicles is intuitively in terms of installed monitoring and diagnostic systems and depends on the number of available variables that can be acquired to assess the vehicle parameters. As illustrated below (**Figure 3**), under the Industry 4.0 framework, it is shown a general scheme where are presented different problems (challenges) to be solved under the Industry 4.0 framework.

Therefore, this work presents a systematic report related to the new trends and challenges that are associated with condition monitoring strategies used for assessing the state-of-charge in batteries under the Industry 4.0 framework. Precisely, in this work are presented those classic and significant techniques of analysis that have led to high-performance signal processing, as well as those artificial intelligence techniques that are implemented in experimental and model-based assessing approaches. Additionally, in this work are included the most important aspects that have to be theoretically considered whether a condition monitoring strategy is intended to be implemented for the assessment of the battery's condition.

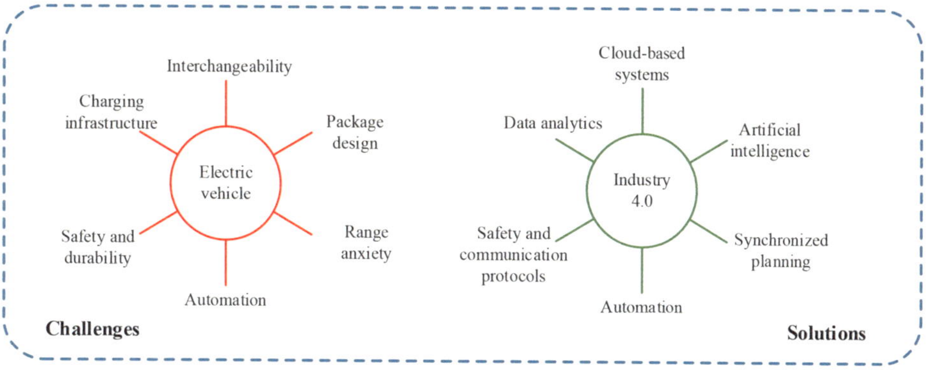

Figure 3.
Challenges to be faced under an Industry 4.0 framework presented in some published research works ([3]).

2. Theoretical background

In this section, a summary of the most common battery technologies nowadays, as well as an overview of the main components and functions that must be accomplished by a BMS (Battery Management System) to guarantee the proper operation of any battery system, is presented.

2.1 Different battery technologies

Batteries are electrochemical devices that can receive and store energy to be used at a later moment. Although there are more energy-storage devices, batteries have gained popularity due to their capability of providing high power and energy efficiency at a relatively low cost with a long life cycle and a rapid response [13]. **Figure 4** illustrates the general construction of any type of battery. It is composed of two electrochemical cells that can turn chemical energy into electricity. Each cell consists of a positive electrode, or cathode, a negative electrode or anode, and an electrolyte that is commonly a fluid that allows the flow of the ions (i+) from one electrode to another. This way, the electric current flows outside, and it can be used to feed any load.

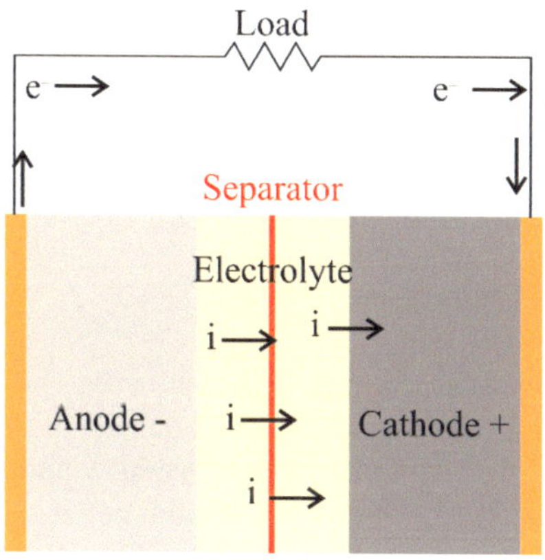

Figure 4.
Representation of the basic internal composition of a battery.

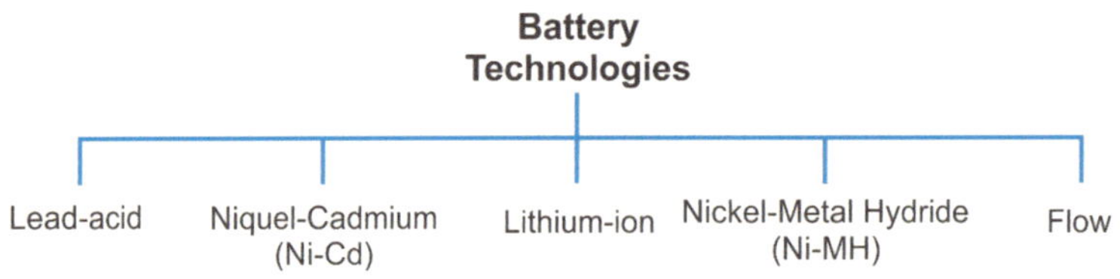

Figure 5.
Main technologies used in the internal composition of a battery.

Due to the key role that batteries play in important emergent technologies such as electric vehicles and renewable generation sources, a big effort is put into the development of a wide variety of batteries with different characteristics. This situation is achieved by using different chemical elements and construction strategies resulting in a wide variety of battery technologies. Next, the main technologies used in batteries are shown in **Figure 5** and also addressed and briefly described. Although there exist several battery technologies, the ones that are presented in this section represent the most used in applications such as renewable generation and electric vehicles.

2.2 Lead-acid batteries

This is one of the oldest technologies used for the development of batteries. Therefore, the lead-acid technology for batteries is mature and widely spread. These types of batteries are characterized to be low cost and very reliable; thus, it is a proficient technology for applications that require an uninterrupted power supply with high quality [16]. In lead-acid batteries, the positive electrode (cathode) is composed of lead dioxide (PbO_2) and a negative electrode (anode) of metallic lead (Pb). Additionally, they consider a sulfuric acid solution (H_2SO_4) as an electrolyte. At the anode, the Pb reacts with a sulfate ion to obtain lead sulfate ($PbSO_4$) as shown in Eq. (1):

$$Pb + SO_4^{2-\rightarrow 2e^{-}+PbSO_4} \tag{1}$$

It is observed in Eq. (1) that two electrons are released at the lead electrode conferring it the negative charge. On its part, the PbO_2 of the cathode reacts with the electrolyte yielding $PbSO_4$ and water according to Eq. (2):

$$PbO_2 + 4H^{++SO_4^{2-}+2e^{-}\rightarrow PbSO_4+2H_2O} \tag{2}$$

Finally, the total reaction can be expressed with Eq. (3):

$$Pb + PbO_2 + 2H_2SO_4 \Leftrightarrow 2PbO_2 + H_2O \tag{3}$$

Eq. (3) shows that the reaction is reversible allowing the battery to be repeatedly charged and discharged. Commonly, a lead-acid battery is composed of several pairs of electrodes that are placed in separate compartments. Each one of these compartments is called a cell. The negative electrode of each cell is connected with the positive electrode of the next cell leaving free the cathode of the first cell and the anode of the last cell, and the result is a battery whose voltage is the sum of the individual voltages of each cell. It is important to mention that each cell of a lead-acid battery handles typical voltages of $E_0 \approx 2.048V$ and typical configurations consider three, six, and 12 cells for a complete battery [17].

2.3 Lithium-ion batteries

This technology is more recent, it was first introduced in the 1990s, but it is recently widely used in electronic devices, smart grids, and electric vehicles [18]. Lithium-ion batteries have gained a lot of popularity because they are the main type of storage system used by all mobile devices as smartphones and tablets. Notwithstanding, they are also highly used in electric vehicle applications as well as in grids containing renewable energy generation. These types of batteries can provide a higher energy density than most of the other available technologies since they operate at voltages around 4 V per cell, while other systems operate at 2 V per cell [19]. Lithium-ion batteries use anodes and cathodes based on insertion-compound materials. In the case of the anode, a carbonaceous material [20] is required; therefore, the preferred compound is graphite formed by one lithium atom per six carbon atoms LiC_6. On its part, for the construction of the cathode, it is used a metal oxide and the available materials are mainly three: the layered $lim\,O_2$ ($M = Mn$,Co and) [21], spinel $lim\,n_2O_4$ [22] and olivine $LiFePO_4$ [23]. Additionally, these batteries use water-free organic liquid electrolytes such as $LiPF_6$ salt dissolved in a mixture of ethylene carbonate (EC). In fact, the use of this type of electrolytes is the reason why lithium-ion batteries are capable of handling 4 V per cell. Finally, this technology incorporates a separator that allows only the lithium ions to flow from one side to another in the battery. During the charging process, some of the lithium ions leave the positive electrode and flow through the electrolyte to the negative electrode. When the lithium ions reach the graphite, they are inserted between the atomic layers of that material, where they recombine with the electrons, leaving the lithium deposited there. When the ions stop flowing, the battery is completely charged. On the other hand, when the battery is discharging, the lithium ions flow back through the electrolyte from the graphite anode to the cathode.

2.4 Niquel-Cadmium (Ni-Cd) batteries

This is another technology that has been on the market for many years. These batteries use a cathode of nickel hydroxide and an anode of cadmium hydroxide. In this case, the electrolyte is an alkaline substance and the charge and discharge process can be described by Eq. (4):

$$2NiOOH + 2H_2O + Cd \Leftrightarrow 2\ni(OH)_2 + Cd(OH)_2 E^0 = 1.29V \quad (4)$$

where E^0 represents the voltage of a single Ni-Cd cell.

These batteries are famous because they can operate at a wide temperature range and they are easy to maintain. However, their manufacturing is complex, making these batteries expensive. But probably the biggest issue related to this technology relays in the fact that it contains cadmium, which is a heavy metal well known for its toxicity [24].

2.5 Nickel-metal hydride (Ni-MH) batteries

This type of battery operates in a way similar to the Ni-Cd one, and this technology is preferred in hybrid electric vehicles (HEV) due to its high-power density and tolerance to overcharge/over-discharge processes [25]. In this case, the Ni-MH technology considers that the active material of the positive terminal is nickel oxyhydroxide (NiOOH) and the active material that constitutes the negative terminal is hydrogen in the form of a metal hydride, which allows the hydrogen produced during the charging process to be stored and released during the discharge process [24]. This type of electrode is responsible for providing greater capacity per volume unit compared to a Ni-Cd battery. A common metal alloy (M) in Ni-MH batteries is an alloy made up of a mixture of zirconium or titanium hydride with another metal such as nickel, cobalt, or aluminum. And the electrolyte in these batteries is mainly made up of potassium hydroxide, which also makes it a type of alkaline battery. The chemical reaction that occurs inside these batteries is described by Eq. (5):

$$MH + NiOOH \Leftrightarrow M + (OH)_2 E^0 = 1.35V \tag{5}$$

Again, as in the Ni-Cd battery, the term E^0 refers to the voltage of a single battery cell. Compared to its cadmium counterpart, this technology is less harmful to the environment. However, its disposal at the end of its lifecycle must be cautious since it still uses corrosive salts.

2.6 Flow batteries

This is a technology that considers systems of two connected tanks, both containing electrolytic liquids: one with a positively charged cathode and the other with a negatively charged anode. Electricity passes from one electrolytic liquid to another through a membrane between the tanks. There are two main types of commercial flow batteries: Vanadium redox batteries (VRB) and Zinc-Bromine (Zn-Br). The VRB uses sulfuric acid containing V5+/V4+ and V3+/V2+ redox couples as the positive and negative half-cell electrolytes. The reaction that describes the charge/discharge process is described by Eq. (6):

$$VO_2^{+ +2H^{+ +V^{2+ \Leftrightarrow VO^{2+ +H_2O+V^{3+ E^0=1.26}}}}} \tag{6}$$

In the case of the Zn-Br battery, its operation principle may be defined by Eq. (7) as follow:

$$Zn + Br_3^{- \Leftrightarrow ZnBr_2 + Br^{- E^0=1.85}} \tag{7}$$

Despite this technology having technical advantages, such as potentially separable liquid reservoirs and almost unlimited longevity over most conventional rechargeable batteries, current implementations are relatively less powerful and require more sophisticated electronics [26].

2.7 Battery management system (BMS)

To ensure the safe and reliable operation of any battery, it is important to keep the operating conditions within a range known as the safe operating area (SOA). **Figure 6** shows a diagram of the different operating conditions that can be observed in a battery.

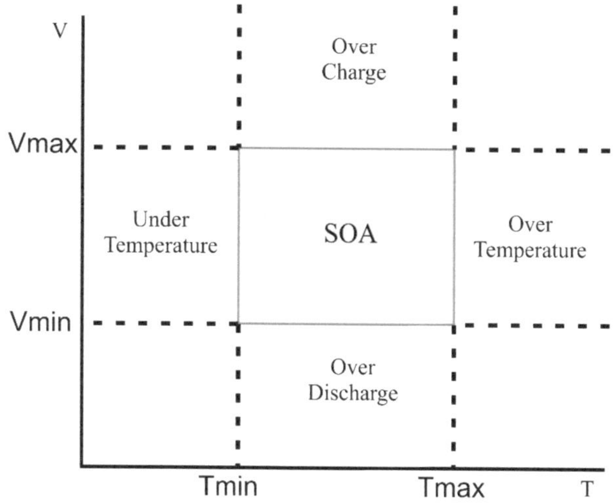

Figure 6.
Common diagram of the SOA for a battery that depicts different states during the charging procedure.

The SOA considers that the voltage and temperature of the battery must not exceed or fall below very specific values. These values are different for any battery, and they must be specified by the manufacturer. However, they can be addressed as the maximum voltage (Vmax), minimum voltage (Vmin), maximum temperature (Tmax), and minimum temperature (Tmin). If Vmax is exceeded, the battery presents an overcharge; when the battery reaches voltages lower than Vmin, it has reached the over-discharge state; for the case of a temperature superior to Tmax, the battery shows an over-temperature state; and finally, if the temperature is lower than Tmin and under temperature condition is achieved. All these last four conditions must be avoided because they can lead to severe damage to the battery, and they can result in safety risks for the final users. On the other hand and as observed, a single-cell battery delivers a small voltage value; therefore, a common battery is confirmed by a series of cells that can deliver a higher voltage together. This situation supposes some challenges, for instance, it is important to guarantee that all the cells perform the charge/discharge operations at the same rate so the complete system is balanced. Additionally, it is necessary to regulate the amount of current that is delivered or received by each cell to avoid damages associated with a misuse of the batteries. In this sense, the battery management system (BMS) plays an important role to keep the battery pack operating safely, reliably, and efficiently [27]. The BMS can be described as a black box model as depicted in **Figure 7**. To accomplish its purpose, the BMS takes the temperature (T), voltage (V), and current (I) of the battery pack and use them to perform different algorithms for controlling the operational conditions of the battery to extend its life and guarantee a safe operation. Additionally, the BMS provides an accurate estimation of the

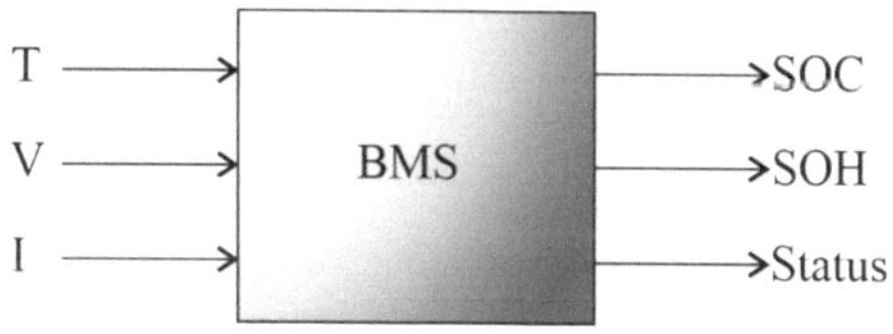

Figure 7.
Black box diagram of a BMS.

State of Charge (SOC) and the State of Health (SOH) of the battery pack, and based on all these parameters, the BMS can deliver information regarding the status of the battery pack and detect if a fault condition is present in the storage system.

The SOC is a parameter that can be defined both: in terms of the battery capacity or energy consumption. In renewable energy generation and EVs applications, it is more common to define the SOC as the ratio of the remaining energy (E_r) and the total energy (E_T) of the battery pack, and it is expressed as a percentage. The mathematical definition can be observed in Eq. (8):

$$SOC_E = \frac{E_r}{E_T} \times 100 \tag{8}$$

On the other hand, the SOH can be defined as the current total capacity that can be performed by the battery compared with the total capacity of the battery at the beginning of its life. As in the case of SOC, this parameter is defined as a percentage, and it is mathematically defined by Eq. (9):

$$SOH = \frac{C_T}{C_{BOL}} \times 100 \tag{9}$$

Where C_T is today's total capacity, and C_{BOL} is the capacity at the beginning of life. In the following section, the most common approaches for the implementation of BMS are presented. A more detailed diagram of how a BMS is composed can be observed in **Figure 8**.

3. Approaches and technologies for the implementation of BMS

In order to ensure the reliable and safe operation of electric vehicles, the accurate application of fault diagnosis schemes over the battery system is mandatory, in which the most relevant elements are composed of the sensors, the systems and components, and the actuators. Hence, different methods have been reported in the literature to

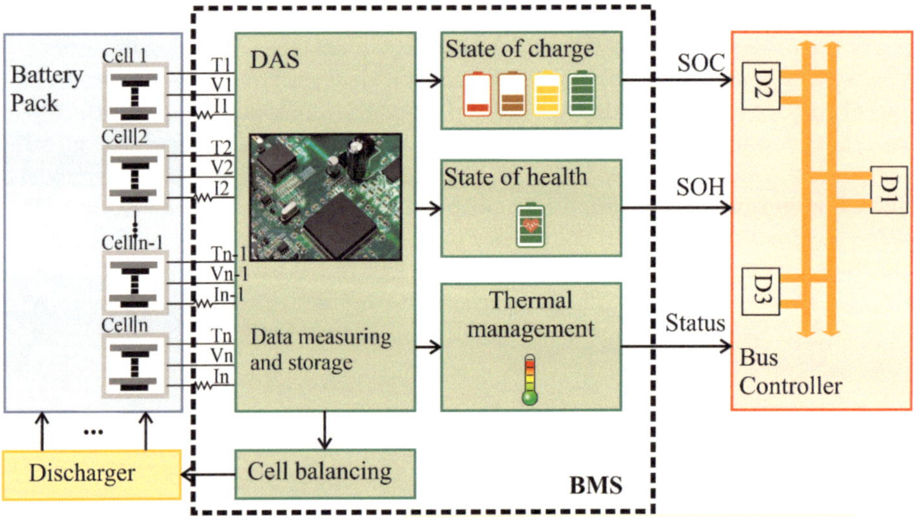

Figure 8.
Detailed diagram of a BMS showing the main and minimal components.

implement different tasks that must be performed by a BMS. In general, all the developed methodologies can be classified into two groups: experimental approaches and model-based approaches. The first one considers that several tests must be performed several times to obtain the information regarding the condition of the battery pack, whereas the second one considers that there exists a series of parameters that describe the battery state, and they focus on finding such parameters [28].

3.1 Experimental approaches

First, it is important to mention that most of the BMSs focus on performing an accurate estimation of the consumed capacity. If this task is correctly performed, it is possible to estimate the SOC and the SOH of a battery pack accurately and reliably. Therefore, most of the works reported in the literature pay special attention to this matter. The most common solution for this issue is the method known as the Coulomb counting [29], which considers the used capacity as the area behind the curve defined by the discharging current over time. When this value is subtracted from the total capacity, it is possible to know the remaining capacity in the battery pack. This method can be mathematically described by Eq. (10):

$$SOC(t) = SOC(t_0) - \frac{1}{C_T}\int_{t_0}^{t} i(t)dt \tag{10}$$

Where $SOC(t)$ is the current SOC; $SOC(t_0)$ is the initial SOC that is commonly considered as 100%; C_T is the nominal capacity of the battery; and $i(t)$ is the discharge current extracted from the battery. Accordingly, the implementation of the aforementioned method can be experimentally performed by means of following the flowchart of **Figure 9**, where the SOC starts by carrying out the real-time data acquisition,

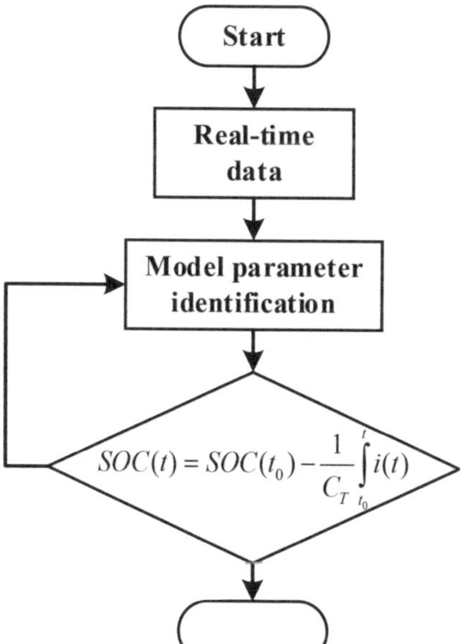

Figure 9.
General flowchart that may be followed to apply the assessment and achieve the SOC in batteries through experimental-based models.

then in a second step, the model parameter identification is achieved, and subsequently, the SOC is estimated in terms of the collected data by applying Eq. (10). Despite this approach being preferred, the implementation of this method has a technical drawback that is related to the use of a sensor for the current measuring. The sensors used for this purpose are usually shunted resistors or Hall effect transducers. These types of instruments introduce an error in the estimation due to the drift. Therefore, the Coulomb counting must be complemented with another technique to compensate for this effect. In this sense, the use of the open circuit voltage (OCV) [30] allows the analysis of energy changes in the electrodes of the battery, and therefore, there exists a direct relationship between the OCV and the SOC of the battery. In the experimental approaches, the OCV is sometimes obtained from the specifications given by the manufacturers. Notwithstanding, the information given by the manufacturer is not as detailed as required to perform an accurate estimation of the SOC.

Thus, the use of methodologies such as the low current test and the incremental current test results is helpful to solve this issue. The low current test considers that the battery must be initially charged using a constant current rate of 1C, considering that 1C means that the complete energy of the battery is taken in intervals of 1 hour. Next, the battery is discharged at a constant rate of C/20, and then, recharging the battery uses this same last rate (C/20). In this test, the voltage between electrodes is constantly measured and recorded during the entire test. This process is repeated several times and the average of all the tests is taken as the OCV [31]. On its part, the incremental current test considers that the battery must be completely charged to represent a 100% SOC. Then, a negative pulse current relaxation is used to discharge the battery and the voltage between terminals is measured every 10% of the discharge. When the battery has been completely discharged, the process is applied in reverse, i.e., the battery is charged with a positive pulse current and the voltage between terminals is measured every 10% of charge. This process must be repeated several times and the OCV curve is obtained by linear interpolation [32]. These techniques provide a good approximation of the OCV that can be easily related to the SOC and SOH of the battery. However, they are considered aggressive tests that may cause damage to the batteries; moreover, they suffer from the polarization effect due to the constant current discharge. In this sense, another widely spread methodology for the estimation of the SOC and SOH in batteries is the use of the impedance measurement [28]. This method takes advantage of the fact that the internal resistance of a battery determines its power capacity. Thus, the internal resistance is calculated using Ohm's law considering the voltage drop over the electrodes when a current is demanded. The so far mentioned algorithms calculate the SOC and SOH directly using their definition stated by Eqs. (8) and (9), respectively. But there is also possible to perform an indirect estimation of the SOC and SOH of the battery using the incremental capacity analysis (ICA) and the differential voltage analysis (DVA). These techniques allow to find a curve coming from the gradient of charged/discharged capacity concerning the cell voltage according to Eq. (11) and another one derived as the gradient of the cell voltage for the battery capacity as shown by Eq. (12):

$$IC = \frac{\Delta Q}{\Delta V} = \frac{dQ}{dV} \tag{11}$$

$$DV = \frac{\Delta V}{\Delta Q} = \frac{dV}{dQ} \tag{12}$$

Where *IC* is the incremental capacity feature, *DV* is the differential voltage feature, Q is the cell capacity, and V is the cell voltage. These curves present peaks at specific values and locations, and as the battery degrades, the amplitude and location of the peaks change. This situation is used for determining the SOH of the battery accurately and reliably [33].

3.2 Model-based approaches

The experimental methods provide a good tool for BMS to perform its task. However, they present the disadvantage of requiring a repeated number of tests to deliver their results. Therefore, they are not recommendable for an online implementation since BMS is expected to monitor the condition of the battery in real time, the model-based solutions seem to be a more appropriate tool. These approaches consider that certain parameters as the capacity and resistance of the battery can be calculated based on a mathematical model. In this regard, batteries have been described using an equivalent circuit model (ECM). This methodology states that a battery can be described by three main parameters: resistance, inductance, and capacitance. By finding these parameters, it is possible to determine the SOC and SOH of the battery in the function of the variations in the nominal values of the parameters. Here, the Kalman filter algorithm turns out to be particularly good for the estimation of the parameters of the battery [34]. This model delivers good results; however, it does not consider what happens inside the battery and may lead to errors if parameters such as the temperature are not taken into account. To overcome this situation, some works propose the development of an electrochemical model (EM). This way, the operation principle of the battery and its dynamic are modeled getting a more reliable and accurate representation. But this increment in the accuracy is not for free, the complexity of the model and the number of parameters increase, making the proper parameter identification more difficult. For instance, in [35], the use of different types of parameters: geometric, transport, kinetic, and concentration is proposed. The result is a mathematical model that comprises a total of 26 parameters. With this model, the SOC and the SOH are calculated considering not only the electric performance but also the composition and internal reactions of the battery. Thereby, SOC and SOH are commonly proposed and/or designed as a condition monitoring scheme that accomplishes stages such as data acquisition or monitoring, feature extraction or signal processing, and the fault diagnosis task in which the fault detection, isolation, and estimation are executed. **Figure 10** shows the flowchart of a condition monitoring scheme used for the implementation of a SOC.

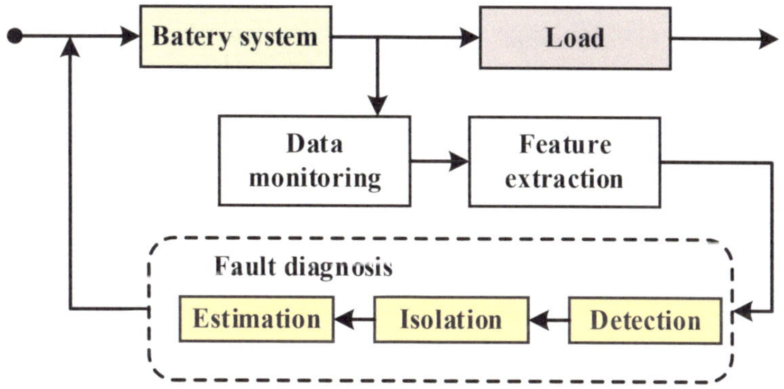

Figure 10.
Flowchart of a condition monitoring-based scheme used for performing the fault diagnosis in battery systems.

Another approach that is gaining popularity is the use of data-driven methodologies based on machine learning. These methodologies model the battery as a black box and develop software that uses example data or past experiences for learning how to solve a problem [28]. Here, support vector machines (SVMs) have proven to be effective for the estimation of parameters such as the SOC of a battery. For instance, in [36], the authors use voltage, current, and cell temperature as inputs of an SVM and with a least square algorithm, they estimate the SOC based on the behavior of the input parameters. A similar implementation is carried out in [37], the difference is that in this work the use of an SVM and the least square approximation are replaced by a deep neural network that estimates the battery condition using as inputs the voltage, current, and temperature. On their part, the authors in [38] propose the use of an ECM, and they use a fuzzy logic system to perform the parameter estimation. At this point, it is important to mention that all the machine learning approaches can be appreciated as a hybrid of the experimental and the model-based methods because they require a series of previous experiments before being implemented; additionally, they use a mathematical model but the model does not describe the system but the conditions required for the system to meet a specific state.

4. New applications and trends in BMS devices

According to recent research works and studies, it has been determined that the BMS (Battery Management System) is the key element in applications such as electric vehicles and renewable energy, this assert is due to the BMS being responsible for managing the energy consumption totally or partially, and it is also responsible for managing the energy storage. Although there exist different types of BMS that allow achieving an effective energy exploitation, nowadays new trends are emerging aiming to contribute to the development of innovative solutions. In this regard, the trend of new research will continue to consider a general diagnostic framework, and these will be based on the flowchart of **Figure 11** as a common base, where the data monitoring, data processing, data analysis, and diagnosis comprise the four general steps.

Accordingly, regarding the ***Data monitoring*** step, the most accepted approaches are those that perform the assessment by means of experimental and/or model-based implementations, which are also known as data-driven approaches. Despite these proposals differing whether experimental data and/or simulated data are used, in both cases may exist similar aspects that are taken into account and that lead to new proposals. In case that data are acquired through experimental tests, the monitoring procedure consists of recording physical magnitudes such as voltage levels, current consumption, and reached temperature; in fact, these signals are commonly acquired for the whole battery

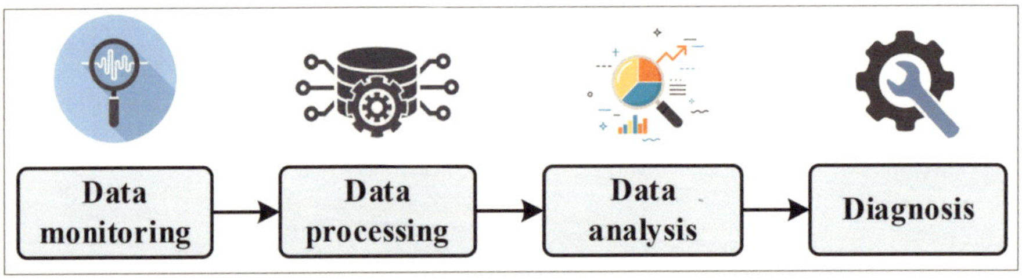

Figure 11.
General flowchart that may be followed to perform the assessment of batteries.

bank and are also individually acquired for each cell [39]. On the other side, equivalent circuit models are considered into account as the theoretical models when the data used are generated through simulation procedures, where the battery dynamics remain the most important aspect to be considered during the simulation [40].

Subsequently, the ***Data processing*** step may probably represent the most important stage since all the acquired data are processed with specific techniques, in this sense, the data processing may consider the simplest signal processing procedures such as the data normalization, data sub-sampling, data organization and may also consider the most complex signal processing procedures such as those techniques based on time domain, frequency domain, and time-frequency analysis [41]. The main objective of the Data processing step relies on the characterization and modeling of the acquired data, therefore, the processing of each acquired signal is performed in order to achieve a specific task, for example, the voltage signal may be processed aiming to give the current percentage or level of charge of the bank battery, the current signals are used to estimate the energy that may be supplied to all cells of the bank battery during the charging process and/or to estimate the energy consumption during the discharge procedure; and the temperature signals are taken into account as an additional variable that is implemented in most of the state-of-health monitor approaches to take care of the current state of the battery bank and to extend its useful life as much as possible [42].

Afterward, the ***Data Analysis*** and ***Diagnosis*** steps are commonly implemented as a part of the process that leads achieving the state estimation of the bank battery, as well as the remaining useful life, the level of charge, or in general is implemented to provide the SOH (state-of-health). Commonly, the *Data Analysis* stage includes Machine Learning techniques to process the available data [43], whereas the *Diagnosis* stage comprises intelligent algorithms to perform the automatic assessment task, in this regard, the most used techniques and algorithms are dimensionality reduction and/or feature extraction techniques, Support Vector Machines (SVM), Neural Networks such as Recurrent Neural Networks (RNN) and Fed-Forward Neural Networks (FNN), as well as regression models that may be based on Fuzzy algorithms; additionally, the use of genetic algorithms (GI) as a part of the assessing structures when the optimization of parameters is required [44]. On the other hand, it should be mentioned that for both stages, *Data analysis* and *Diagnosis*, most of the proposed approaches compute numerical values such as the Maximum Absolute Error (MAE), the Root Mean Square (RMSE), the Mean Square Error (MSE), and the goodness-of-fit R2, where these values are used as a quantitative measurement that depicts the effectiveness of the designed approaches [45]. An important aspect that must be also highlighted for the *Data analysis* stage is the estimation of the most representative set of features that allows a high-performance characterization of the processed signals. Finally, the use of Neural Networks is preferred in most of the designed predictors or SOH approaches due to their versatility and the low computational burden for their implementation in real-time applications. Thus, the selection of an appropriate signal processing technique, the use of Machine Learning techniques, and the implementation of Artificial Intelligence may represent the most important aspects to be considered during the proposal of novel strategies applied to assess the state-of-charge in batteries for multiple applications.

5. Conclusions

Modern society is undergoing an important transition toward new forms of transportation and energy generation that are sustainable and that allow reducing the emission of gasses that cause the greenhouse effect and global warming. In this sense, batteries play an important role because they allow energy storage with high power and energy efficiency at a relatively low cost. However, to ensure their proper operation and to extend their lifecycle as much as possible, the use of a BMS is mandatory. BMS allows the battery pack to perform its task safely and reliably by estimating parameters that provide information regarding the condition of the batteries. Several methodologies have been developed to allow the BMS to fulfill its task reliably and accurately. The experimental approaches can provide an estimation of the battery status using a simple but effective method. However, they require the implementation of several tests to properly work becoming these techniques suitable mainly for offline implementations. On the other hand, the model-based approaches can perform the same task that the experimental techniques robustly and reliably can be implemented for online condition monitoring, at the cost of higher complexity. Finally, the machine learning techniques provide a hybrid between the experimental and the model-based methodologies that uses artificial intelligence techniques for identifying the condition of the batteries based on the behavior of some inputs that are commonly the electric parameters of the battery pack. These implementations require a set of experiments to be performed before they can be implemented; however, once they have been properly trained, they can operate in online systems. All the methodologies used for BMS deliver accurate and reliable results, and this work aims to be a tool for the readers to know different options so they can select the one that better fits their needs.

Acknowledgements

This work has been partially supported by the FONDEC-UAQ2022.

Conflict of interest

The authors declare no conflict of interest.

Author details

Juan Jose Saucedo-Dorantes, David Alejandro Elvira-Ortiz,
Carlos Gustavo Manriquez-Padilla, Arturo Yosimar Jaen-Cuellar
and Angel Perez-Cruz*
Engineering Faculty, Autonomous University of Queretaro, San Juan del Rio, Mexico

*Address all correspondence to: angel.perez@uaq.mx

References

[1] Athanasopoulou L, Bikas H, Papacharalampopoulos A, Stavropoulos P, Chryssolouris G. An industry 4.0 approach to electric vehicles. International Journal of Computer Integrated Manufacturing. 2022;**1**:1-25. DOI: 10.1080/0951192X.2022.2081363

[2] Bongomin O, Yemane A, Kembabazi B, Malanda C, Mwape MC, Mpofu NS, et al. Industry 4.0 disruption and its neologisms in major industrial sectors: A state of the art. Journal of Engineering. 2020;**2020**:1-25. DOI: 10.1155/2020/8090521

[3] Mastinu GRM, Cadini F, Gobbi M. Industry 4.0 and automotive 4.0: Challenges and opportunities for designing new vehicle components for automated and/or electric vehicles, SAE Technical Paper 2019-01-0504. 2019. DOI: 10.4271/2019-01-0504

[4] Catelani M, Ciani L, Fantacci R, Patrizi G, Picano B. Remaining useful life estimation for prognostics of lithium-ion batteries based on recurrent neural network. IEEE Transactions on Instrumentation and Measurement. 2021. Art no. 3524611;**70**:1-11. DOI: 10.1109/TIM.2021.3111009

[5] Iftikhar A, Lim MH, Ahmed MA, Syed AI, Leong MS. Scopes, challenges and approaches of energy harvesting for wireless sensor nodes in machine condition monitoring systems: A review. Measurement. 2021;**183**:1-13

[6] Qian L, Jun W, Rui X, Weixiang S, Hongwen H. Towards a smarter battery management system: A critical review on optimal charging methods of lithium ion batteries. Energy. 2019;**183**:220-234

[7] Bektas O, Jones JA, Sankararaman S, et al. A neural network filtering approach for similarity-based remaining useful life estimation. International Journal of Advanced Manufacturing Technology. 2019;**101**:87-103. DOI: 10.1007/s00170-018-2874-0

[8] Zunya S, Abdallah C. A dual-LSTM framework combining change point detection and remaining useful life prediction. Reliability Engineering & System Safety. 2021;**205**:107257

[9] Zheng Y, He X, Wang H, et al. Well-to-wheels greenhouse gas and air pollutant emissions from battery electric vehicles in China. Mitigation and Adaptation Strategies for Global Change. 2020;**25**:355-370. DOI: 10.1007/s11027-019-09890-5

[10] Ning Z, Huang J, Wang X, Rodrigues JJPC, Guo L. Mobile edge computing-enabled internet of vehicles: Toward energy-efficient scheduling. IEEE Network. 2019;**33**(5):198-205. DOI: 10.1109/MNET.2019.1800309

[11] Khan F, Ali Y, Khan AU. Sustainable hybrid electric vehicle selection in the context of a developing country. Air Quality, Atmosphere and Health. 2020;**13**:489-499. DOI: 10.1007/s11869-020-00812-y

[12] Monteiro V, Afonso JA, Ferreira JC, Afonso JL. Vehicle electrification: New challenges and opportunities for smart grids. Energies. 2019;**12**:118. DOI: 10.3390/en12010118

[13] Chen H, Chen S, Jiang S. Optimal game-based energy management with renewable energy for secure electric vehicles charging in internet of things. Mathematical Problems in Engineering.

2021, Article ID 6078149, 2021:19. DOI: 10.1155/2021/6078149

[14] Gayathri MN. A smart bidirectional power interface between smart grid and electric vehicle. In: Vinoth Kumar B, Sivakumar P, Rajan Singaravel M, Vijayakumar K, editors. Intelligent Paradigms for Smart Grid and Renewable Energy Systems. Algorithms for Intelligent Systems. Singapore: Springer; 2021. DOI: 10.1007/978-981-15-9968-2_5

[15] Anna N, Cheng C, Bin l, Andrew B, Matthew S. Fully electrified land transport in 100% renewable electricity networks dominated by variable generation. Renewable Energy. 2022;**182**: 562-577

[16] Zou C, Zhang L, Hu X, Wang Z, Wik T, Pecht M. A review of fractional-order techniques applied to lithium-ion batteries, lead-acid batteries, and supercapacitors. Journal of Power Sources. 2018;**390**:286-296

[17] Saminathan RK. Lead Acid Battery. Attacking Sulphate Passivation and Cyclability Problems. Munich: GRIN Publishing; 2017

[18] Xiong R, Zhang Y, Wang J, He H, Peng S, Pecht M. Lithium-ion battery health prognosis based on a real battery management system used in electric vehicles. IEEE Transactions on Vehicular Technology. 2018;**68**(5):4110-4121

[19] Manthiram A. An outlook on lithium ion battery technology. ACS Central Science. 2017;**3**(10):1063-1069

[20] Xiong R, Pan Y, Shen W, Li H, Sun F. Lithium-ion battery aging mechanisms and diagnosis method for automotive applications: Recent advances and perspectives. Renewable and Sustainable Energy Reviews. 2020; **131**:110048

[21] Luo D, Li G, Fu C, Zheng J, Fan J, Li Q, et al. LiMO2 (M= Mn, Co, Ni) hexagonal sheets with (101) facets for ultrafast charging–discharging lithium ion batteries. Journal of Power Sources. 2015;**276**:238-246

[22] Zhang S, Deng W, Momen R, Yin S, Chen J, Massoudi A, et al. Element substitution of a spinel LiMn 2 O 4 cathode. Journal of Materials Chemistry A. 2021;**9**(38):21532-21550

[23] Yu Z, Jiang L. Olivine LiFePO4 nanocrystals grown on nitrogen-doped graphene sheets as high-rate cathode for lithium-ion batteries. Solid State Ionics. 2018;**325**:12-16

[24] Fan X, Liu B, Liu J, Ding J, Han X, Deng Y, et al. Battery technologies for grid-level large-scale electrical energy storage. Transactions of Tianjin University. 2020;**26**(2):92-103

[25] Zhou W, Zhu D, Liu K, Li J, Wu C, Chen Y. Long-life Ni-MH batteries with high-power delivery at lower temperatures: Coordination of low-temperature and high-power delivery with cycling life of low-Al AB5-type hydrogen storage alloys. International Journal of Hydrogen Energy. 2018; **43**(46):21464-21477

[26] Lourenssen K, Williams J, Ahmadpour F, Clemmer R, Tasnim S. Vanadium redox flow batteries: A comprehensive review. Journal of Energy Storage. 2019;**25**:100844

[27] Rahimi-Eichi H, Ojha U, Baronti F, Chow MY. Battery management system: An overview of its application in the smart grid and electric vehicles. IEEE Industrial Electronics Magazine. 2013; 7(2):4-16

[28] Xiong R, Li L, Tian J. Towards a smarter battery management system: A critical review on battery state of health monitoring methods. Journal of Power Sources. 2018;**405**:18-29

[29] Liu K, Li K, Peng Q, Zhang C. A brief review on key technologies in the battery management system of electric vehicles. Frontiers of Mechanical Engineering. 2019;**14**(1):47-64

[30] Zhang R, Xia B, Li B, Cao L, Lai Y, Zheng W, et al. A study on the open circuit voltage and state of charge characterization of high capacity lithium-ion battery under different temperature. Energies. 2018; **11**(9):2408

[31] Lipu MH, Hannan MA, Hussain A, Hoque MM, Ker PJ, Saad MM, et al. A review of state of health and remaining useful life estimation methods for lithium-ion battery in electric vehicles: Challenges and recommendations. Journal of Cleaner Production. 2018;**205**: 115-133

[32] Zheng F, Xing Y, Jiang J, Sun B, Kim J, Pecht M. Influence of different open circuit voltage tests on state of charge online estimation for lithium-ion batteries. Applied Energy. 2016;**183**: 513-525

[33] Zheng L, Zhu J, Lu DDC, Wang G, He T. Incremental capacity analysis and differential voltage analysis based state of charge and capacity estimation for lithium-ion batteries. Energy. 2018;**150**: 759-769

[34] Park J, Lee M, Kim G, Park S, Kim J. Integrated approach based on dual extended Kalman filter and multivariate autoregressive model for predicting battery capacity using health indicator and SOC/SOH. Energies. 2020;**13**(9): 2138

[35] Li W, Cao D, Jöst D, Ringbeck F, Kuipers M, Frie F, et al. Parameter sensitivity analysis of electrochemical model-based battery management systems for lithium-ion batteries. Applied Energy. 2020;**269**:115104

[36] Li J, Ye M, Meng W, Xu X, Jiao S. A novel state of charge approach of lithium ion battery using least squares support vector machine. IEEE Access. 2020;**8**: 195398-195410

[37] How DN, Hannan MA, Lipu MSH, Sahari KS, Ker PJ, Muttaqi KM. State-of-charge estimation of li-ion battery in electric vehicles: A deep neural network approach. IEEE Transactions on Industry Applications. 2020;**56**(5): 5565-5574

[38] Zheng W, Xia B, Wang W, Lai Y, Wang M, Wang H. State of charge estimation for power lithium-ion battery using a fuzzy logic sliding mode observer. Energies. 2019;**12**(13):2491

[39] Abd EB, Farid M, Belkacem OB, Saad M. Bond graph modeling, design and experimental validation of a photovoltaic/fuel cell/electrolyzer/ battery hybrid power system. International Journal of Hydrogen Energy. 2021;**46**(47):24011-24027

[40] Dao VQ, Dinh M-C, Kim CS, Park M, Doh C-H, Bae JH, et al. Design of an effective state of charge estimation method for a lithium-ion battery pack using extended Kalman filter and artificial neural network. Energies. 2021; **14**:2634. DOI: 10.3390/en14092634

[41] Panwar NG, Singh S, Garg A, Gupta AK, Gao L. Recent advancements in battery management system for li-ion batteries of electric vehicles: Future role of digital twin, cyber-physical systems, battery swapping technology, and nondestructive testing. Energy

Technology. 2021;**9**:2000984. DOI: 10.1002/ente.202000984

[42] Long Z, Long H, Yuejiu Z, Xin L, Minggao O, Languang L. Massive battery pack data compression and reconstruction using a frequency division model in battery management systems. Journal of Energy Storage. 2020;**28**:101252

[43] Samanta A, Chowdhuri S, Williamson SS. Machine learning-based data-driven fault detection/diagnosis of lithium-ion battery: A critical review. Electronics. 2021;**10**:1309. DOI: 10.3390/electronics10111309

[44] Qaisar SM, AbdelGawad AEE. Prediction of the Li-Ion Battery Capacity by Using Event-Driven Acquisition and Machine Learning, 2021 7th International Conference on Event-Based Control, Communication, and Signal Processing (EBCCSP). 2021. pp. 1-6. DOI: 10.1109/EBCCSP53293.2021.9502399.

[45] Surya S, Rao V, Williamson SS. Comprehensive review on smart techniques for estimation of state of health for battery management system application. Energies. 2021;**14**:4617. DOI: 10.3390/en14154617

Chapter 5

Marine Robotics 4.0: Present and Future of Real-Time Detection Techniques for Underwater Objects

Meng Joo Er, Jie Chen and Yani Zhang

Abstract

Underwater marine robots (UMRs), such as autonomous underwater vehicles, are promising alternatives for mankind to perform exploration tasks in the sea. These vehicles have the capability of exploring the underwater environment with onboard instruments and sensors. They are extensively used in civilian applications, scientific studies, and military missions. In recent years, the flourishing growth of deep learning has fueled tremendous theoretical breakthroughs and practical applications of computer-vision-based underwater object detection techniques. With the integration of deep-learning-based underwater object detection capability on board, the perception of underwater marine robots is expected to be enhanced greatly. Underwater object detection will play a key role in Marine Robotics 4.0, i.e., Industry 4.0 for Marine Robots. In this chapter, one of the key research challenges, i.e., real-time detection of underwater objects, which has prevented many real-world applications of object detection techniques onboard UMRs, is reviewed. In this context, state-of-the-art techniques for real-time detection of underwater objects are critically analyzed. Futuristic trends in real-time detection techniques of underwater objects are also discussed.

Keywords: underwater marine robots, deep learning, real-time object detection

1. Introduction

In the age of Industry 4.0, revolutions based on artificial intelligence have increased by leaps and bounds in various sectors [1–3]. In the community of marine science and engineering, many underwater exploration tasks are usually executed by Underwater Marine Robots (UMRs), such as Remotely Operated Underwater Vehicles (ROVs) and Autonomous Underwater Vehicles (AUVs), as shown in **Figure 1**. These marine robots have significantly overcome many difficulties in underwater exploration tasks thanks to their distinct capability of operating round the clock. As a matter of fact, they have been widely used in the community of marine science and engineering extensively.

These UMRs, which are available in different shapes and sizes, are capable of performing a wide variety of tasks and are widely employed in many sectors. In the

(a) (b)

Figure 1.
Underwater marine robots: (a) remotely operated underwater vehicle (ROV), (b) autonomous underwater vehicle (AUV). (images from the internet).

civilian sector, UMRs are used for aquaculture, such as providing important information for feeding, surveillance and security, and early warning of diseases [4]. Furthermore, UMRs have been exploited in seafood collection, e.g., picking holothurian, sea urchin, scallop, and other marine products, and have made significant contributions to the economy [5]. UMRs are also a promising choice to perform maintenance and cleaning works on underwater hulls, which is important to maintaining health conditions of a ship [6]. In other applications, UMRs have been employed for scientific research of the ocean, including ocean observation, underwater inspection, and monitoring of marine ecosystems. Furthermore, UMRs have been employed in the military and security sector for specific missions, such as surveillance, underwater monitoring, mine detection, and countermeasure [7].

Superior perception is highly desired for UMRs to perform assigned tasks successfully. Cameras and sonars are two kinds of sensors that UMRs typically rely on for environmental perception. There are distinct advantages and disadvantages in employing cameras and sonars for exploration tasks. However, it should be noted that both optical and sonar images share the same technology stack of processing. In recent years, flourishing development of artificial intelligence, especially deep learning, has fueled tremendous theoretical breakthroughs and practical applications [8, 9]. On one hand, development of deep learning is inseparable from exponential growth of data, which has spawned a lot of research works related to data mining [10–12]. On the other hand, artificial intelligence has been successfully applied to various fields, such as smart city [13, 14] and intelligent transportation [15, 16]. However, to our knowledge, most of these applications are on the land; underwater applications with artificial intelligence have not been fully explored yet. In the age of Industry 4.0, underwater object detection is one of the important applications that employ artificial intelligence techniques. Object detection is crucial for environmental perception which resolves around "what objects are located at where". With the adoption of deep-learning-based underwater object detection techniques on board, the perception capability of UMRs is expected to be enhanced greatly.

However, due to the constraints of existing technology, UMRs can only be equipped with embedded computing platforms, such as the Raspberry Pi, as shown in **Figure 2**-(a), which has extremely limited computing power. A more high-end computing platform is the NVIDIA Jetson, provided by NVIDIA Corporation, and is shown in **Figure 2**-(b). However, it also has limited computing power.

In order to circumvent the scarcity of limited computing resources, programs executed on such platforms must be significantly lightweight and efficient. However, existing deep learning models are usually computationally expensive. According to [17],

DOI: http://dx.doi.org/10.5772/intechopen.107409

Figure 2.
Embedded computing platforms for UMRs: (a) raspberry pi, (b) NVIDIA Jetson. (images from the internet).

a standard ResNeXt-50 has about 25.0×10^6 parameters and 4.2×10^9 FLOPS on 8 GPUs of NVIDIA M40. This demonstrates that deep learning models are not suitable for deployment on embedded platforms, and they pose a critical research challenge for underwater object detection. In order to circumvent this limitation, deep-learning-based underwater object detection algorithms should be efficient so that they are implementable. As such, viable real-time detection techniques of underwater objects are highly desired.

Real-time detection of underwater objects, as one of the key challenges in Marine Robotics 4.0, i.e., Industry 4.0 for Marine Robots, is critically reviewed in this chapter. To facilitate a full understanding of the subject matter, we have comprehensively and systematically reviewed and analyzed related techniques for real-time detection of underwater objects. Futuristic trends in real-time detection of underwater objects are also discussed.

2. Preliminaries

Underwater object detection not only needs to recognize all objects of interest, but also locate their positions in underwater images. As shown in **Figure 3**, position

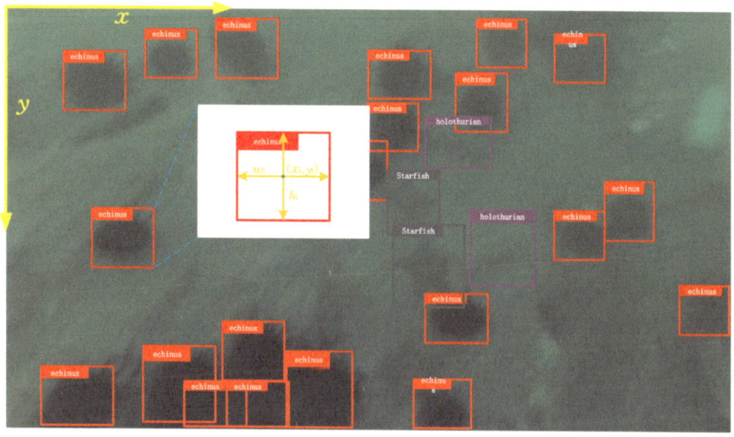

Figure 3.
Underwater object detection. The detection result is presented by a bounding box with a label on it, where (x_i, y_i) denotes the coordinates of i-th object, and (w_i, h_i) denotes the width and height of box. (x, y) is the frame of axes for detection results, with origin at the top left corner of the image (image from the DUO dataset [18]).

information is generally represented by a rectangular bounding box defined by (x_i, y_i, w_i, h_i), where (x_i, y_i) denotes center-point coordinates of $i - th$ object, and (w_i, h_i) is the width and height of the box. The frame of axes (x, y) for the detection result is presented in yellow with the origin $(0 - indexed)$ at the top left corner of the image. In addition, category label of the object is attached to the bounding box.

The underwater object detection problem can be formulated as follows:

$$X \overset{f(\theta)}{\rightarrow} \{(p_i, c_i, x_i, y_i, w_i, h_i) \mid i \in (1, \dots, N)\} \tag{1}$$

where $f(\theta)$ indicates an object detector that is based on any neural networks parameterized by θ. The function $f(\theta)$ takes an image X as its input, and outputs N predictions for objects in that image. The term N denotes the number of objects detected in that image. Each prediction contains a confidence indicator p_i, the category label c_i that the object belongs to, and the position information encoded in the bounding box (x_i, y_i, w_i, h_i). It is well-known that underwater object detection can provide valuable information for semantic understanding of the underwater environment, and it is a fundamental research topic in the community of marine science and engineering.

3. State of the arts using deep learning

Deep-learning-based object detection methods are typically associated with large model sizes, are usually sophisticated, and cannot match real-time requirements when applied on UMR platforms. However, as far as actual use of underwater object detection in shallow water for mission execution is concerned, real-time detection is the most important prerequisite. As such, deep-learning-based detectors for UMR platforms must be as efficient as possible. The key idea that underpins the lightweight model is to create an elegant and practical lightweight network architecture while achieving excellent performance. In the field of object detection, this is a never-ending quest for research excellence.

The development of underwater object detection techniques suitable for real-time performance has a long history. In this context, we will review representative literatures on real-time detection techniques, which can be categorized into three categories, namely two-stage detectors, one-stage detectors, and anchor-free detectors.

3.1 Two-stage detectors

The R-CNN (Regions with CNN features) for object detection [19] is the first successful two-stage deep learning object detector developed in the object detection community, but it is not suitable for real-time detection. As illustrated in **Figure 4**, it begins with a selective search [20] to extract a collection of object candidates (region proposals). Next, to extract features, each proposal is re-scaled to a fixed-size picture and input to a Convolutional Neural Network (CNN) which is pre-trained on ImageNet [21]. Finally, linear SVM classifiers are utilized to predict the existence of an object and to distinguish object types inside each region based on the features extracted by CNN.

However, the R-CNN applies CNN to each potential region for extracting features. There are a lot of overlaps, resulting in many redundant computations and resulting in very sluggish detection speed. In order to alleviate this problem, the Fast R-CNN [22]

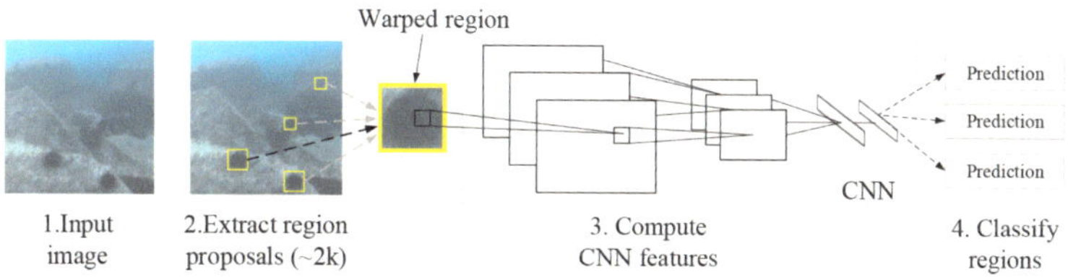

Figure 4.
Network architecture of R-CNN, where CNN features extraction is applied on each candidate region (image from [19]).

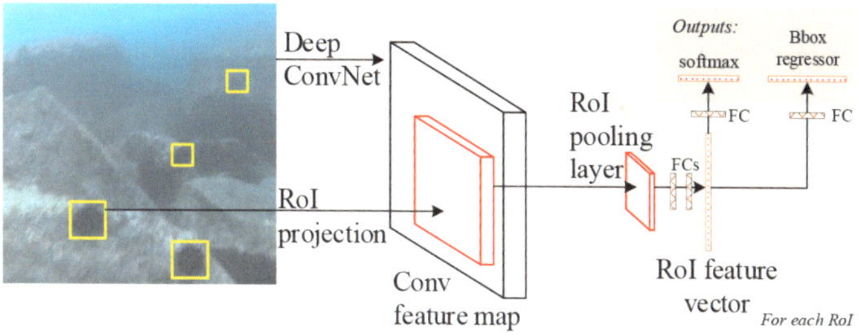

Figure 5.
Network architecture of fast R-CNN, where features extraction is applied to the entire image only once (figure from [22]).

employ CNN to extract features from the entire picture only once and obtains features for each candidate region via a Region of Interest (ROI) pooling operation, as illustrated in **Figure 5**. In comparison with the R-CNN, it achieves superior accuracy on various benchmark datasets but improve image processing speed by 146 times under the same conditions and reduces the training time by 9 times.

In [23], Fast R-CNN is trained to detect underwater objects in sonar images. By using Bayesian optimization, which follows the Automated Machine Learning (AutoML) principle, the hyperparameter configuration of Fast R-CNN was set to be optimum. In [24], encouraged by the powerful detection performance obtained by CNNs on generic datasets, Fast R-CNN is applied to a domain-specific underwater environment for accurate identification and recognition of fish. At the time, Fast R-CNN was widely used in underwater object detection.

However, Fast R-CNN continues to employ complicated selective search approach for the generation of candidate region proposals, which turns out to be time-consuming. Ren *et al.* [25] propose a Region Proposal Network (RPN) that predicts candidates directly from the shared feature maps, as illustrated in **Figure 6**. This new

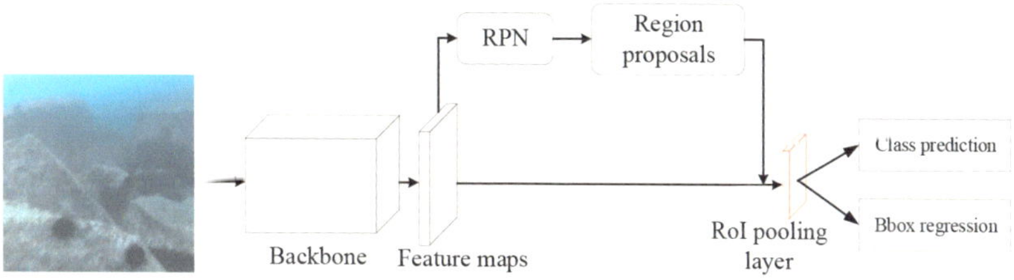

Figure 6.
Network architecture of faster R-CNN, where region proposal network (RPN) is proposed for extraction of region candidates based on the shared feature maps (figure from [25]).

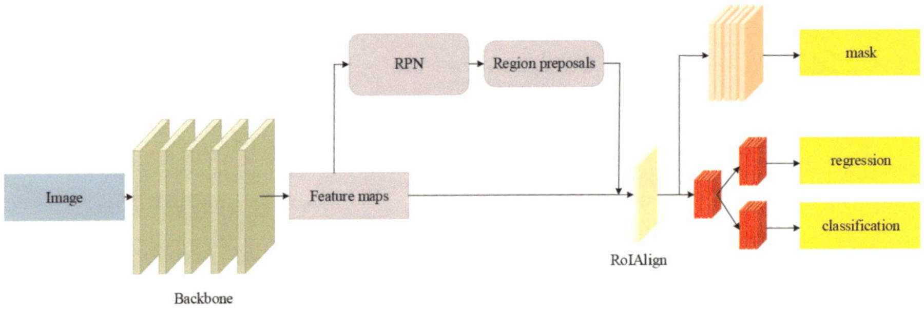

Figure 7.
Network architecture of mask R-CNN (figure from [33]).

architecture is dubbed Faster R-CNN. Typical processing time of each picture in selective search is around $1 - 2s$, but the RPN requires only approximately $10ms$, resulting in tremendous increase in detection speed.

In [26], for faster detection and recognition of fishes by sharing CNNs with objectness learning, the backbone of Faster R-CNN is substituted with a pre-trained ZFNet [27]. In [28], the Faster R-CNN is enhanced to detect underwater organisms, which is exposed to many challenges, such as low-quality images, varying sizes or forms, and overlapping or occlusion objects. The backbone is replaced with ResNet [29]. For multi-scale feature fusion, the BiFPN architecture proposed in [30] is adopted. Finally, to minimize the amount of redundant bounding boxes in the training data, the EIoU (Effective IoU) [31] is utilized to replace IoU. On the URPC2018 dataset [32], the accuracy of the modified Faster R-CNN is 8.26% higher than the original version of Faster R-CNN. Faster R-CNN has dominated underwater object detection for a long time.

After that, the Faster R-CNN is extended by Mask R-CNN, which adds a branch for predicting an object mask in parallel with the current branch for bounding box identification [33], as illustrated in **Figure 7**. It can recognize objects in a picture quickly while also creating a high-quality segmentation mask for each instance. Thanks to the benefits of multi-task learning, Mask R-CNN outperforms all existing single-model entries on a wide range of computer vision tasks by adding only a minor overhead to Faster R-CNN.

In [34], to identify and separate underwater objects from forward-looking sonar pictures, a modified Mask R-CNN is proposed by replacing the Resnet backbone. The modified Mask R-CNN reduces the number of network parameters significantly while maintaining the detection performance. It is suitable for real-time detection. The Mask R-CNN is also utilized to identify common fishery species (yellowfin bream, *Acanthopagrus australis*) for animal movement studies to assess ecosystem health, comprehend ecological dynamics, and address management and conservation problems [35].

In this section, we have reviewed several representative two-stage detectors. By discarding the complicated module with high computational complexity, the detection speed improves significantly.

3.2 One-stage detectors

The aforementioned detectors are members of the R-CNN family of two-stage algorithms, which frame the detection as a "coarse-to-fine" process [36]. They are well-known for their excellent detection precision but low detection speed [37].

Another family of detectors, the YOLOs (You Only Look Once) [38–40] foregoes extraction of candidate region proposals and predicts detection outcomes directly from shared feature maps of CNN. These approaches are also known as one-stage detectors. The inference time is reduced to 50 ms by using a one-stage approach while maintaining relatively high accuracy, whereas other competitive models need more than 200 ms. This is a bigger leap forward in terms of real-time detection.

In 2015, R. Joseph *et al.* proposed the YOLO detector [38]. The key idea of the YOLO detector is to split the picture into grids and predict bounding boxes and probabilities for each cell by using a CNN directly. As illustrated in **Figure 8**, it splits the picture into a $S \times S$ grid, and predicts B bounding boxes with 1 confidence per box, and C class probabilities for each grid cell. The final predictions are encoded in a $S \times S \times (B * 5 + C)$ output tensor directly by the convolutional network.

In [41], a YOLO detector is trained on generating realistic sonar pictures by GANs [42] for underwater object recognition, which is required to automate activities like shipwreck investigation, mine clearance, and landmark-based navigation. Later, R. Joseph produced a series of enhancements to YOLO and offered its v2 and v3 editions [39, 40], which improved detection accuracy while maintaining fast detection speed.

YOLO v2 is an enhanced version of YOLO, with batch normalization [43], removal of fully connected layers, and the use of excellent anchor boxes acquired using k-means and multiscale training, in addition to the custom GoogLeNet network [44] being replaced by the simpler DarkNet19 network. In [45], YOLO v2 is presented as a coarse pre-detection module in the pipeline of rotational object detection using forward-looking sonar in underwater applications, where detection results of YOLO v2 are clipped from the sonar picture and fed to a more fine-grained detector.

The most extensively utilized approach in the industry is YOLO v3, where the Darknet-53 backbone harvests features, and three detection heads fuse different scale feature maps for object detection with different sizes. In [46], experiments to detect and classify sea cucumber, scallop, and sea urchin from underwater photos were carried out, and the results demonstrate that the YOLO v3 algorithm has a mAP value 6.4% higher and a recall rate 13.9% higher than Faster R-CNN. Furthermore, YOLO v3 has a detection speed of 20 frames per second, which is 12 frames per second faster

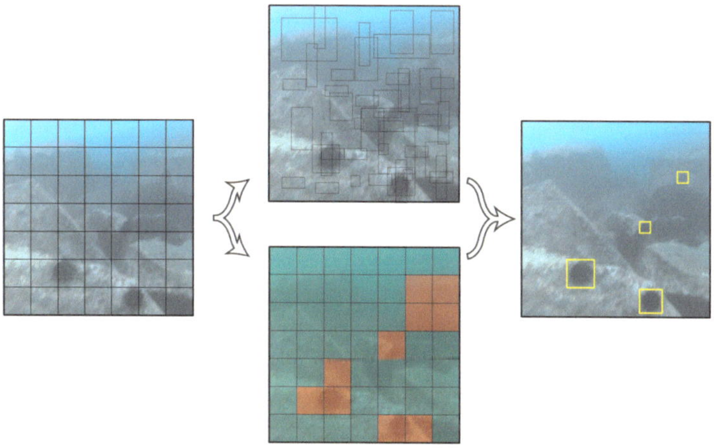

Figure 8.
The YOLO detector is depicted as a regression issue in this picture. It splits the picture into a $S \times S$ grid, predicting B bounding boxes with 1 confidence per box, and C class probabilities for each grid cell. The tensor $S \times S \times (B * 5 + C)$ encodes these predictions.

than Faster R-CNN. In [47], YOLOv3 is integrated into an underwater manipulator (BlueROV2) to identify objects for grabbing.

YOLO v4 [48] has put to the test a large variety of strategies that are supposed to enhance accuracy of a CNN. Finally, it combines techniques such as Weighted-Residual-Connections [30], Cross-Stage-Partial-Connections [49], Cross mini-Batch Normalization [50], Self-adversarial-training [51], Mish activation [52], Mosaic data augmentation, DropBlock regularization [53], and CIoU loss [54] to achieve optimal object detection speed and accuracy. In [55], to construct a lightweight underwater object detector, YOLO v4 is combined with a multi-scale attentional feature fusion module. For real-time performance, it also replaces the CSPDarknet53 backbone [49] with MobileNet [56].

From two-stage detectors to one-stage detectors, the YOLO series has gained a qualitative leap in real-time underwater object detection. Leveraging meticulous design in the network architecture, one-stage detectors will improve performance and detection speed significantly.

3.3 Anchor-free detectors

Another significant paradigm shift in real-time object detection is from anchor-based to anchor-free techniques. The majority of the aforementioned approaches are anchor-based, whereby anchors of various sizes and aspect ratios are established on the picture, allowing object detection to predict related offsets. The usage of anchor boxes has long been thought to be a secret to successful detection [57].

Thousands of pre-defined anchor boxes are placed on the picture in anchor-based techniques, and the model predicts which anchor box will respond to the ground-truth. However, the generation of anchors via region proposal network [25] or k-means clustering [40] is a time-consuming process. Undoubtedly, anchor-based approaches will also result in duplicate predictions, necessitating the use of a non-maximum suppression algorithm [58] to eliminate undesirable outcomes. Unfortunately, non-maximum suppression is also an expensive operation, which slows down the speed of object detection significantly.

Anchor-free detectors aim to eliminate expensive operations that are related to anchor mechanism. Without the necessity for non-maximum suppression, anchor-free techniques remove the computation load raised by anchors and regress the category and position of the object directly by convolutional networks [57, 59]. They remove anchor-related computations like anchor clustering, allowing for even more real-time efficiency.

One of the most canonical anchor-free detectors, CenterNet [59], represents an object as a single point – the center-point of its bounding box. As illustrated in **Figure 9**, the neural network predicts the center-point heatmaps $\hat{Y}$, offsets $\hat{O}$ and sizes $\hat{S}$ of bounding boxes. By using key point estimation, CenterNet determines the center point of objects and regresses all other object parameters, such as size. The bounding box at position (x_i, y_i) may be generated from predictions at inference as follows:

$$\left(\hat{x}_i + \delta\hat{x}_i - \hat{w}_i, \hat{y}_i + \delta\hat{y}_i - \hat{h}_i, \hat{x}_i + \delta\hat{x}_i + \hat{w}_i, \hat{y}_i + \delta\hat{y}_i + \hat{h}_i,\right) \tag{2}$$

where $(\delta\hat{x}_i, \delta\hat{y}_i) = \hat{O}_{\hat{x}_i,\hat{y}_i}$ is the offset prediction and $\left(\hat{w}_i, \hat{h}_i\right) = \hat{S}_{\hat{x}_i,\hat{y}_i}$ is the size prediction. Without the use of IoU-based non-maxima suppression or other post-processing operations, all outputs are generated directly from key point estimations.

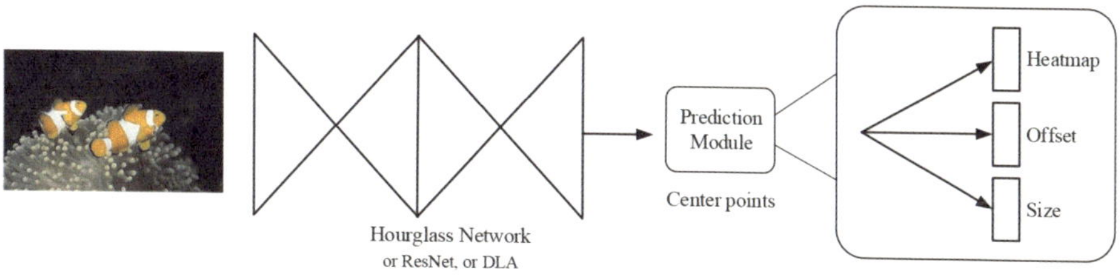

Figure 9.
Architecture of CenterNet (figure from [59]).

Contrary to complicated computation experienced in anchor mechanism, the detection speed of anchor-free models is improved over one-stage detectors significantly while maintaining superior detection accuracy. Anchor-free models have become the de facto solution for real-time detection [57]. For example, the AquaNet [5] and MRF-Net [60] are improved based on the anchor-free model termed CenterNet for underwater detection, and the efficiency and effectiveness are both verified by comprehensive experiments.

4. Futuristic trends

The limited computing resources of UMRs is the main factor that prevents the deployment of deep-learning-based models for real-time detection in underwater environment. Meanwhile, difficulties of communication in underwater environment prevent the possibility of exploring other cloud computing solutions. As a consequence, reducing model size seems to be the only feasible method moving forward.

In the literatures, the two strategies to achieve real-time underwater object detection, namely lightweight network design and model compression, have been proposed. Lightweight network design aims at developing some effective low-complexity network architecture, while model compression attempts to remove redundant parameters of a pre-trained model.

4.1 Lightweight network design

In the development of deep learning algorithms, by discarding or replacing the most complicated module in a model, both accuracy and inference speed in deep-learning-based object detection have been improved [44, 56, 61]. Re-designing fundamental components in the neural network architecture is another option for achieving light-weighting model.

GoogLeNet [44] presented an Inception block made up of 4 convolution paths in various configurations. Convolution with 1×1 kernel is extensively utilized in the Inception block to minimize the computational complexity. The network becomes more efficient by approximating the predicted ideal sparse structure using conveniently accessible dense construction pieces. In SqueezeNet [62], 1×1 convolutions are also utilized to replace 3×3 convolutions. It reduces the number of input channels to 3×3 convolutions and postpones the down-sampling operations in the network architecture. Finally, with the same detection accuracy, SqueezeNet is $50\times$ smaller than AlexNet [63] in size, resulting in higher detection speed.

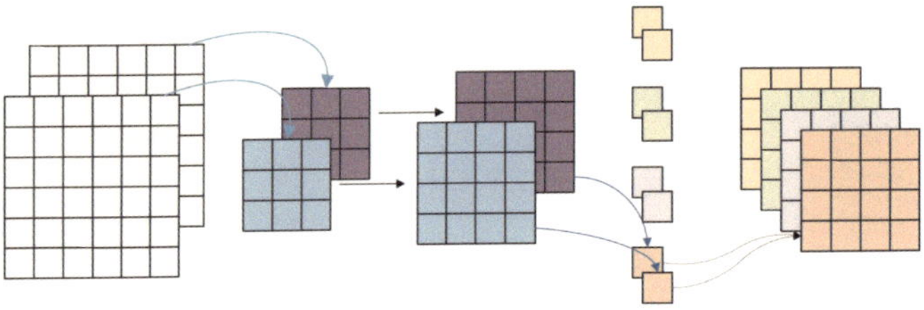

Figure 10.
Illustration of depth-wise separable convolution.

In contrast with conventional convolution, MobileNet [56] proposed depth-wise separable convolutions, which are a type of factorized convolution that factorizes a standard convolution into a depth-wise convolution and a 1×1 point-wise convolution, as shown in **Figure 10**, saving a significant amount of mult-adds operations and parameters while reducing accuracy by only 1%. ShuffleNet [64], on the other hand, makes use of two novel operations, point-wise group convolution and channel shuffle, to drastically reduce computational costs while preserving moderate detection accuracy. Xception [65], ResNeXt [17], and ChannelNet [66] are also wonderful works that adopt depth-wise separable convolution.

Depth-wise separable convolution, 1×1 convolution, and Max-pooling procedure are all employed extensively in the deep neural network presented in [61] to reduce computational complexity and model size. They also constructed an efficient receptive module inspired by Inception v3 architecture [67] to compensate for the inadequately retrieved features, as illustrated in **Figure 11**. Taking advantage of lightweight design, the proposed method outperforms or is comparable to state-of-the-art methods in terms of the *mAP* metric, and it significantly outperforms existing methods in terms of detection speed metrics, such as *GFLOPs*, processing time per image, and *FPS*. Experimental results demonstrate that the proposed algorithm can be executed on *RaspberryPi*, achieving real-time underwater object detection.

The underlying theory of lightweight network design is low-rank approximation. When information is encoded in data matrix X, a full-rank matrix $\hat{X}$, which is constructed by the linearly independent columns (or rows) of matrix X, can be obtained. It is quite conceivable (and rather frequent) for the rank of a matrix to be smaller than the total number of column vectors in the matrix. This means there are some redundant columns that can be generated by scaling and concatenating multiple

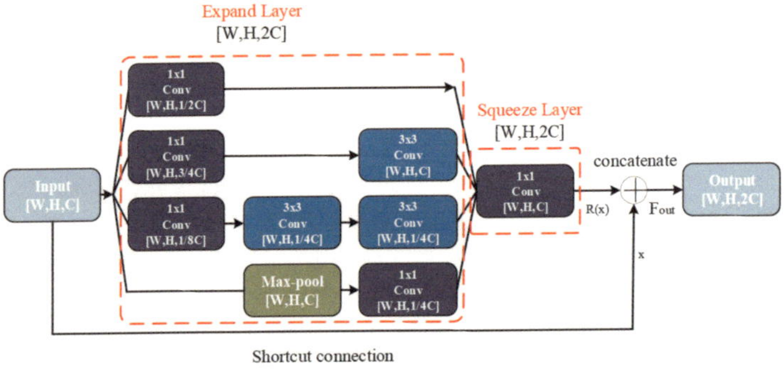

Figure 11.
Receptive module inspired by inception block (figure from [61]).

columns from the full-rank matrix $\hat{X}$. In other words, when a matrix contains redundant information, it can be represented by using fewer bits with little-to-no loss in information. Based on the theory of low-rank approximation, different effective and efficient techniques can be employed to design lightweight network architectures. Undoubtedly, it will play a pivotal role in realizing real-time detection of underwater objects.

4.2 Model compression

Another key method to achieve real-time detection is model compression [68], which aims to remove redundant parameters (or neurons) in the pre-trained models. Existing research has shown that deep networks exhibit parameter redundancy, which is useless for final prediction [69]. This serves as a theoretical foundation for compressing of deep learning models. Various compression methods have been proposed over the years, each of which has its pros and cons. Network pruning [70], knowledge distillation [71], and parameter quantization [72] are some of the most prominent strategies used to reduce network complexity.

Neural networks are typically over-parameterized, i.e., there are significant redundant parameters or neurons [73]. Based on this observation, we can reduce redundancy without compromising substantial performance degradation. In network pruning, the importance of neurons (or parameters) is first evaluated based on some metrics, such as the number of times it was not zero on a given dataset, the absolute values or the lifetime of the neurons, etc. Next, neurons that are of less importance will be removed.

With pruning, the model's performance is expected to drop. In general, performance degradation can be recovered by fine-tuning using the training dataset [74]. Network pruning can be applied at multiple granularities by different implementations, such as weight pruning, neuron pruning, kernel pruning, channel pruning, etc. By removing redundancy in the network, model complexity can be reduced, and generalization can be improved. Based on network pruning, even over 90% of the model size can be removed with little-to-no performance loss, and the computation speed of the model is improved significantly. In fact, network pruning has become a prerequisite for the deployment of deep learning on edge devices.

Knowledge distillation is another important technique for model compression. In general, training multiple distinct models on the same dataset and then averaging their predictions is a fairly easy technique to enhance the performance of almost any machine learning algorithm [75]. It is also widely believed that a large neural network usually outperforms a small one before over-fitting. Knowledge distillation compresses the knowledge in an ensemble (or a large model, known as a "Teacher Model") into a single small model (known as a "Student Model"), which is much easier to deploy on edge devices that are limited in computing resources [71]. It is achieved by minimizing the distance of predictive distribution between the Teacher Model and Student Model. The predictive distribution output by Teacher Model usually contains some implicit knowledge from the training dataset, which is helpful to guide model learning, easing out the optimization process. Through knowledge distillation, we can maintain superior performance of the larger model while reducing model size and consumption of computing resources.

Parameter quantization is concerned with re-organization of network parameters. The main objective of parameter quantization is to represent the neural network with fewer bits [76]. For example, by compressing the 16-bit float parameters into 8-bit integers, one can halve the memory cost with little loss in performance [77]. However, the most commonly used quantization technique is parameter clustering [78, 79], where the parameters in a network are first clustered by clustering methods (e.g., k-means), and then every parameter is represented by the centroid of the corresponding cluster. Based on parameter clustering, the entire neural network can be represented by a cluster index table and the centroids. Each index is denoted by 2-bit unsigned integers. Hence, the deep learning model can be compressed significantly. In the extreme case, we can convert a network to a binary connect model, where all parameters are +1 or −1 [80]. Last but not least, some information encoding methods, such as Huffman encoding, that represents frequent clusters with fewer bits and rare clusters with more bits [81], can also be used as quantization techniques, since they are efficient encoding strategies.

In this section, we have reviewed two key techniques that help to reduce the model size but maintain moderate performance with only slight degradation. Through model reduction, the memory cost and computational complexity are reduced significantly, which makes real-time detection on resource-constrained devices more feasible. Indeed, lightweight network design and model compression are complementary and should be applied iteratively to obtain a more elegant model.

5. Conclusions

UMRs play a significant and pivotal role in ocean exploration in the era of Industry 4.0. Real-time object detection will equip UMRs with superior perception capabilities. In this chapter, we have identified real-time object detection as a key challenge of ocean exploration while using UMRs. Towards this end, crucial techniques pertaining to real-time detection of underwater objects have been critically reviewed and systematically analyzed based on the evolution in deep learning techniques. Three categories of detectors, namely two-stage detectors, one-stage detectors, and anchor-free detectors, have been reviewed and analyzed. Furthermore, futuristic trends of real-time detection, including lightweight network design and model compression, have been proposed and intensively discussed. It is hoped that readers will find this survey informative and useful in helping them to understand recent advancements in real-time detection of underwater objects, and will guide them in research in this exciting area, which will have a long-lasting impact to the mankind.

Acknowledgements

The authors would like to acknowledge the support of Fundamental Research Funds for the Central Universities under Grant 3132019344 and Leading Scholar Grant, Dalian Maritime University under Grant 00253007.

Author details

Meng Joo Er*, Jie Chen and Yani Zhang
Institute of Artificial Intelligence and Marine Robotics, College of Marine Electrical Engineering, Dalian Maritime University, Dalian, China

*Address all correspondence to: mjer@dlmu.edu.cn

References

[1] Gordan M, Razak HA, Ismail Z, Ghaedi K. Recent developments in damage identification of structures using data mining. Latin American Journal of Solids and Structures. 2017;**14**: 2373-2401

[2] Ghaedi K, Gordan M, Ismail Z, Hashim H, Talebkhah M. A literature review on the development of remote sensing in damage detection of civil structures. Journal of Engineering Research and Reports. 2021;**20**(10): 39-56

[3] Gordan M, Sabbagh-Yazdi S-R, Ismail Z, Ghaedi K, Carroll P, McCrum D, et al. State-of-the-art review on advancements of data mining in structural health monitoring. Measurement. 2022:**193**:110939

[4] Li J, Xu C, Jiang L, Xiao Y, Deng L, Han Z. Detection and analysis of behavior trajectory for sea cucumbers based on deep learning. IEEE Access. 2019;**8**:18832-18840

[5] Liu C, Wang Z, Wang S, Tang T, Tao Y, Yang C, et al. A new dataset, poisson Gan and aquanet for underwater object grabbing. IEEE Transactions on Circuits and Systems for Video Technology. 2022;**32**:2831-2844

[6] Song C, Cui W. Review of underwater ship hull cleaning technologies. Journal of Marine Science and Application. 2020;**19**(3): 415-429

[7] Hoadley DS and Lucas NJ. Artificial intelligence and national security. Congressional Research Service. 2018

[8] Gordan M, Chao OZ, Sabbagh-Yazdi S-R, Wee LK, Ghaedi K, Ismail Z. From cognitive bias toward advanced computational intelligence for smart infrastructure monitoring. Frontiers in Psychology. 2022;**13**:846610-846610

[9] Talebkhah M, Sali A, Marjani M, Gordan M, Hashim SJ, Rokhani FZ. Iot and big data applications in smart cities: Recent advances, challenges, and critical issues. IEEE Access. 2021;**9**:55465-55484

[10] Gordan M, Razak HA, Ismail Z, Ghaedi K, Tan ZX, Ghayeb HH. A hybrid ann-based imperial competitive algorithm methodology for structural damage identification of slab-on-girder bridge using data mining. Applied Soft Computing. 2020;**88**:106013

[11] Gordan M, Ismail Z, Razak HA, Ghaedi K, Ibrahim Z, Tan ZX, et al. Data mining-based damage identification of a slab-on-girder bridge using inverse analysis. Measurement. 2020;**151**:107175

[12] Gordan M, Ismail ZB, Razak HA, Ghaedi K, Ghayeb HH. Optimization-based evolutionary data mining techniques for structural health monitoring. Journal of Civil Engineering and Construction. 2020;**9**(1):14-23

[13] Tan ZX, Thambiratnam DP, Chan TH, Gordan M, Abdul Razak H. Damage detection in steel-concrete composite bridge using vibration characteristics and artificial neural network. Structure and Infrastructure Engineering. 2020;**16**(9):1247-1261

[14] Gordan M, Sabbagh-Yazdi S-R, Ghaedi K, Thambiratnam DP, Ismail Z. Introduction to monitoring of bridge infrastructure using soft computing techniques. In: Applied Methods in Design and Construction of Bridges, Highways and Roads - Theory and Practice. London, UK: IntechOpen; 2022 ch. 4

[15] Prakash A, Behl A, Ohn-Bar E, Chitta K, Geiger A. Exploring data aggregation in policy learning for vision-based urban autonomous driving. In: Proceedings of the IEEE/CVF Conference on Computer Vision and Pattern Recognition. 2020. pp. 11763-11773. DOI: 10.1109/CVPR42600.2020.01178

[16] Kendall A, Hawke J, Janz D, Mazur P, Reda D, Allen JM, et al. Learning to drive in a day. In: Proceedings of the International Conference on Robotics and Automation (ICRA). 2019. pp. 8248-8254. DOI: 10.1109/ICRA.2019.8793742

[17] Xie S, Girshick R, Dollár P, Tu Z, He K. Aggregated residual transformations for deep neural networks. In: Proceedings of the IEEE Conference on Computer Vision and Pattern Recognition. 2017. pp. 1492-1500. DOI: 10.48550/arXiv.1611.05431

[18] Liu C, Li H, Wang S, Zhu M, Wang D, Fan X, et al. A dataset and benchmark of underwater object detection for robot picking. In: Proceedings of the IEEE International Conference on Multimedia & Expo Workshops. 2021. pp. 1-6. DOI: 10.1109/ICMEW53276.2021.9455997

[19] Girshick R, Donahue J, Darrell T, Malik J. Rich feature hierarchies for accurate object detection and semantic segmentation. In: Proceedings of the IEEE Conference on Computer Vision and Pattern Recognition. 2014. pp. 580-587. DOI: 10.1109/CVPR.2014.81

[20] Uijlings JR, Van De Sande KE, Gevers T, Smeulders AW. Selective search for object recognition. International Journal of Computer Vision. 2013;**104**(2):154-171

[21] Jia D, Wei D, Richard S, Li JL, Kai L, and Li FF. Imagenet: A large-scale hierarchical image database. In: Proceedings of the IEEE Conference on Computer Vision and Pattern Recognition. 2009. pp. 248-255. DOI: 10.1109/CVPR.2009.5206848

[22] Girshick R. Fast r-cnn. In: Proceedings of the IEEE International Conference on Computer Vision. 2015. pp. 1440-1448. DOI: 10.1109/ICCV.2015.169

[23] Karimanzira D, Renkewitz H, Shea D, Albiez J. Object detection in sonar images. Electronics. 2020;**9**(7):1180

[24] Li X, Shang M, Qin H, Chen L. Fast accurate fish detection and recognition of underwater images with fast r-cnn. In: Proceedings of the IEEE Conference on OCEANS. 2015. pp. 1-5. DOI: 10.23919/OCEANS.2015.7404464

[25] Ren S, He K, Girshick R, Sun J. Faster r-cnn: Towards real-time object detection with region proposal networks. IEEE Transactions on Pattern Analysis and Machine Intelligence. 2016;**39**(6):1137-1149

[26] Li X, Shang M, Hao J, Yang Z. Accelerating fish detection and recognition by sharing cnns with objectness learning. In: Proceedings of the IEEE Conference on OCEANS. 2016. pp. 1-5. DOI: 10.1109/OCEANSAP.2016.7485476

[27] Zeiler MD, Fergus R. Visualizing and understanding convolutional networks. In: Proceedings of the European Conference on Computer Vision. 2014. pp. 818-833. DOI: 10.1007/978-3-319-10590-1_53

[28] Shi P, Xu X, Ni J, Xin Y, Huang W, Han S. Underwater biological detection

algorithm based on improved faster-rcnn. Water. 2021;**13**(17):2420

[29] He K, Zhang X, Ren S, Sun J. Deep residual learning for image recognition. In: Proceedings of the IEEE Conference on Computer Vision and Pattern Recognition. 2016. pp. 770-778. DOI: 10.1109/CVPR.2016.90

[30] Tan M, Pang R, Le QV. Efficientdet: Scalable and efficient object detection. In: Proceedings of the IEEE/CVF Conference on Computer Vision and Pattern Recognition. 2020. pp. 10781-10790. DOI: 10.48550/arXiv.1911.09070

[31] Zhang YF, Ren W, Zhang Z, Jia Z, Wang L, Tan T. Focal and efficient iou loss for accurate bounding box regression. Neurocomputing. 2022;**506**: 146-157

[32] D. U. o. T. National Nature Science Foundation of China. China Underwater Robot Predessional Contest [Online]. Available: http://www.urpc.org.cn/

[33] He K, Gkioxari G, Dollár P, Girshick R. Mask r-cnn. In: Proceedings of the IEEE international Conference on Computer Vision. 2017. pp. 2961-2969. DOI: 10.1109/ICCV.2017.322

[34] Fan Z, Xia W, Liu X, Li H. Detection and segmentation of underwater objects from forward-looking sonar based on a modified mask rcnn. Signal, Image and Video Processing. 2021;**15**:1135-1143

[35] Lopez Marcano S, Jinks EL, Buelow CA, Brown CJ, Wang D, Kusy B, et al. Automatic detection of fish and tracking of movement for ecology. Ecology and Evolution. 2021;**11**(12): 8254-8263

[36] Zou Z, Shi Z, Guo Y, Ye J. Object detection in 20 years: A survey. arXiv preprint arXiv:1905.05055. 2019

[37] Yan D, Li G, Li X, Zhang H, Lei H, Lu K, et al. An improved faster r-cnn method to detect tailings ponds from high-resolution remote sensing images. Remote Sensing. 2021;**13**(11):2052

[38] Redmon J, Divvala S, Girshick R, Farhadi A. You only look once: Unified, real-time object detection. In: Proceedings of the IEEE Conference on Computer Vision and Pattern Recognition. 2016. pp. 779-788. DOI: 10.1109/CVPR.2016.91

[39] Redmon J, Farhadi A. Yolo9000: Better, faster, stronger. In: Proceedings of the IEEE Conference on Computer Vision and Pattern Recognition. 2017. pp. 7263-7271. DOI: 10.1109/ CVPR.2017.690

[40] Redmon J, Farhadi A. Yolov3: An incremental improvement. arXiv preprint arXiv:1804.02767, 2018

[41] Sung M, Kim J, Lee M, Kim B, Kim T, Kim J, et al. Realistic sonar image simulation using deep learning for underwater object detection. International Journal of Control, Automation and Systems. 2020;**18**(3): 523-534

[42] Goodfellow I, Pouget-Abadie J, Mirza M, Xu B, Warde Farley D, Ozair S, et al. Generative adversarial networks. Communications of the ACM. 2020;**63** (11):139-144

[43] Ioffe S and Szegedy C. Batch normalization: Accelerating deep network training by reducing internal covariate shift. In: Proceedings of the International Conference on Machine Learning. 2015. pp. 448-456. DOI: 10.5555/3045118.3045167

[44] Szegedy C, Liu W, Jia Y, Sermanet P, Reed S, Anguelov D, et al. Going deeper with convolutions. In:

Proceedings of the IEEE Conference on Computer Vision and Pattern Recognition. 2015. pp. 1-9. DOI: 10.1109/CVPR.2015.7298594

[45] Neves G, Ruiz M, Fontinele J, Oliveira L. Rotated object detection with forward-looking sonar in underwater applications. Expert Systems with Applications. 2020;**140**:112870

[46] Yang H, Liu P, Hu Y, Fu J. Research on underwater object recognition based on yolov3. Microsystem Technologies. 2021;**27**(4):1837-1844

[47] Haugaløkken BOA, Skaldebø MB, Schjølberg I. Monocular vision-based gripping of objects. Robotics and Autonomous Systems. 2020;**131**:103589

[48] Bochkovskiy A, Wang C-Y, Liao H-YM. Yolov4: Optimal speed and accuracy of object detection. arXiv preprint arXiv: 2004.10934. 2020

[49] Wang CY, Liao HYM, Wu YH, Chen PY, Hsieh JW, Yeh IH. Cspnet: A new backbone that can enhance learning capability of cnn. In: Proceedings of the IEEE/CVF Conference on Computer Vision and Pattern Recognition Workshops. 2020. pp. 390-391. DOI: 10.1109/CVPRW50498.2020.00203

[50] Yao Z, Cao Y, Zheng S, Huang G, Lin S. Cross-iteration batch normalization. In: Proceedings of the IEEE/CVF Conference on Computer Vision and Pattern Recognition. 2021. pp. 12331-12340

[51] Chen K, Chen Y, Zhou H, Mao X, Li Y, He Y, et al. Self-supervised adversarial training. In: Proceedings of the IEEE International Conference on Acoustics, Speech and Signal Processing. 2020. pp. 2218-2222. DOI: 10.1109/ICASSP40776.2020.9054475

[52] Misra D. Mish: A self regularized non-monotonic neural activation function. arXiv preprint arXiv: 1908.08681. 2019;**4**:2

[53] Ghiasi G, Lin TY, Le QV. Dropblock: A regularization method for convolutional networks. Advances in neural information processing systems. 2018;**31**

[54] Zheng Z, Wang P, Liu W, Li J, Ye R, Ren D. Distance-iou loss: Faster and better learning for bounding box regression. In: Proceedings of the AAAI Conference on Artificial Intelligence. 2020. pp. 12993-13000. DOI: 10.1609/aaai.v34i07.6999

[55] Zhang M, Xu S, Song W, He Q, Wei Q. Lightweight underwater object detection based on yolo v4 and multi-scale attentional feature fusion. Remote Sensing. 2021;**13**(22):4706

[56] Howard AG, Zhu M, Chen B, Kalenichenko D, Wang W, Weyand T, et al. Mobilenets: Efficient convolutional neural networks for mobile vision applications. arXiv preprint arXiv: 1704.04861. 2017

[57] Tian Z, Shen C, Chen H, He T. Fcos: Fully convolutional one-stage object detection. In: Proceedings of the IEEE/CVF International Conference on Computer Vision. 2019. pp. 9627-9636. DOI: 10.1109/ICCV.2019.00972

[58] Hosang J, Benenson R, and Schiele B. Learning non-maximum suppression. In: Proceedings of the IEEE Conference on Computer Vision and Pattern Recognition. 2017. pp. 4507-4515. DOI: 10.1109/CVPR.2017.685

[59] Zhou X, Wang D, Krähenbühl P. Objects as points. arXiv preprint arXiv: 1904.07850. 2019

[60] Qin R, Zhao X, Zhu W, Yang Q, He B, Li G, et al. Multiple receptive field network (mrf-net) for autonomous underwater vehicle fishing net detection using forward-looking sonar images. Sensors. 2021;**21**(6):1933

[61] Yeh CH, Lin CH, Kang LW, Huang CH, Lin MH, Chang CY, et al. Lightweight deep neural network for joint learning of underwater object detection and color conversion. IEEE Transactions on Neural Networks and Learning Systems. 2021:1-15. DOI: 10.1109/TNNLS.2021.3072414

[62] Iandola FN, Han S, Moskewicz MW, Ashraf K, Dally WJ, Keutzer K. Squeezenet: Alexnet-level accuracy with 50x fewer parameters and< 0.5 mb model size. arXiv preprint arXiv: 1602.07360. 2016

[63] Krizhevsky A, Sutskever I, Hinton GE. Imagenet classification with deep convolutional neural networks. Advances in Neural Information Processing Systems. 2012;**25**:1097-1105

[64] Zhang X, Zhou X, Lin M, Sun J. Shufflenet: An extremely efficient convolutional neural network for mobile devices. In: Proceedings of the IEEE Conference on Computer Vision and Pattern Recognition. 2018. pp. 6848-6856. DOI: 10.1109/CVPR.2018.00716

[65] Chollet F. Xception: Deep learning with depthwise separable convolutions. In: Proceedings of the IEEE Conference on Computer Vision and Pattern Recognition. 2017. pp. 1251-1258. DOI: 10.1109/CVPR.2017.195

[66] Gao H, Wang Z, Cai L, Ji S. Channelnets: Compact and efficient convolutional neural networks via channel-wise convolutions. IEEE Transactions on Pattern Analysis and Machine Intelligence. 2021;**43**(08): 2570-2581

[67] Szegedy C, Vanhoucke V, Ioffe S, Shlens J, Wojna Z. Rethinking the inception architecture for computer vision. In: Proceedings of the IEEE Conference on Computer Vision and Pattern Recognition. 2016. pp. 2818-2826. DOI: 10.1109/CVPR.2016.308

[68] Cheng Y, Wang D, Zhou P, Zhang T. Model compression and acceleration for deep neural networks: The principles, progress, and challenges. IEEE Signal Processing Magazine. 2018;**35**(1):126-136

[69] Cheng Y, Yu FX, Feris RS, Kumar S, Choudhary A, Chang S. An exploration of parameter redundancy in deep networks with circulant projections. In: Proceedings of the IEEE International Conference on Computer Vision. 2015. pp. 2857-2865. DOI: 10.1109/ICCV.2015.327

[70] Liu Z, Sun M, Zhou T, Huang G, Darrell T. Rethinking the value of network pruning. arXiv preprint arXiv: 1810.05270. 2018

[71] Hinton G, Vinyals O, Dean J. Distilling the knowledge in a neural network. arXiv preprint arXiv: 1503.02531. 2015

[72] Han S, Mao H, Dally WJ. Deep compression: Compressing deep neural networks with pruning, trained quantization and huffman coding. arXiv preprint arXiv:1510.00149. 2015

[73] LeCun Y, Denker J, Solla S. Optimal brain damage. Advances in Neural Information Processing Systems. 1989;**2**: 598-605

[74] Liang T, Glossner J, Wang L, Shi S, Zhang X. Pruning and quantization for

deep neural network acceleration: A survey. Neurocomputing. 2021;**461**: 370-403

[75] Dietterich TG. Ensemble methods in machine learning. In: Proceedings of the International Workshop on Multiple Classifier Systems. 2000;**1578**:1-15

[76] Cheng Y, Wang D, Zhou P, Zhang T. A survey of model compression and acceleration for deep neural networks. arXiv preprint arXiv:1710.09282. 2017

[77] Vanhoucke V, Senior A, Mao MZ. Improving the speed of neural networks on cpus. In: Proceedings of the Deep Learning and Unsupervised Feature Learning Workshop. Granada Spain: NIPS; 2011

[78] Gong Y, Liu L, Yang M, Bourdev L. Compressing deep convolutional networks using vector quantization. arXiv preprint arXiv:1412.6115. 2014

[79] Wu J, Leng C, Wang Y, Hu Q, Cheng J. Quantized convolutional neural networks for mobile devices. In: Proceedings of the IEEE Conference on Computer Vision and Pattern Recognition. 2016. pp. 4820-4828. DOI: 10.48550/arXiv.1512.06473

[80] Courbariaux M, Bengio Y, David J-P. Binaryconnect: Training deep neural networks with binary weights during propagations. Advances in Neural Information Processing Systems. 2015; **28**:3123-3131

[81] Erdal E, Ergüzen A. An efficient encoding algorithm using local path on huffman encoding algorithm for compression. Applied Sciences. 2019; **9**(4):782

Chapter 6

Virtual Sensors for Smart Data Generation and Processing in AI-Driven Industrial Applications

Maddi Etxegarai, Marta Camps, Lluís Echeverria, Marc Ribalta, Francesc Bonada and Xavier Domingo

Abstract

The current digitalisation revolution demonstrates the high importance and possibilities of quality data in industrial applications. Data represent the foundation of any analytical process, establishing the fundamentals of the modern Industry 4.0 era. Data-driven processes boosted by novel Artificial Intelligence (AI) provide powerful solutions for industrial applications in anomaly detection, predictive maintenance, optimal process control and digital twins, among many others. Virtual Sensors offer a digital definition of a real Internet of Things (IoT) sensor device, providing a smart tool capable to face key issues on the critical data generation side: i) Scalability of expensive measurement devices, ii) Robustness and resilience through real-time data validation and real-time sensor replacement for continuous service, or iii) Provision of key parameters' estimation on difficult to measure situations. This chapter presents a profound introduction to Virtual Sensors, including the explanation of the methodology used in industrial data-driven projects, novel AI techniques for their implementation and real use cases in the Industry 4.0 context.

Keywords: virtual sensors, artificial intelligence, machine learning, innovative sensing strategies, internet of things, industry 4.0

1. Introduction

Digitalisation and data exploitation are two of the fundamental driving forces of the new paradigm defined by the Industry 4.0 (I4.0) revolution. Recent developments in sensors, Cyber-Physical Systems (CPS), automation, and quality inspection, among others, are motivating the digitalisation of the manufacturing and non-manufacturing industries, making available large amounts of data that may capture the nature of the process and its variability. These data streams become of utmost importance when targeting enhanced productivity, flexibility, competitiveness, and environmental impact. Hence, these large data streams not only represent a valuable opportunity but also introduce a substantial challenge for industries to digest and extract value from them, without losing focus on their day-to-day operations. Data-driven solutions, including Data Mining, Big Data, or Artificial Intelligence

(AI), provide the right tools and functionalities to digest these large amounts of data, create value, and impact manufacturing operational Key Performance Indicators (KPIs). Moreover, AI-based solutions can also support knowledge discovery actions and enrich experts' industrial knowledge by discovering previously unknown process parameter correlations that can have a big impact on industrial operations.

The perceived value of data exploitation techniques, mainly powered by AI solutions, has increased in line with the growing available data in nearly all processes and sectors. The development of data-centred and data-driven solutions has become a crucial element as a tool for not only managing but also taking advantage of the incoming process data. Nevertheless, an important issue must be considered: do available or captured data accurately represent the scenario, the process, and the environment? In most cases, the answer is no. Not all relevant or key process parameters can be physically measured, or the associated cost for direct measurement is not sustainable. Thus, the need for computing or estimating these key process parameters based on measured data has become more relevant as data availability has increased and production excellence has become progressively more demanding.

Traditionally, relying on the data provided by physical sensors has been a recurring challenge due to several limitations: the cost of the sensor, accuracy, stability, and impossibility to measure specific parameters due to physical, spatial, or environmental constraints. These challenges have commonly been addressed by using analytical approaches based on physical and mathematical expressions. While this strategy can increase the underlying physics knowledge of the process and provides a general solution, it also requires extensive experimental validation and the definition of accurate assumptions and boundary conditions. Recent AI and Machine Learning (ML) advances allow for novel data-driven approaches to estimate key process parameters. The so-called Virtual Sensors (VS), also known as Soft Sensors or Software Sensors, represent a software layer that provides indirect measurements of a process variable based on the data gathered by physical (or other virtual) sensors leveraging a fusion function [1]. The exponential growth of data during the last decade has entailed the rise of data-driven solutions powered by AI and ML algorithms, correlating input data (measurable parameters) with output targets by heuristic and probabilistic models.

This chapter aims to explain the potential of Virtual Sensors for industrial process monitoring and provide an introduction to their development. Two real industrial use cases are presented, focused on High Pressure Die Casting and wastewater treatment, to illustrate and highlight the capabilities of this technology.

2. Industrial applications of Virtual Sensors

The decision-making process in industrial applications (logistics, planning, quality control, predictive maintenance, etc.) is driven and influenced by the evolution of key parameters along the production process value chain. In most cases, this set of key parameters is obtained by deploying sensors along the process chain. For instance, placing a thermocouple sensor to monitor the temperature in a foundry or a flow meter in a complex water distribution system pipe. The monitoring data captured along the production line is used to compute KPIs that measure the operational performance of the industrial process or equipment over time. Industrial KPIs are of utmost importance for informed decision-making, as well as for measuring and targeting an objective accomplishment. Some of the most relevant KPIs are:

- **Throughput**: the number of produced units per time unit.
- **Scrap ratio**: the number of defective parts over the total production.
- **Availability**: the ratio between uptime and production downtimes.
- **Overall Equipment Effectiveness (OEE)**: The percentage of manufacturing time that is genuinely productive, combining aspects of quality, performance, and availability in a single KPI.

Data accuracy and reliability are of great importance since the decision-making process relies on KPIs computed from data gathered at the production chain. In case of sensor failure, malfunction, drift, or need for recalibration, industrial KPIs may not confidently represent the process performance anymore. This situation could lead to two non-optimal scenarios: poor decision-making due to the lack of reliable information or production breakdowns due to equipment failure. Furthermore, equipment, infrastructure, material, or even people involved (technicians, staff, etc.) may be threatened due to the malfunction of the monitoring systems. Thus, mitigation strategies should be considered to reduce this risk. Robust and accurate data-driven solutions leveraging production data can provide resilience capabilities to operate in non-optimal conditions. Virtual Sensor offers an appropriate solution since they increase the reliability and agility of the system at a low operational cost, providing an indirect measurement for non-measurable physically properties.

AI and data-driven Virtual Sensor can significantly impact industrial applications by providing valuable process insights that support and enrich informed decision-making processes, as shown in **Figure 1**, where the schematic design of two Virtual Sensors is introduced.

Within the industrial applications, the three key objectives of Virtual Sensors are:

- **Expand knowledge:** To compute extra parameters derived from real sensors that are impossible or not sustainable to measure (at full-scale), thus contributing to a better understanding of the process.

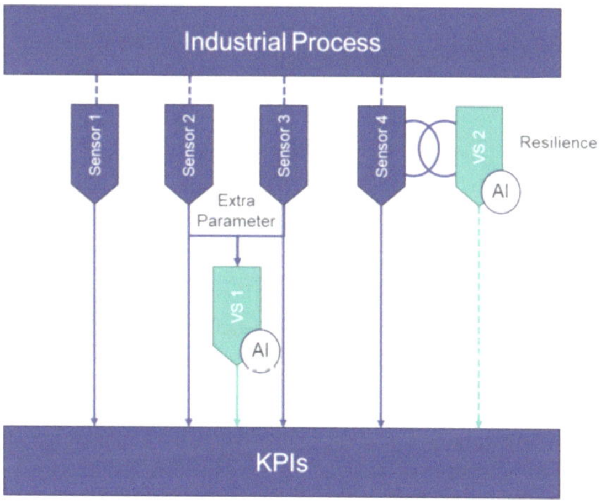

Figure 1.
Virtual sensors applications in industry.

- **Resilience:** To simulate real sensor outputs that mitigate production breakdowns due to equipment failure or even planned maintenance.

- **Accuracy:** To remove and replace the occurrence of outliers in real sensor readings and detect sensors drifts and recalibration needs.

Industrial applications can benefit from the Virtual Sensor functionalities: increasing the knowledge of the process, reducing the operational costs of the monitoring strategy, and offering a cost-effective solution enhancing monitoring system resilience.

Even though Virtual Sensors are a relatively recent research topic, their industrial applications are becoming increasingly relevant. A promising example is the usage of Virtual Sensor in Smart Factories and digitalised manufacturing facilities where devices, machinery and production systems are interconnected to enhance decision-making and management [2]. Dobrescu et al. [3] presented the development of services and computing resources for hybrid simulation of Virtual Manufacturing systems, providing a sensor-cloud interface where the end-user can virtualise multiple Virtual Sensors. The adoption of robots and their interactions with humans in Smart Factories was studied by Indri et al. [4], where Virtual Sensors were used to enhance the knowledge of the robot operation.

The applications of Virtual Sensor in the manufacturing industry are very heterogeneous. Maschler et al. [5] estimated the combustion duration on a large gas engine using just the rotational speed as input data. They studied in this work the importance of pre-processing the data for greater accuracy, showing different results for the use of Principal Component Analysis, Fast Fourier Transformation, or just a simple smoothing of the measured rotational speed. Alonso et al. [6] aimed to calculate the cooling power estimation to enable the replacement of the expensive portable measuring system. They used a model based on a Deep Learning architecture that involved data from the chiller's thermodynamic variables (temperature and pressure) and data from the refrigeration circuit (pressure power).

Other studies focus on the malfunctioning of the system instead. Zenisek et al. [7] presented an approach to stabilise and optimise the metal deposition process, merging information from various sources. The ML-based method generates a valid data stream from heterogeneous sources and can mitigate the problem of data merging through the knowledge of domain experts. Finally, they presented a real use case where they estimated the current weld bead height, one of the principal performance indicators of the process. Aware of the problems that could generate a sensor failure and the consequent interruption of information flow, Ilyas et al. [8] introduced a framework capable of finding Internet of Things (IoT) sensors in the surrounding environment and replacing faulty sensors in an automated way. The framework selects the data source based on metadata description, pre-processes historical data, and trains and ranks machine learning algorithms with great results without human intervention. They tested the model predicting the output of a solar power plant.

Tegen et al. [9] proposed Dynamic Intelligent Virtual Sensors (DIVS). The idea was to combine a broader (and not fixed) set of heterogeneous data sources based on Machine Learning to involve the user in the loop. The dynamic part of the concept can be interesting for industrial applications: evaluating the inputs of the Virtual Sensor in terms of information quality (for instance, noise, entropy, etc.) and deciding whether a data source (physical sensor) should be removed or added to the Virtual Sensor. Moreover, the online incremental learning concept was also applied, looking for a Virtual Sensor that relies not only on traditional batch learning but can be dynamically adjusted involving user labelling.

Virtual Sensor can also be applied in multiple areas of the industrial water domain covering the whole water cycle. Djerioui et al. [10] implemented a Virtual Sensor of the chlorine parameter in water treatment plants using the conductivity, dissolved oxygen, suspended solids, and pH variables as input data. The study compares the performance of a Support Vector Machine (SVM) and an Extreme Learning Machine (ELM) ML algorithm, showing better behaviour using ELM. Pattanayak et al. [11] developed a Virtual Sensors to predict in real-time the Chemical Oxygen Demand (COD) of the river Ganga using the input quality parameters of ammonia, total suspended solids, nitrate, pH, and dissolved oxygen. They evaluated different algorithms, finally building a predictive model based on K-Nearest Neighbours, which was used to predict the water quality at the treatment plant's discharge point.

Wastewater treatment is a process where factors such as energy cost or climate footprint are directly related to the process optimisation. Virtual Sensor enables monitoring key parameters in situations where the physical sensors may lead to error due to the constant contact with wastewater. Foschi et al. [12] proposed a Virtual Sensor for the *E. Coli* value for wastewater disinfection using the data from conventional wastewater physical and chemical indicators (such as COD, nitrate, and ammonia). Their research obtains a predictive model trained using an artificial neural network, which could save up to 57% of disinfectant. Pisa et al. [13] showed a Virtual Sensor to predict ammonium and total nitrogen to control effluent violations at the treatment plant using input flow, input ammonium, temperature, and internal recycle flow data. They accomplished the generation of a predictive model using a deep neural network with Long-Short Term Memory neurons, capable of predicting the nitrogen-derived parameters with good accuracy.

3. Methodology

In this chapter, we focus on the Machine Learning domain, currently one of the most trending areas under the Artificial Intelligence umbrella. Machine Learning aims to develop smart models based on data-driven algorithms that can accurately generate predictions without the explicit necessity to program them for that objective. It can be seen as learning (or training) a function (f) that maps input variables (X) to output variables (Y). Once defined, function f can be used to generalise the learned behaviour and make predictions (Y′) given a new unseen instance of input variables X'. Here, a data-driven approach depends on existing data sets to infer the unknown function f based on parametric or non-parametric algorithms.

More specifically, we propose the use of the regression-type of the Supervised Learning family of algorithms for the Virtual Sensor implementation, as shown in **Figure 2**. These algorithms rely on labelled datasets providing both input variables X

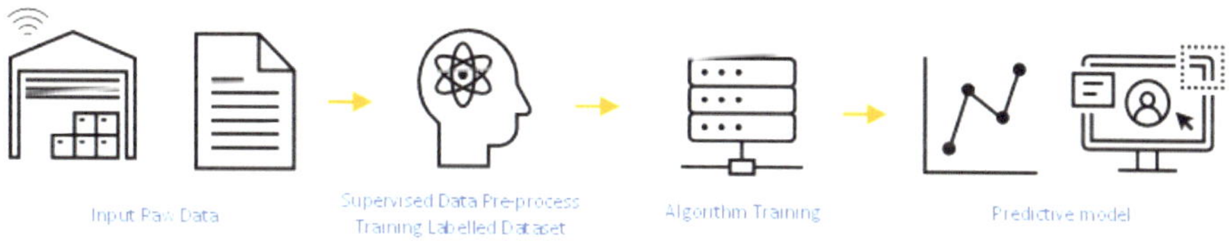

Figure 2.
Supervised learning paradigm.

and output variables Y to infer the function f. Moreover, in regression problems, the output variables Y are continuous values instead of the categorical data type required in classification problems.

In this scenario, to successfully conduct a data-driven project, it is of utmost importance to follow a standardised method to translate business problems into tasks, suggest data transformations, or provide means for evaluating the final results and reporting the process, among other objectives. The Cross Industry Standard Process for Data Mining (CRISP-DM) methodology provides this flexible framework [14] and it is organised into seven well-differentiated phases, as shown in **Figure 3**. In this sense, the data mining process is generally cyclic, since it is usually necessary to go back and forth between stages until a valid solution that meets the quality criteria is found. At this point, it is usually a common misunderstanding across the community to consider that the work is finished. Even when the solution is finally deployed and integrated into a production environment, the performance of the underlying models needs to be continuously checked. This is due to the data-driven nature of the concept, which could make a model unfeasible, for example, in those cases where the baseline conditions of the studied process change or evolve over time. This effect makes the learned function f not valid for new scenarios since the relation between input variables X and output variables Y has changed. An innovative solution in this scenario considers an online CRISP-DM model to retrain and validate the predictive models periodically over time.

The CRISP-DM process starts with understanding the business perspective, objectives, and requirements to design the project plan together with the field expert. Once the goals are defined, the initial data are collected and processed with activities channelled to familiarise with them. This first analysis can help identify data quality problems or detect interesting subsets to enable hypotheses for hidden information. Next, the data preparation phase aims to construct the final dataset, which will be used to feed and validate the algorithms. Usually, a significant amount of effort is devoted to this task since it is the most time-consuming and delicate stage that generates one of the most critical outcomes, the training dataset. This is important because data must be consistent and reliable in the Data Science domain since it defines the basis of all the solutions. Data cleaning, feature engineering, feature selection, or data scaling are some of the common processes carried out in this stage and require experienced and creative data scientists for a successful implementation.

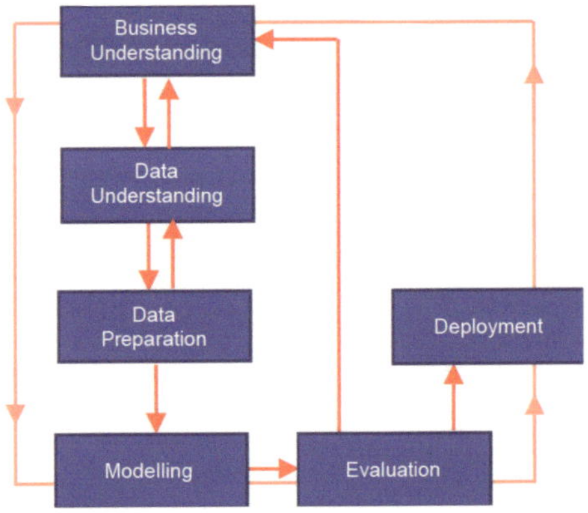

Figure 3.
Phases of the CRISP-DM process.

Different Machine Learning algorithms are selected, trained, and calibrated in the modelling phase to achieve optimal performance. The reason behind trying different algorithms is that each one is based on several techniques, has different mathematic fundamentals, and makes different assumptions. Thus, it does not exist one general solution to all the problems and each case needs to be analysed independently, given the fact that underlying data and patterns are different [15].

Then, even though the algorithms are independently evaluated in the modelling phase, during the evaluation phase, the whole model, all the stages, and all the algorithms that appear should be thoroughly assessed and reviewed, as well as the business objectives defined in the initial business understanding phase. Furthermore, a comparison across different models is required to identify the most successful ones. Finally, for the deployment, the model and the knowledge gained are organised and presented in a way that the final customer can understand, use, and maintain.

Usually, the model training, selection and evaluation stages follow a well-established methodology in the Data Science domain, as shown on the left in **Figure 4**. First, in case of parametric Machine Learning algorithms, the model training step is aimed at learning and validating the parameters of the function f (e.g., the coefficients in regression or the weights of a neural network). Separate training and testing datasets must be used across these phases. Otherwise, the model would suffer from overfitting. In this case, a model that reproduces training labels Y during the validation would present a perfect score but would not be able to make good predictions on new data X', since it would not have learned the authentic data patterns.

Splitting data into training and test datasets is known as the Cross-Validation (CV) process, and K-fold CV defines its most basic implementation. The idea is to split the training dataset into k folds, train k models using k-1 different folds (as training datasets) and validate them on the remaining fold. Several methodology variations have been proposed depending on the data type, the basic idea of this concept is shown on the right in **Figure 4**. The final training performance corresponds to the average of the k individual models' performance.

The training step also considers the evaluation and search of the most optimal algorithm hyperparameters given a training dataset. In this context, the hyperparameters are those algorithm parameters that by changing their value, are used to manage the learning process (e.g., the learning rate in Gradient Descent-based approaches). Similar to the CV procedure, several methodologies were used to this end [16]. To mention some, Grid Search proposes an exhaustive search on all hyperparameter combinations given a set of predefined values, while Randomised Search samples any given number of candidates from a parameter space following a specified distribution.

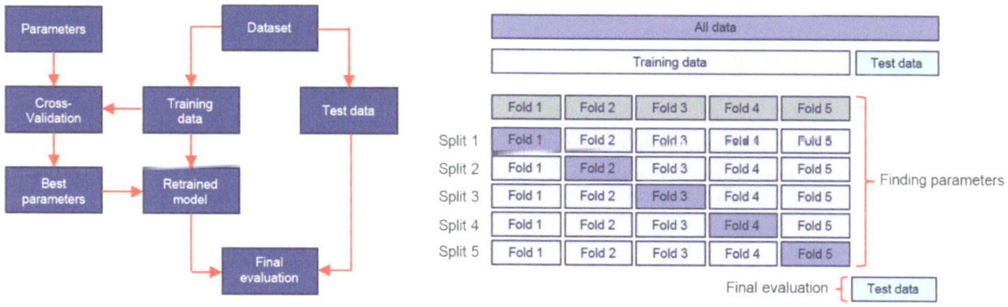

Figure 4.
Left: Cross-validation flow in ML models training. Right: K-folds CV approach.

Finally, to correctly understand the presented Virtual Sensor case study's performance, it is also essential to introduce the validation metrics used to evaluate and compare the models. The following regression metrics are proposed:

- **Mean Absolute Error (MAE) regression loss**: computes the averaged absolute difference (error) between the ground truth and the model predictions.

$$MAE = \frac{1}{N}\sum_{i=1}^{N}\left|y_i - \hat{y}_i\right| \quad (1)$$

where N is the test dataset size, y_i is the ground truth value of the i_{st} entry in the test dataset and $\hat{y}_i$ is the model prediction of the i_{st} entry in the test dataset.

- **R^2 or the coefficient of determination:** computes the proportion of variance explained by the independent variables in the model.

$$R^2\left(y_i, \hat{y}_i\right) = \frac{\sum_{i=1}^{N}\left(y_i - \hat{y}_i\right)^2}{\sum_{i=1}^{N}\left(y_i - \overline{y}\right)^2} \quad (2)$$

where N is the test dataset size, y_i is the ground truth value of the i_{st} entry in the test dataset, $\hat{y}_i$ is the model prediction of the i_{st} entry in the test dataset, and $\overline{y}$ is the average ground truth value.

4. Case studies

Virtual Sensors are a flexible and versatile technology that can be found in multiple sectors of the industry. In this section, two real use cases are introduced. The first case is related to mould injection of metallic pieces in the manufacturing industry. The second case is related to the wastewater treatment industry.

4.1 Aluminium mould injection use case

High-Pressure Die Casting (HPDC) is a process in which a molten metallic alloy is forced under pressure into a locked metal mould cavity, formed by the cover die half and the ejector die half, where a powerful press holds it until the metal solidifies. After solidifying, the ejector die half opens, and the piece is ejected. Finally, the dies are closed again, ready for the next cycle. The casting process is composed of 3 stages:

- Prefill or slow shot stage: the plunger advances at low speed until the metal starts to fill the dies cavity.

- Fill or quick shot stage: once the metal reaches the gate of the die, the plunger speed is sharply increased, between 4 and 10 times.

- Consolidation or solidification stage: once the dies cavity is filled with about 95–98% of its volume, the plunger reduces its speed, and the controlling variable is switched from plunger position to pressure, inducing a high pressure during the metal solidification process.

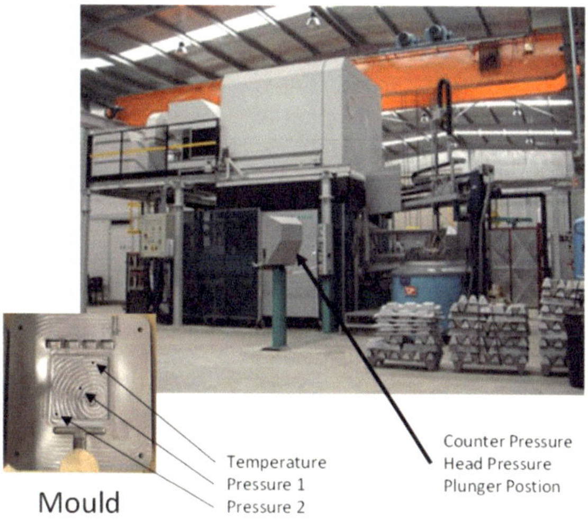

Figure 5.
HPDC Bühler machine with the three machine sensors (counter pressure, head pressure, plunger position) and an image of the mould with the holes of the three mould sensors (temperature, pressure 1 and pressure2).

The HPDC machine incorporates many sensors to track its activity. However, the mould, which must be redesigned for each new piece or batch, should include additional sensors if its sensorization is needed. As mould sensors are expensive, difficult to instal, and their integration may affect the product's finish, the proposed solution is to replace the in-mould sensors with Virtual Sensor, inferred using external machine sensors data. The Virtual Sensors allow to monitor the process and to apply corrective and preventive actions. These Virtual Sensors are developed using AI and ML methods, enabling a richer and more profound understanding of the process. The HPDC machine used for these experiments, the mould and the sensors are shown in **Figure 5**.

4.1.1 Data

The experimental campaign is carried out in the Bühler Evolution D53 machine, where aluminium L2630 is injected into tray-shaped moulds. During the lapse of two days, 256 pieces are cast at 13 different machine configurations. For each machine configuration at least 10 samples are manufactured. During each batch, the data from six sensors is recorded at a 2 kHz frequency. The change of the three in-mould sensors, two for the cavity pressure and one for the cavity temperature is shown on the left graphic in **Figure 6**. The temporal evolution of the three machine sensors: plunger position, head pressure and counter pressure is shown on the right plot in **Figure 6**.

The dataset recorded during the first day (132 tests) is used to train the model while the dataset of the second day (126 tests) is used for the test phase.

4.1.2 Methods

As previously explained, the in-mould sensors are expensive and may affect the shape and result of the final piece. Therefore, in this section, the in-mould sensors: a temperature sensor and two pressure sensors, from now on referred to as pressure 1 and pressure 2, are predicted using machine sensors: plunger position, velocity, head pressure and counter pressure. This part exemplifies the Virtual Sensor forecasting.

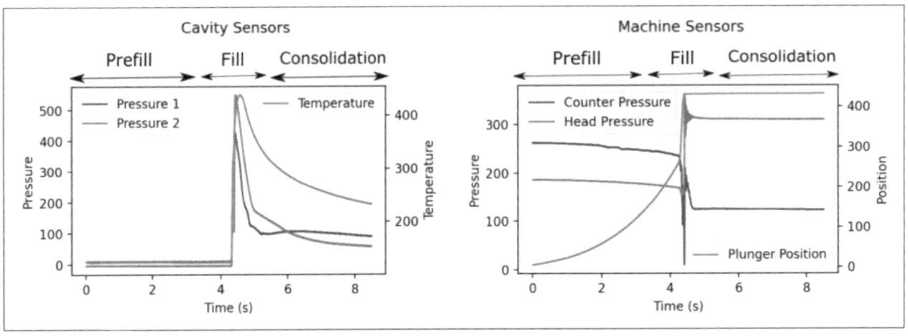

Figure 6.
Schematic representation of an HPDC shot sleeve and an injection curve with the 3 different phases: Prefill, fill and consolidation.

Following the CRISP-DM methodology, the following phase is the data preparation, essential to arrange the input data that is later fed to the algorithms. The Pearson's correlation analysis [17] demonstrates that the plunger position, counter pressure, and head pressure are highly correlated. Thus, the products of these three sensors, in pairs, are added as variables: counter pressure x head pressure, counter pressure x plunger position and head pressure x plunger position. This technique enables the use of highly related variables while preserving their influence.

To predict an instant value of any of the three virtual samples defined, the three original sensors, the three products explained above, the derivative of the position (the velocity), and 2 or 5 back samples are given as input, iterating through the results to find the most suitable input parameters for this use case.

The training dataset is split randomly in a stratified way, keeping the same percentage of machine configurations in each. The 80% of data are used for the training dataset, and the remaining 20% are employed in the validation dataset. Finally, all the data are scaled using the *MinMaxScaler*, which transforms the data into the 0–1 range. Training data are first fitted and, afterwards, train and validation datasets are converted.

The CV grid search methodology with the aforementioned K-fold split is implemented to train an evaluate different models based on the following ML algorithms:

- **Decision Tree:** an algorithm that predicts the target value by learning simple decision rules inferred from the data in a flowchart-like tree structure, with decision nodes and leaves. The chosen hyperparameters to tune are the maximum depth of the tree that will be created, and the maximum number of features required for each split [18].

- **Random Forest:** an ensemble regression algorithm that computes the output by randomly generating a multitude of decision trees and averaging the predictions of all the trees. The chosen hyperparameters to tune are, like the Decision Trees algorithm, the maximum depth, and the maximum number of features. Additionally, the number of trees in the forest (the number of estimators) has also been chosen [19].

- **KNN:** the k-Nearest Neighbour algorithm predicts the output by storing all the training data and calculating the distance between the new and stored data.

The most important parameters are the number of neighbours used to predict each data point and the weight function used to determine the importance given to the neighbour data [20].

- **SVR:** Support Vector Regression algorithm is a variation of the classifier Support Vector Machine but adjusted for regression problems. Instead of separating data into classes by means of a hyperplane, the data are adjusted to the mentioned hyperplane with a certain degree of tolerance given (ε), where the best fit is the hyperplane with the maximum number of points. Therefore, the hyperparameter ε needs to be tuned, together with the C parameter, which determines de regularisation applied to the algorithm [21].

4.2 Wastewater treatment plant use case

The Activated Sludge Process (ASP) [22] is usually a critical stage in a Wastewater Treatment Plant (WWTP) and has a direct impact on the effluent water quality as well as on the greenhouse gas (GHG) emissions, demanding considerable quantities of energy. Specifically, the ASP Nitrification step is the biological process of converting ammonia to nitrate in wastewater tanks using aerobic autotrophic bacteria. The process requires proper working conditions such as enough biomass concentrations, specific environmental conditions, a minimum residence time to process the water, and a great amount of oxygen. Any variation in these conditions directly affects the amount of ammonia being treated, thus in the effluent water quality.

In this scenario, the airflow system controls the oxygen injection, one of the key processes with the highest resource consumption and impact in the treatment plant. The water operators manage the air blowers to optimise the process (i.e., the effluent water quality reaches the expected criteria, while energy consumption and GHG emissions are minimised), thus the use of sensors to monitor in real-time these quality parameters enable an online control. Ammonia is another key parameter that needs to be adequately treated. In case its monitoring gathers non-real values, the blower's management is directly influenced, resulting in elevated costs, climate impacts and issues in the effluent water quality. Implementing a Virtual Sensor enables continuous monitoring of the ammonia parameter which enables the: i) detection of sensors' malfunction or drift in measurements (due to the constant contact with wastewater), and ii) implementation of maintenance actions without the need to stop dependent systems, therefore ensuring correct and continuous WWPT operations.

This use case focuses on the WWTP ASP treatment tanks within its corresponding lanes. It operates in the following manner:

- The wastewater enters the first phase of the primary treatment, where the sediment is clarified.
- The clarified water enters an anaerobic tank, where water gets digested.
- The water slowly moves to the aerobic tank, where the nitrification process happens.
- Finally, the water leaves the tank and other processes are applied, such as second clarification or disinfections.

4.2.1 Data

The data available comprises historical information on three sensors located inside the treatment lane, as shown in **Figure 7**:

- Dissolved Oxygen (DO), located at the entrance of the aerobic tank.

- Water flow, placed at the entrance of the anaerobic tank.

- Ammonia level, set at the final part of the aerobic tank.

These sensors extract the information every 5 minutes, and the dataset spans two years of registers, with regular and irregular values that need to be checked and filtered. Furthermore, due to the sensors being located at different parts of the reaction tank and the water taking time to flow between the inner tanks, it is required to study the time correlation between sensors.

The train set contains 80% of the data, and the test set the remaining 20%. This second set includes the latest data gathered.

4.2.2 Methods

The first phase of the CRISP-DM cycle (Business Understanding) covers the analysis of the problem and the definition of the data-driven approach. The approach focuses on predicting the real-time value of the ammonia parameter using the past and real-time values of the DO and water flow variables, and the past values of ammonia.

Following the CRISP-DM methodology, data are preprocessed, cleaned and new variables are created. To decide which timestamps are used as input features for the model, it is crucial to understand the correlation between them and the objective variable. Pearson's correlation, autocorrelation and cross-correlation techniques [23] are applied to decide the features.

The autocorrelation plot for ammonia is shown on the left graphic in **Figure 8**. The most important lags (previous values) are the ones nearest to the present time, and past hour lags are used as input variables for the model. The cross-correlation among the sensors' data also shows the most important lags. The cross-correlation between the ammonia and water flow variables is shown on the right graph in **Figure 8**, indicating the correlation of any lag from the water flow sensor with the present value of the ammonia sensor. The most important lags are from the previous three hours (−30 lags * 5 minutes per lag), which coincides with the time the water spends moving inside the

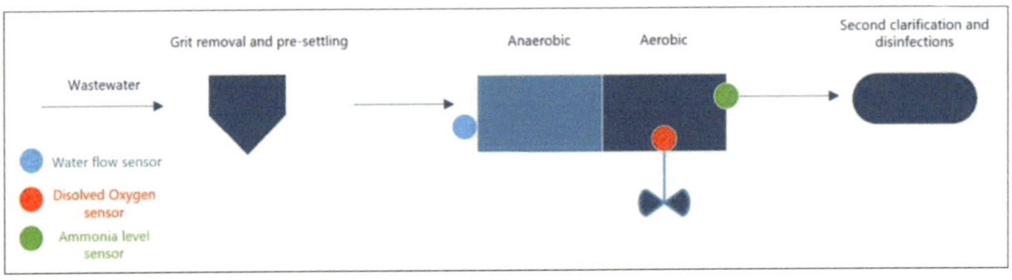

Figure 7.
Wastewater treatment plant lane. Visual sensor location.

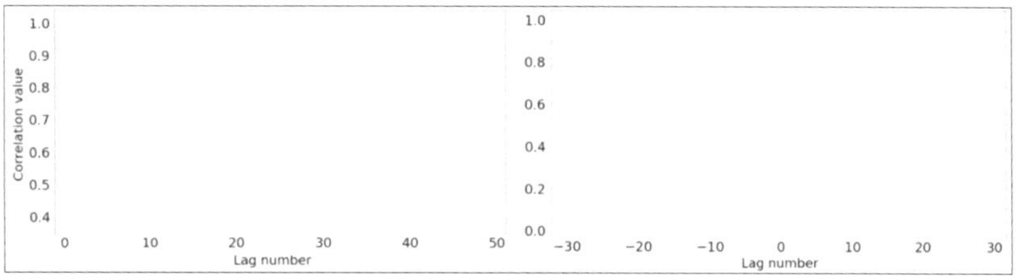

Figure 8.
Left: Autocorrelation for the ammonia parameter. Right: Cross-correlation between the ammonia and water flow parameters.

reaction tank. The DO lag selection follows the same strategy, but in this case, the present values are the most related.

To use the data of the different water parameters, the registers need to have a similar scale of values, so the weight assigned to a feature by the predictive model is not affected by higher or lower values. In this case, the standard score (or Z-score) [24] is used, setting the mean to 0 and scaling the variance to 1.

In the final iterations of the CRISP-DM process, a Long-Short Term Memory (LSTM) [25]. Artificial Neural Network [26] algorithm has been used to deal with the process nonlinearities and multiple input time series data, and ultimately, to implement the Ammonia Virtual Sensor. LSTM is a Recurrent Neural Network (RNN) [27] that has feedback connections and can process data sequences such as videos, text, or time series. The inner structure of the LSTM stores the output activations from the different layers of the network. Then, the next time an input is fed, the previously obtained outputs are used as inputs, concatenating the stored information with the new input thus simulating some kind of memory system. The LSTM differentiates from other types of RNNs in the capability of storing multiple iterations of output activations without losing information through time, being the best reason to use this architecture when numerous lags are used. To generate an LSTM architecture, several parameters need to be considered and iterated over. The most important ones are:

1. Number of layers: Number of hidden recurrent layers, to treat the non-linearities of the entering features.

2. Number of neurons: Number of neurons in each layer. Each neuron computes the outputs of the previous layer and sends the result to the next layer.

3. Dropout: Dropout is a regularisation method that probabilistically excludes LSTM units from activating and updating the weight while training, reducing overfitting conditions and therefore improving the model performance. In this use case, the architectures have a dropout of 10%.

To decide the best algorithm hyperparameters (e.g. neural network layer and neurons per layer), several training iterations are done using the Cross-Validation grid search technique over the training dataset to ensure the model is not overfitting. Afterwards, several combinations are compared to find out which combination obtains better results in the test set. The scoring metrics used are the MAE and R^2.

5. Results and discussion

5.1 Aluminium mould injection use case

Using 2 and 5 back samples as additional input variables for the algorithms does not improve the results. Neither the R^2 score nor the MAE score nor the performance improve, but the additional samples hugely increase the prediction time and computational power needed. Therefore, only the same instant sensors' samples, their interactions and the velocity are considered as input variables of the final model.

The predictions of all ML algorithms used in each Virtual Sensor development compared with the real sensor values (black lines) are shown in **Figures 9–11**. For better visual clarity, only four cycles are depicted for each sensor. The prediction and the real values of the first pressure sensor are shown in **Figure 9**. The SVR algorithm (light blue line) and KNN (yellow line) are the algorithms with the lowest R^2 error and highest MAE error for all three sensors. On the contrary, the other two algorithms, Decision Tree (red line) and Random Forest (dark blue line) both present higher R2 errors and lower MAE errors for all three sensors. These metrics can be seen in **Table 1**.

The pressure 2 virtual sensor predictions compared with the real values are shown in **Figure 10**. The results are generally worse in this case than in the pressure 1 sensor. Even though the Random Forest algorithm adjusts more closely to the real sensor, the third and fourth cycle predictions show an example of a fair disparity in the results. It should be kept in mind that the graphic only depicts 4 sample cycles and not the totality of the data predicted. The metrics of the predictions can be found in **Table 2**.

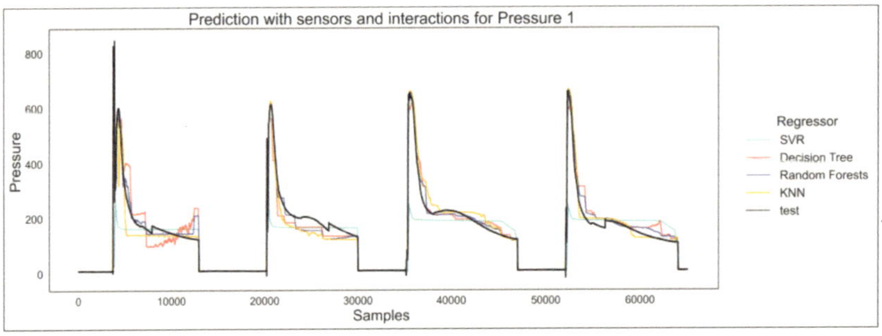

Figure 9.
VS performance comparison for pressure 1 variable simulation.

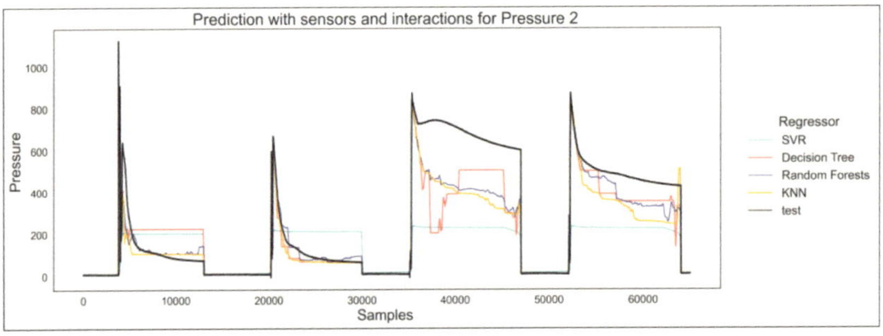

Figure 10.
VS performance comparison for pressure 2 variable simulation.

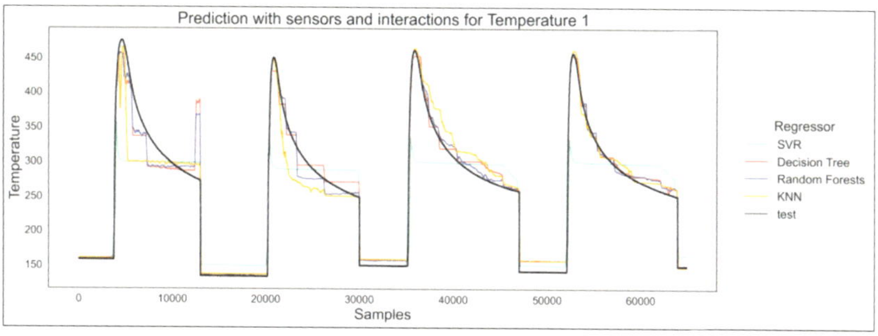

Figure 11.
VS performance comparison for temperature variable simulation.

	Algorithm	Hyperparameters	Train	Validation	Re-train	Test
R2	SVR	C = 1 Epsilon = 0.1	0.709	0.732	—	—
	Decision Tree	Max_depth = 10 Max_features = auto	0.991	0.968	—	—
	Random Forest	N_estimators = 100 Max_ features = 2 Max_depth = 25	0.998	0.972	0.997	0.903
	KNN	N_neighbors = 20 Weights = Distance	0.998	0.717	—	—
MAE	SVR	C = 1 Epsilon = 0.1	35.1	30.2	—	—
	Decision Tree	Max_depth = 10 Max_features = auto	5.19	10.1	—	—
	Random Forest	N_estimators = 100 Max_ features = 2 Max_depth = 25	2.13	9.12	3.12	22.9
	KNN	N_neighbors = 20 Weights = Distance	2.28	23.4	—	—

Table 1.
Performance of each algorithm for the temperature sensor in both datasets.

The results for the temperature sensor are shown in **Figure 11**. In this case also, the SVR predicts almost constant values during the consolidation stage. Unlike the other Virtual Sensor, the prediction during the prefill stage fails to fit closely to the real sensor in all the algorithms.

Tables 1–3 show the main results in R^2 and MAE for the three Virtual Sensor models and for each algorithm employed. The algorithm with the highest R^2 error and the lowest MAE error is the Random Forest regressor for all three in-mould sensors. Therefore, Random Forests with the mentioned fine-tuned hyperparameters is chosen as the best algorithm. Following the train/test methodology explained beforehand, the performances of the test dataset are also shown in **Tables 1–3**.

Both the temperature and pressure 1 sensors obtain high R^2 errors and low MAE errors for the Virtual Sensors predictions. Pressure 2 also gets a high R^2, but high overfitting behaviour can be assumed due to the lower values in the validation and test dataset contrary to the train errors. To illustrate the distribution of the predicted VS values, the counts of the real values versus the predicted ones for the three in-mould

	Algorithm	Hyperparameters	Train	Validation	Re-train	Test
R2	SVR	C = 1 Epsilon = 0.01	0.480	0.461	—	—
	Decision Tree	Max_depth = 10 Max_features = log2	0.966	0.926	—	—
	Random Forest	N_estimators = 120 Max_features = 3 Max_depth = 10	0.998	0.950	0.965	0.820
	KNN	N_neighbors = 20 Weights = Distance	0.997	0.337	—	—
MAE	SVR	C = 1 Epsilon = 0.01	42.1	43.7	—	—
	Decision Tree	Max_depth = 10 Max_features = log2	12.0	20.7	—	—
	Random Forest	N_estimators = 120 Max_features = 3 Max_depth = 10	2.84	16.3	13.7	29.5
	KNN	N_neighbors = 20 Weights = Distance	2.99	44.4	—	—

Table 2.
Performance of each algorithm for the pressure 1 sensor in both datasets.

	Algorithm	Hyperparameters	Train	Validation	Re-train	Test
R2	SVR	C = 0.01 Epsilon = 1	0.381	0.327	—	—
	Decision Tree	Max_depth = 10 Max_features = log2	0.931	0.677	—	—
	Random Forest	N_estimators = 90 max_features = 2 max_depth = 10	0.999	0.775	0.886	0.071
	KNN	N_neighbors = 20 Weights = Distance	0.999	0.482	—	—
MAE	SVR	C = 0.01 Epsilon = 1	64.4	104	—	—
	Decision Tree	Max_depth = 10 Max_features = log2	22.7	57.9	—	—
	Random Forest	N_estimators = 90 max_features = 2 max_depth = 10	2.27	51.0	33.8	97.7
	KNN	N_neighbors = 20 Weights = Distance	2.23	75.9	—	—

Table 3.
Performance of each algorithm for the pressure 2 sensor in both datasets.

sensors are shown in **Figure 12**, using the test dataset. The prediction of pressure 1 is more accurate than pressure 2. In this figure, it can also be observed that although the prediction of pressure 2 is far from making a good prediction, it is worth noting that

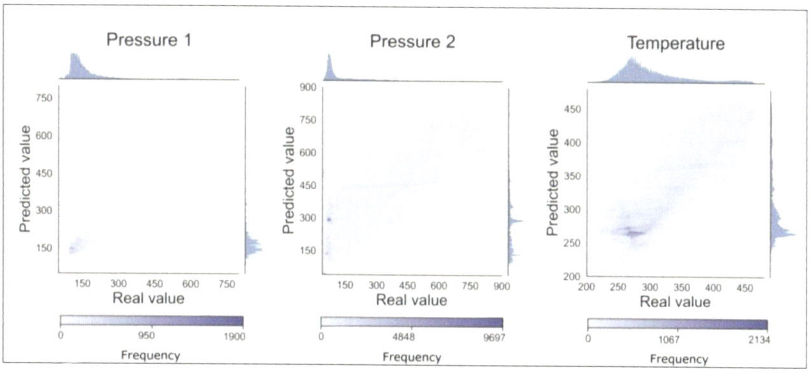

Figure 12.
Heat map of the predicted value vs. real values of each virtual sensor. The colourmap indicates the frequency of repetition.

its errors are mostly due to an erroneous prediction around 0 values, the 'stand-by' value. For the temperature sensor, most values are inside an error of 50 degrees.

5.2 Wastewater treatment plant use case

The train and test processes resulted in the three LSTM architectures outputting the best results are shown in **Table 4**, displaying the scores for the final test set. Similar performances are achieved, but the third model presents the highest R^2. Therefore, the selected architecture is the last one, with 3 hidden layers and 25 neurons on each layer.

The model's response also needs to be validated in situations with a high increase in the ammonia parameter. The Virtual Sensor acting in two cases where the predictions correctly follow the increase of ammonia is shown in **Figure 13**. As it can be seen, the error also increases in these situations since the model is predicting unusual conditions.

To detect possible flaws in the model at a more individual level, the evaluation of registers is done by means of a scatter plot, as shown in **Figure 14**. It compares the predicted and real values, plotting the regression line of all the values to give a general perspective of the overall correlation. It can be observed that, within the predictions, there are no individual registers with a great error, but the general error detected previously is confirmed here. The predictions are lower than the real values, and that is a general flaw of the model trained.

Architectures	MAE	R^2
Number of layers = 4 Number of neurons = 20	0.202	0.960
Number of layers = 3 Number of neurons = 30	0.018	0.970
Number of layers = 3 Number of neurons = 25	0.020	0.975

Table 4.
LSTM architectures and their scoring using the final test set.

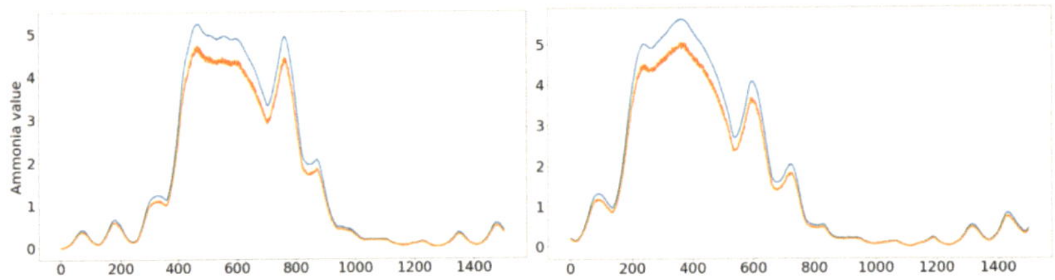

Figure 13.
Real ammonia value, in blue, versus predicted virtual sensor value, in orange. Two cases of a sudden increase in ammonia.

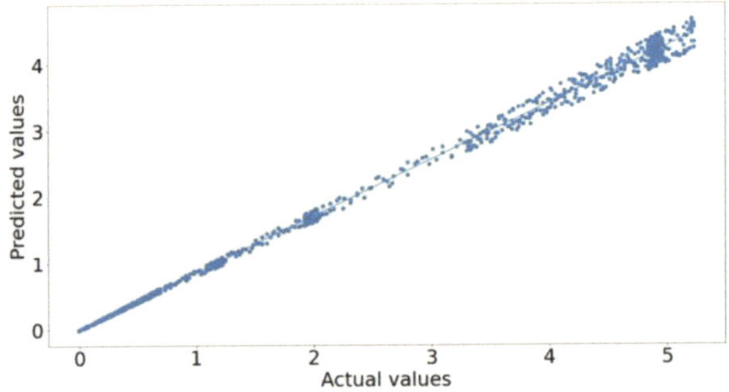

Figure 14.
Scatter plot of the predictions, comparing the individual predictions with the real values.

6. Conclusion

Artificial Intelligence is becoming a key element in the 'must have' technology stack for industries that embrace the challenges and opportunities of the Industry 4.0 paradigm. Smart exploitation of the production chain parameters and data is key for informed decision-making that can impact relevant industrial Key Performance Indicators.

This chapter focuses on a novel approach that utilises Artificial Intelligence and data-driven solutions to expand the production process knowledge base and provide more resilient and robust monitoring systems. The so-called Virtual Sensors allow the creation of indirect measurements of process variables, creating virtual replicas of the real sensors that can detect and mitigate sensors drifts, malfunctions, inaccuracies, etc. Furthermore, new parameters that are difficult or impossible to measure can be estimated by combing inputs of different sensors by means of AI-driven models.

The use of standard methodologies and good practices is considered when describing how the Cross Industry Standard Process for Data Mining can be put in place for developing Virtual Sensor for industrial applications. Additionally, two use cases are presented and described: High Pressure Die Casting (HPDC) and Wastewater Treatment Plant. In the HPDC use case, three Virtual Sensors are implemented to predict two different pressures and the temperature inside the mould cavity. The final models based on Random Forest algorithms offer an R^2 error of 0.903 for the temperature sensors, 0.820 for the pressure 1 sensor and 0.071 for the pressure 2 sensor. The predicted curves follow the real trend, especially for the pressure 1 and temperature sensors, positioning the Virtual Sensors as a trustworthy technology to avoid the implementation of cavity sensors that increase the cost and can affect the shape of the final piece.

In the Wastewater Treatment Plant case, a Virtual Sensors is implemented to improve and ensure the continuous monitoring of the Ammonia parameter in the Activated Sludge Process stage. In this way, the dependence on online real sensor measurements is considerably reduced, which enables an uninterrupted WWTP optimal control. Long-Short Term Memory Deep Neural Network architectures are introduced as algorithms capable to deal with non-linear process behaviours, showing a Deep Learning architecture that correctly adapts to the needs of time series data, which is a good match for Virtual Sensors development. The model benchmarks show a low predictive error, offering a R^2 score of 0.975, thus demonstrating the capacities of such technologies in these complex scenarios.

Acknowledgements

This work was financially supported by the Catalan Government through the funding grant ACCIÓ-Eurecat.

Author details

Maddi Etxegarai*, Marta Camps, Lluís Echeverria, Marc Ribalta, Francesc Bonada and Xavier Domingo
Eurecat, Centre Tecnològic de Catalunya, Unit of Applied Artificial Intelligence, Barcelona, Spain

*Address all correspondence to: maddi.etxegarai@eurecat.org

References

[1] Martin D, Kühl N, Satzger G. Virtual Sensors. Business and Information Systems Engineering. 2021;**63**:315-323. DOI: 10.1007/s12599-021-00689-w

[2] Pech M, Vrchota J, Bednář J. Predictive maintenance and intelligent sensors in smart factory: Review. Sensors. 2021;**21**:1470. DOI: 10.3390/s21041470

[3] Dobrescu R, Merezeanu D, Mocanu S. Process simulation platform for virtual manufacturing systems evaluation. Computers in Industry. 2019;**104**:131-140. DOI: 10.1016/j.compind.2018.09.008

[4] Indri M, Lachello L, Lazzero I, Sibona F, Trapani S. Smart sensors applications for a new paradigm of a production line. Sensors. 2019;**19**(3):650. DOI: 10.3390/s19030650

[5] Maschler B, Ganssloser S, Hablizel A, Weyrich M. Deep learning based soft sensors for industrial machinery. Procedia CIRP. 2021;**99**:662-667. DOI: 10.1016/j.procir.2021.03.115

[6] Alonso S, Morán A, Pérez D, Reguera P, Díaz I, Domínguez M. Virtual sensor based on a deep learning approach for estimating efficiency in chillers. In: International Conference on Engineering Applications of Neural Networks. Cham: Springer; 2019. pp. 307-319. DOI: 10.1007/978-3-030-20257-6_26

[7] Zenisek J, Gröning H, Wild N, Huskic A, Affenzeller M. Machine learning based data stream merging in additive manufacturing. Procedia Computer Science. 2022;**200**:1422-1431. DOI: 10.1016/j.procs.2022.01.343

[8] Ilyas EB, Fischer M, Iggena T, Tönjes R. Virtual sensor creation to replace faulty sensors using automated machine learning techniques. In: 2020 Global Internet of Things Summit (GIoTS). Dublin, Ireland: IEEE; 2020. pp. 1-6. DOI: 10.1109/GIOTS49054.2020.9119681

[9] Tegen A et al. Collaborative sensing with interactive learning using dynamic intelligent virtual sensors. Sensors. 2019;**19**(3):477. DOI: 10.339/s19030477

[10] Djerioui M, Bouamar M, Ladjal M, Zerguine A. Chlorine soft sensor based on extreme learning machine for water quality monitoring. Arabian Journal for Science and Engineering. 2019;**44**:2033-2044. DOI: 10.1007/s13369-018-3253-8

[11] Pattanayak AS, Pattnaik BS, Udgata SK, Panda AK. Development of chemical oxygen on demand (COD) soft sensor using edge intelligence. IEEE Sensors Journal. 2020;**20**:14892-14902. DOI: 10.1109/JSEN.2020.3010134

[12] Foschi J, Turolla A, Manuela A. Soft sensor predictor of E. coli concentration based on conventional monitoring parameters for wastewater disinfection control. Water Research. 2021;**191**:116806. DOI: 10.1016/j.watres.2021.116806

[13] Pisa I, Santín I, Lopez J, Morell A, Vilanova R. ANN-based soft sensor to predict effluent violations in wastewater treatment plants. Water. 2019;**19**(6):1280. DOI: 10.3390/s19061280

[14] Wirth R, Hipp J. CRISP-DM: Towards a standard process model for data mining. In: Proceedings of the 4th International Conference on the Practical Applications of Knowledge Discovery and Data Mining. Vol. 1. NY, USA: 2000. pp. 29-39

[15] Wolpert DH, Macready WG. No-free-lunch theorems for optimization. IEEE Transactions on Evolutionary Computation. 1995;**1**:67. DOI: 10.1109/4235.585893

[16] Claesen M, De Moor B. Hyperparameter search in machine learning. The XI Metaheuristics International Conference. 2015:1-4. DOI: 10.48550/ARXIV.1502.02127

[17] Benesty J et al. Pearson correlation coefficient. In: Noise Reduction in Speech Processing. Berlin, Heidelberg: Springer; 2009. pp. 1-4. DOI: 10.1007/978-3-642-00296-0_5

[18] Quinlan JR. Induction of decision trees. Machine Learning. 1986;**1**(1): 81-106. DOI: 10.1007/BF00116251

[19] Ho TK. Random decision forests. In: Proceedings of 3rd International Conference on Document Analysis and Recognition. Montreal, QC, Canada: IEEE; 1995. pp. 278-282. DOI: 10.1109/ICDAR.1995.598994

[20] Altman NS. An introduction to kernel and nearest-neighbor nonparametric regression. The American Statistician. 1992;**46**(3):175-185. DOI: 10.1080/00031305.1992.10475879

[21] Vapnik V. The nature of statistical learning theory. Springer Science & Business Media. 1999. DOI: 10.1007/978-1-4757-2440-0

[22] Metcalf L, Eddy HP, Tchobanoglous G. Wastewater Engineering: Treatment, Disposal, and Reuse. Vol. 4. New York: McGraw-Hill; 1991

[23] Rabiner LR, Gold B, Yuen CK. Theory and application of digital signal processing. IEEE Transactions on Systems, Man, and Cybernetics. Feb 1978;**8**(2):146-146. DOI: 10.1109/TSMC.1978.4309918

[24] Gross E. Practical statistics for High Energy Physics. CERN Yellow Reports: School Proceedings. 2017;**4**:165-186. DOI: 10.23730/CYRSP-2017-004.165

[25] Hochreiter S, Schmidhuber J. Long short-term memory. Neural Computation. 1997;**9**(8):1735-1780. DOI: 10.1162/neco.1997.9.8.1735

[26] McCulloch WS, Pitts W. A logical calculus of the ideas immanent in nervous activity. The Bulletin of Mathematical Biophysics. 1943;**5**(4): 115-133. DOI: 10.1007/BF02478259

[27] Rumelhart DE, Hinton GE, Williams RJ. Learning internal representations by error propagation. Parallel Distributed Processing: Explorations in the Microstructure of Cognition. 1986;**1**:318-362. DOI: 10.5555/104279.104293

Chapter 7

Artificially Intelligent Super Computer Machines and Robotics: Apprehensions and Challenges – A Call for Responsible Innovation Framework

Khalid Rasheed Memon and Say Keat Ooi

Abstract

"Industrial revolution 4.0" is a term that is becoming increasingly popular among academics. A number of articles have been carved to emphasize the beneficial aspects of the stated issue under many titles such as cyber-physical systems, internet of things, artificial intelligence, smart manufacturing, digitalization of industrial production, and so on. However, few academics have delved into the negative or dark side of such a profound technological paradigm change, especially the artificially intelligent robotics, creating a large knowledge vacuum. Because of this, little is known about the negative repercussions of artificial intelligence (AI), a key component of the Fourth Industrial Revolution (or IR 4.0). It is an open secret now that AI machines may have serious impacts on human autonomy, fairness, justice, and agency. These unanticipated consequences have resulted in the development of an emerging concept, that is, responsible innovation. The responsible innovation framework binds the firm ethically, morally, and socially to be responsible, environmentally friendly, humanitarian, and business-oriented while developing innovative products. The current study proposes an integrated responsible innovation framework that acts as a science governance mechanism and considers organizations and stakeholders collectively responsible for upcoming technological innovations. This study has suggested several implications for policymakers.

Keywords: artificial intelligence, industrial revolution 4.0, cyber-physical systems, responsible innovation, business ethics

1. Introduction

The fourth industrial revolution, considered as IR 4.0, is ushering in a new era of industry and technological innovation. It will be dominated by manufacturing and industrial processes that use cyber-physical systems, cloud computing, big data & artificial intelligence [1, 2]. Drastic changes are coming to companies across the board in terms of their effect on value generation, business models, and downstream services [3]. Indeed, IR 4.0 is not more than an expansion of information and communication technology, paired with the exponentially grown transmission, computation, and storage capabilities that enable the materialization of incredibly powerful, linked technological systems, dubbed "Cyber-Physical-Systems" [4].

Cyber-physical systems (CPS) integrate computer, networking, and physical processes, utilizing various technologies such as artificial intelligence, robots, big data, and security [5]. These technologies would have a significant influence on industrial output, as well as on our daily lives. It is now common to engage with robots and artificially intelligent devices in a variety of applications [6], including 3D printing, educational learning agents, home health examinations, online vehicle sales systems, gaming and entertainment, and maintenance [7]. Our small and medium enterprises (SMEs) will also be profoundly impacted by this technological breakthrough and the possibility of fusing the virtual and real worlds enabled by these cyber-physical systems [8].

This kind of artificially intelligent technology, in today's networked age, would make it possible for us to access information and services from anywhere, even our hands, cell phones, cars, and other home and personal electronics may all be controlled from a distance. When it comes to air conditioning, we may want to switch on the unit as soon as we get home so that our room is nice and chilly. Coffee machines may even prepare coffee for us while we are asleep, saving our time and effort in the morning. To make repairs on certain devices, remote access may be required. This will allow technicians to find the true source of the problem and provide them with a working spare part. Using an efficient communication system, even its own system may order the required spares [9]. Scalability, accuracy, efficiency, and long-term sustainability are all attributes these artificially intelligent robots possess [10].

Artificial Intelligence (AI) is a term frequently used to refer to the branch of research that aims to equip robots with cognitive abilities such as logic, reasoning, planning, learning, and perception. Despite the reference to "machines" in this description, it is applicable to "any sort of living intellect" [11]. Similarly, as it is present in primates and other remarkable creatures, the definition of intelligence may be expanded to include an interconnected collection of capacities, such as creativity, emotional awareness, and self-consciousness [12]. Until the late 1980s, "symbolic AI" was strongly connected with the phrase artificial intelligence. To address some of the constraints of symbolic AI, sub-symbolic approaches such as neural networks, fuzzy systems, evolutionary computing, and other computational models began to gain favor, resulting in the emergence of the branch of AI known as computational intelligence [13]. Currently, the word AI embraces the entire notion of an intelligent computer, including its operational and societal implications.

A practical definition is that offered by Russell et al. [14]: "Artificial Intelligence is the study of human intelligence and actions replicated artificially, such that the resultant bears to its design a reasonable level of rationality." This concept can be further improved by specifying that, for specified and well-defined activities, the degree of rationality may even surpass that of humans.

Current AI technologies are utilized in internet advertising, driving, aviation, health, and picture identification for personal support. Recent advances in AI have captivated both the scientific community and the general audience. This is shown by automobiles with automated steering systems, commonly known as autonomous cars [10]. Each vehicle is outfitted with a collection of lidar sensors and cameras that enable detection of its three-dimensional environment and give the capability to make intelligent judgments regarding moves in changeable, real-world traffic situations. The authors Perez et al. [15] cited that the Alpha-Go, built by Google Deepmind to play the board game Go, is another example. Last year, Alpha-Go became the first computer to defeat a professional player when it defeated the Korean grandmaster, Lee Sedol. More recently, it defeated the current world number one, Ke Jie, in China.

Another recent illustration includes Microsoft's Tay, an artificial intelligence robot built to carry on discussions on social networks. It had to be deactivated shortly after its debut since it could not discern between positive and bad human contact [16]. The emotional intelligence of AI is likewise restricted. AI can only recognize fundamental human emotional states such as anger, happiness, sorrow, fear, suffering, and tension. Emotional intelligence is one of the next frontiers of greater customization. True and full AI does not yet exist. At this stage, AI will replicate human cognition to the extent that it will be capable of dreaming, thinking, feeling emotions, and having its own objectives [12]. Although there is no indication that this type of genuine AI will emerge before 2050, the computer science concepts propelling AI ahead are evolving quickly, and it is vital to analyze its implications from not only a scientific stance, but also from a social, ethical, and legal one [15].

Artificially intelligent technology also provides enormous societal advantages in nearly every part of life by doing activities autonomously (via robots), reducing costs and time without human interaction, standardizing services, and assisting people with tedious and dangerous duties [17]. We'll have self-driving automobiles when the rest of civilization is fully automated [18]. But this would not stop here since the world is moving towards "persuasive computing" which would manipulate our minds through the use of sophisticated algorithms on our data and we would be steered through free internet offerings or complex work processes; even these would be used in politics as the governments like to steer their citizens. Especially during elections, whosoever will control and use this technology for the manipulation of undecided voters, can win the elections whereas the said controlling of minds would be difficult to detect [19]. Thus, artificially intelligent devices and robots, in particular, have the potential to do terrible harm to the globe [20]. Machines with artificial intelligence are predicted to overtake humans in all aspects of life between 2020 and 2060. However, prominent scientists and technology experts like Elon Musk, Bill Gates, and Steve Wozniak are predicting that this will pose a serious threat to civilization in the years to come [21]. As a result of these artificially intelligent computers, we will lose our democracies, our autonomous and self-governance decision-making, and our distinctiveness; consequently, we must protect these pillars of our existence as they are the cornerstone for enhanced efficiency and success [12]. As mature information societies, we must be prepared for technology breakthroughs that have social, ethical, economic, and sustainability ramifications, and we must have contingency plans in place. These digital transitions should not occur abruptly and unexpectedly [18].

Numerous initiatives have been launched in Europe and the United States to address these concerns/challenges, including "Technological Assessment Organizations" (TA), "Technological Assessment and Ethical, Legal, and Social Aspects of Emerging Sciences" (ELSA), the "United States Office of Technology Assessment" (OTA), and the "Netherlands Organization for Technology Assessment" (NOTA). Similarly, the "Triple Helix Framework" including university, industry, and government, as well as the "Quadruple Helix Framework" incorporating "Society" as a fourth component, were developed. These movements/frameworks were intended to bridge the divide between society and technological advancements. However, "Responsible Innovation" (RI) is regarded to be far broader than these movements, as it encompasses both societal and governance applications [22–24]. RI has become one of the most critical and paramount areas for scientific empirical research, which gained diminutive attention earlier [5, 17]. However, responsible innovation has suddenly gained traction and momentum even after extreme crises; Europeans believe that sustainable and smart growth can only be achieved with innovation where responsible innovation develops structure and policy for such innovation [4]. RI will then be used to get Europe's strategies out of this economic downturn.

Responsible innovation emphasizes that its high time to understand the relationship between IR 4.0 and sustainability; whereby to ensure responsible citizenship, a well-prepared and planned strategy for technological advancements with social, ethical, economic, and sustainability ramifications is crucial. This study aims to contribute theoretically to a relatively under-researched area by proposing the role of organizational resources and capabilities as the antecedents of responsible innovation, highlighting the often-neglected business responsibility that is expected to form a sustainable competitive advantage, and ultimately resulting in a better sustainability performance.

In short, the following are some of the ways that the present research hopes to contribute to the existing body of knowledge. To begin, it will provide a definition of AI and highlight significant advances in the field. The next step is to offer a comprehensive analysis of the possible dangers and risks posed by AI machines on a global scale. Thirdly, the study will emphasize the importance, efficacy, and significance of a responsible innovation framework to offset all of the upcoming challenges and disasters that will be caused by technological innovations, including AI, and stresses the importance of adopting the framework. Fourthly, the study will put out a proposition for an integrated framework of responsible innovation. This framework is comprised of RI dimensions, the helices of the quadruple helix framework, and the basis of the relationship between all these helices. In the end, the study will discuss future research and limitations, and conclusion.

2. Artificial intelligence, its limitations, and responsible innovation

This section will now define AI, briefly discuss its periodic developments, and then discuss the challenges and apprehensions our world may face as a result of AI. At the conclusion of this section, RI will be presented as the solution for dealing with the impending disaster, catering to all technological innovations in the IR 4.0 era, including AI.

2.1 Defining "artificial intelligence"

Artificial intelligence (AI) is one of the latest fields. The work on AI started soon after World War II, whereas its name was invented in 1956. AI presently comprises many sub-fields that may range from general to very specific, for instance, playing chess, poetry writing, car driving, diagnosing a disease, etc. It's basically about all intellectual tasks [25]. Let us first define what intelligence is then we'll move toward artificial intelligence.

Intelligence has been defined in many ways, and it has been a bit controversial as well [26]. Therefore, we would present the definition from "Mainstream science on intelligence" (1994), which is a collective statement, signed/agreed by 52 researchers (out of 131) who were invited to sign in Wall Street Journal as an op-ed statement:

> *"Intelligence is a very general mental capability that, among other things, involves the ability to reason, plan, solve problems, think abstractly, comprehend complex ideas, learn quickly and learn from experience. It is not merely book learning, a narrow academic skill, or test-taking smarts. Rather, it reflects a broader and deeper capability for comprehending our surroundings—"catching on," "making sense" of things, or "figuring out" what to do" [27].*

Similarly, the concept of artificial intelligence is defined, and it's evident that the incorporation of intelligence in machines would be considered as artificial intelligence. However, it is formally defined as: "The science and engineering of making intelligent machines, especially intelligent computer Programs" [28], whereas Copeland [29] defines AI as "the ability of a digital computer or computer-controlled robot to perform tasks commonly associated with intelligent beings."

2.2 Review of previous works on artificial intelligence

The author of this chapter has highlighted, through sequential data, the overall progression that has taken place within the subject of artificial intelligence (AI) since many readers of this chapter may want a high-level overview of the topic. This would make it simpler, to create links between the many AI sub-fields and to comprehend the incremental development of AI (See **Table 1**). Nevertheless, these new advancements only address a portion of the whole topic and are listed here for your convenience:

2.3 Artificial intelligence-apprehensions and challenges

2.3.1 A threat to world sustenance

Currently, the field of artificial intelligence is thriving. The days of creating code one line at a time are finished, and its time for a change. The world is on its way to becoming intelligent. We will soon have smart homes, smart towns, and smart industries [16]. However, these AI systems are smarter than humans in several ways, including computing, driving automobiles, playing chess, and other strategic games. Scientists are working to create robots that mimic human behavior. This self-reinforcing nature of these robots means that there is a limited amount of time remaining to produce more inventive machines than humans.

However, in the 1960s, the US Defense Department acquired an interest in AI research that had previously focused on problem-solving and symbolic techniques. As a result of these important landmarks, more research and development in this field have led to the development of modern computers such as decision support systems (DSS) and smart computers. However, the frightening image of these robotics is still science fiction, even while it may occur in the future if we do not regulate or establish appropriate strategies for controlling and configuring technological breakthroughs, we can prevent it from occurring [4].

Artificially intelligent robots and computers are predicted to exceed humans in all aspects of life between 2020 and 2060, as previously indicated, despite the dire warnings and predictions of prominent scientists and technologists such as Elon Musk, Bill Gates, and Steve Wozniak [16]. Aside from that, these machines with artificial intelligence have the potential to be used in harmful ways to serve evil ends, making them possibly much more destructive than an atom bomb [7]. Terrorists, criminals,

Year	Development	Source
1923	The play "Rossum's University Robots" by Karel Kapek premiered in London, marking the first time, the word "Robot" was used in English.	[15]
1945	The word "Robotics" was coined by Columbia University alumnus Issac Asimov.	[30]
1950	Alan Turing developed the Turing Test, which measures intellect. Claude Shannon offered a comprehensive examination of chess playing as a search in his book, Chess: A Search for Meaning.	[31]
1956	"Artificial Intelligence" term was coined by John McCarthy.	[25]
1958	LISP, the artificial intelligence programming language created by John McCarthy, was released.	[25]
1964	Danny Bobrow's thesis at MIT demonstrated that computers are capable of accurately solving algebra word problems.	[28]
1979	The "Stanford Cart," the first computer-controlled autonomous vehicle, was created.	[28]
1984	Dennet discussed the frame problem and how it is related to the difficulties arising from attempting to give robots common sense.	[15]
1990	Major advances in AI: 1. The significant demonstrations in Machine Learning. 2. The case-based reasoning 3. The multi-agent planning 4. Scheduling 5. Data mining, web crawler 6. The natural language understanding and translation 7. Vision, virtual reality 8. Games	[32]
1997	World Champion Gerry Kasparov was defeated by the "Deep Blue Chess Program."	[25]
2000	Commercialization of robotic pets that can be interacted with. MIT created a robot named "Kismet" with an expressive face.	[15]
2015	First Humanoid Robot Sophia was developed.	[33]
2016	TAY robot was released by Microsoft as a chatbot for interacting with Twitter users.	[15]

Table 1.
Highlights of incremental developments in the AI field.

and religious extremists have always been drawn to and craved a position of authority. The Pentagon's and the White House's computer networks have already been compromised, so there is no guarantee that robots will not be misused [12]. As a result, instead of building massive, unmanageable computers, it is suggested that intelligent machines be distributed around the world.

2.3.2 The impact of artificial intelligence on jobs, employment, and social life

Jobs and unemployment are a major issue for the general population, with many predicting more deindustrialization [34]. Artificially intelligent systems/robotics will unquestionably modify job roles and may demand more thought-provoking but less technical or professional skills-oriented work tasks and competencies, as well as problem-solving and self-organizing work duties and competences [35]. Research on this subject is extensively available (See [34, 36, 37]).

According to this theory, the ultimate objective of cyber-physical systems and smart manufacturing is not to replace humans with machines, but to link and work with humans in order to accomplish mass customization via their combined effort. A new generation of robots will take the place of low-skilled individuals and technical specialists who do routine activities [35]. Due to the fact that machines can anticipate and correct problems even before they occur, jobs requiring expert planning and monitoring will become more in demand [34, 37], and an increase in the mental requirements for employees will result [37, 38]. The required credentials and talents of employees are, nevertheless, still a source of uncertainty [10, 39]. It is expected that even managers will need extra abilities in order to interact with machines and fulfill the demands and problems of the new era of technology [5]. Therefore, academics and practitioners should also emphasize the lack of competencies and abilities needed to grow up our industries in those specific areas.

Who will need to hire drivers if self-driving cars become common place in everyday life? To a similar extent, robots will take over the boring activities currently performed by humans such as news-reader and typewriter operators as well as file clerks and tellers in banks and other financial institutions. One robot may work for 24 hours continuously without taking a break or changing shifts; for example, it can read the news for 24 hours straight. Consequently, it will ultimately replace people in routine jobs. In the meantime, humans will continue to be needed for jobs that cannot be automated. These include jobs requiring social interaction and creativity as well as jobs involving physical examinations in the medical field, technical jobs (e.g., pipefitters and plumbers), and jobs requiring critical thinking [36].

2.4 Responsible innovation: a pulling strategy for the business arena

The preceding explanation demonstrates that there are increasing risks and uncertainties regarding the future effect of artificially intelligent robots. Apart from this, other technological advances such as those in biotechnology and nanotechnology (some academics and scientists believe that the present pandemic Covid-19 is also the result of such technological breakthroughs) have ensnared and powerless the whole world [4, 40]. Similarly, the literature discusses several other enormous challenges such as poverty, climate change, and sustainability, all of which require extensive involvement and dialog of stakeholders, as well as the formulation of some principles and values to understand better the associated risks, challenges, and uncertainties [41]. Regrettably, some experts feel that critical thresholds have already been crossed, putting the earth's life-sustaining system in jeopardy. Considering these dangers, there is an immediate need for continuous actions to mitigate their impact on global health, security & development [42].

The United Nations, the European Union, international organizations, and individual governments are all tasked with finding answers to these colossal problems. Numerous projects have been launched to involve companies as active participants and foster collaboration between companies, the public sector, and civil society actors to foster sustainable growth. As a result, industries are increasingly regarded as part of such societal concerns and are expected to seek answers as socially responsible organizations [43]. As previously discussed, several initiatives in Europe and the United States have been launched, including "Technological Assessment organizations" (TA), the "United States Office of Technology Assessment" (OTA), "Technological Assessment and Ethical, Legal, and Social Aspects of Emerging Sciences" (ELSA), and the "Netherlands Organization for Technology Assessment" (NOTA). However, the phrase "responsible research" was first used in the sixth framework program in 2002 to create a growing link between ethics and technology worldwide. Later on, the phrase "responsible research and innovation" (RRI) was established in Europe's 7th framework plan in 2013 to foster public trust in scientific discoveries ("Regulation (EU) No 1291/2013", 2013). And today, RRI is often regarded as encompassing these trends, as it encompasses both social and governance applications [22–24].

The framework offered by the authors mainly integrates many previously published strategies that have made significant contributions to various elements, as mentioned earlier, in multiple ways. These points underscore the need to stimulate scientists' reflexivity, extend the range of strategic alternatives, "open up," and infuse a greater capacity for reflection within research work [44–46]. Anticipatory governance [47, 48], technology assessment in all of its forms (constructive and real-time, for example; [49, 50]), upstream engagement [46], socio-technical integration, and midstream modulation [51, 52]. These various instances demonstrate the need of forethought, involvement, and integration [47]. Even if it's blatant plagiarism, responsible innovation does so with reason in some cases. By emphasizing, for example, the role that users play in innovation as well as the use of mechanisms such as patens for innovation governance, applied approaches from the fields of strategic innovation management and innovations studies (including concepts such as the democratization of innovation [53] and open innovation [54] contribute equally significantly.

3. Proposed theoretical framework

3.1 Integrated responsible innovation framework

Physical resources such as land, machineries, manufacturing buildings, and equipment were once seen as critical to a company's success during previous industrial periods. Adam Smith's worldview influenced the neoclassical economic theory, which held that physical assets were the most important source of wealth creation, and so the exploitation of these resources occurred in the midst of this theory. However, a number of academics (e.g., [55–58]) argue that other trends in the financial world, such as the increasing value of service, creativity & innovation, knowledge, expertise in information and communication technologies, digitalization, and the flow of intellectual property, have shifted the focus of financial growth and wealth formation.

The new digital era has fundamentally altered the nature and techniques of manufacturing. Traditional procedures and physical resources are no longer a source of competitive advantage since they are now transparent and susceptible to imitation [59]. As a result, intangible assets and talents, such as brand recognition, innovation and creativity, and organizational culture as well as design, may be used to gain a competitive advantage. Leonidou et al. [60] emphasize the importance of intangible assets and competencies in the quest for social and ethical acceptance. Continuous innovation, cross-functional and stakeholder integration, as well as environmental strategies, are among the skills. Furthermore, Kamasak [61] claims that both physical and intangible resources should be employed jointly to prove the assertion of RBV that resources cannot be used alone since it employs the capabilities that gather, integrate, and manage a lot of resources.

Technological breakthroughs are evaluated for their ethical acceptability, sustainability, and social acceptance under the umbrella of "responsible innovation" [41, 62]. There is also a significant connection between responsible innovation and the resource-based view (RBV) since responsible innovation includes acquiring company resources and skills [63]. Competition and improved performance may be achieved by using an organization's unique resources to produce a value-creating strategy that is not being employed by any other competitor. These resources are uncommon and precious and are inimitable and non-substitutable [64]. Research by Scholten and Van der Duin [65] shows that a competitive advantage may be achieved if stakeholders and consumers work together with enterprises to implement sustainable and ethical manufacturing systems. This demonstrates that a valuable resource for gaining a competitive edge and improving performance is innovative thinking done responsibly [63].

Responsible innovation (RI) establishes a deliberative framework of stakeholder involvement as the core science governance mechanism, with stakeholders considered jointly and highly accountable to the emerging technological innovations ([66], in press). It entails putting the firm's resources and competencies to good use to become the firm's distinguishing competency. While establishing a distinguishing capability of the company, RI may help the company obtain a competitive advantage and improve its performance [63].

In contrast, prior research on RI is only a precursor, and there is a lack of extensive empirical study, therefore nothing is known about its application for economic gains and advantages [67, 68]. Because of the uncertainty around the influence of RI on achieving a competitive edge, its practical application, and its economic advantages and gains, businesses are reluctant to use RI methods. In fact, failing to incorporate a holistic approach while generating responsible innovation may prove to be a fruitless endeavor, given the unique and specific qualities of responsible innovation. Now we would discuss in detail the suggested integrated RI framework (See **Figure 1**).

3.2 Dimensions of responsible innovation as guiding principles

Practitioners and academics have discussed and debated numerous RI dimensions in the literature, which have been split into administrative and scholarly dimensions. As stated by the European Commission, there are six dimensions: ethics, engagement, science education, gender equality, governance, and open access. As a rule of thumb, these are administrative in nature. Stahl [69] focused on realistically implementable dimensions such as actors, norms, and activities, whereas Stilgoe et al. [70] discussed four (4) distinct aspects: anticipation, responsiveness, reflexivity, and inclusiveness. Stilgoe et al. [70] four-dimensional model would be the focus of our investigation.

Indeed, these aspects are guiding principles for the framework and build a basis for the governance mechanism of the RI framework and the RI framework. Furthermore, these concepts should be applied throughout the whole innovation process, not only at the product's launching stage. A controlled science governance structure is therefore established, which promotes the notion of making processes responsible rather than allowing them to be unrestrained and unregulated. Let us take a look at each of these dimensions one by one.

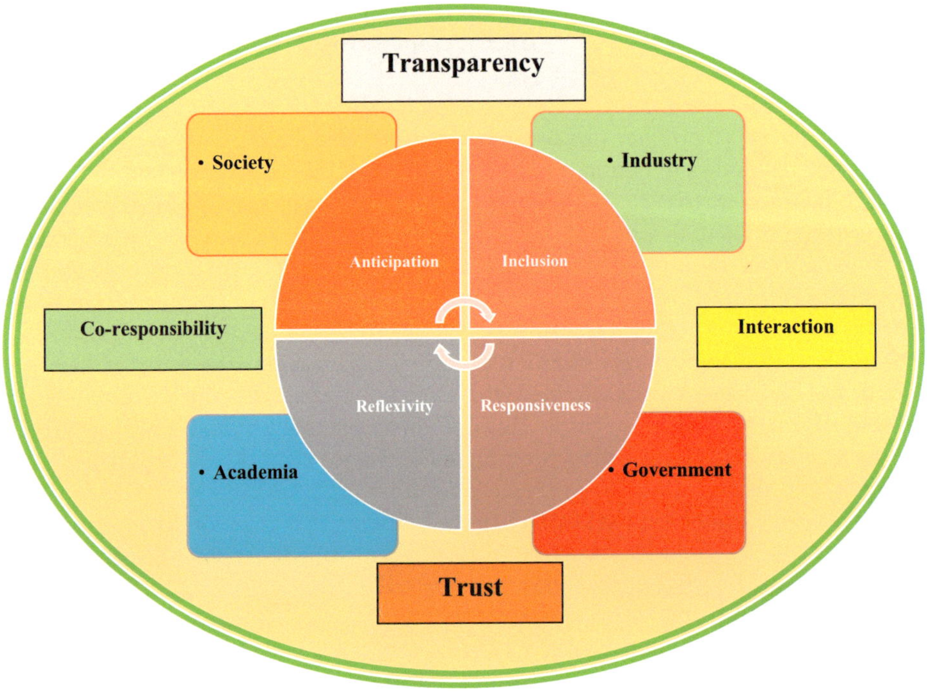

Figure 1.
Integrated responsible innovation framework (source: Authors).

3.2.1 Anticipation

In easy words, it is about identifying, forecasting/foreseeing the potential hazards and harms that may be caused through some technological innovation. The tools to be used for anticipation may be technology assessment, foresight, vision assessment, and horizon scanning. This allows the anticipators to understand future technological dynamics on a timely basis rather than getting too late to suggest a constructive way out for society. Looking at the future well before time would allow for allocating resources towards responsible and desirable future directions [70].

3.2.2 Inclusion

This refers to allowing selected public groups, economic and non-economic societal members, to be part of stakeholder groups so that they may convey their voices on behalf of the general public for the ultimate objective of utilizing science and innovation projects for societal benefit. The scientific innovations would get legitimacy as well by including public groups to take part in its processes. Through this way, public opinion and involvement, and governance mechanisms may be established to keep scientific innovation within limits for the public advantage. To achieve this task, several activities and programs may be arranged like public conferences, dialogs, gatherings, citizen's juries, focus groups, deliberative polling, etc. Accordingly, scientific advisory committees may be constituted through the partnership of a multi-stakeholder approach, and a governance mechanism may be established [70].

3.2.3 Reflexivity

This refers to the phenomenon of self-evaluation, self-judgment, and accountability of oneself and the institution for their activities, assumptions, and commitments for not crossing the defined limits in their conscious and written policies and framework. One should be knowledgeable enough to scrutinize the harmful acts and processes through a self-governing mechanism. This leads to one's moral and ethical value-based system supervising science and innovation research and developing an internal governing mechanism, binding the scientists and organizations to observe moral, ethical, and societal responsibilities. Furthermore, the next level of reflexivity comes through the written code of conduct and policies of the organization or a project. It plays its role as an external governing mechanism of reflexivity. Therefore, reflexivity demands drawing a boundary wall of moral responsibilities that do not allow one to cross through it for performing professional responsibilities only [70].

3.2.4 Responsiveness

The concept of responsiveness emphasizes the combination, inculcation, and implementation of three previously presented approaches of inclusion, anticipation, and reflexivity throughout research & innovation activities while influencing their line of action, course, programs, and relevant policies. Moreover, it involves taking action towards emerging new knowledge and perspectives and the values of various stakeholders and the public [70].

4. Outcomes

4.1 Integration of four dimensions of responsible innovation

When it comes to responsible innovation, it's important to remember that the word "Responsible Innovation" encompasses much more than the narrowly defined concepts that have been popularized in the past, particularly in Europe, for instance, "Technological Assessment and Ethical, Legal, and Social Aspects of emerging sciences" (ELSA). In addition to social, ethical, and environmental considerations, the integrated elements encompass governance applications [22–24]. The focus is not on outcomes but instead on the processes. That's why this mechanism serves as a scientific governance mechanism, which promotes the notion of ensuring that processes are managed properly rather than being uncontrolled and irresponsible [71].

RI concepts and dimensions must be introduced within the company for responsible innovation to be effective. As a result, in this section, the top-down and bottom-up techniques [72] are recommended. An effective top-down strategy to drive the company's daily operations while making optimal use of its resources results from defining and translating RI concepts and dimensions into clear vision and mission statements for the organization as a whole. Meanwhile, a bottom-up approach to create a community-based metric has indicated that large community engagement is the key to the promotion of sustainable competitive enterprises [73].

The incorporation of four dimensions would allow for the anticipation and forecasting of future technological advancements, as well as the assessment and development of these technologically innovative products with the participation of relevant stakeholders. It would also allow for the suggestion and implementation of a self-destruction mechanism in products that would operate automatically due to the corrupt work of, for example, an artificially intelligent robot; suggesting and implementing a self-accountability mechanism that would ensure the right direction of organizational production system and in-line with the stated/promised commitments with various stakeholders; and finally determining and paving the way towards future-oriented technological needs of the business as well as stakeholders while combining the previously stated dimensions, policies, and programs for sustainable and competitive growth of the organization [70, 74].

The integration of RI dimensions would ensure the organizational response towards grand societal challenges and reverting to the public interest and increase organizational ethical and societal acceptability, leading the organization towards sustainable competitive advantage and higher firm performance. Since the firm's main goal is to maximize its shareholders' profitability, the firm can fulfill its targets through a responsible innovation framework ([66], in press).

4.2 Helices of quadruple helix framework as economic and non-economic stakeholders: responsible innovation as deliberative stakeholder involvement approach

Stakeholder and public involvement in innovation processes are well recognized for their value and utility [41]. There is a need for a constructive engagement of stakeholders with competing priorities and value systems in order to better understand the challenges, threats, and uncertainties associated with technologies such as nanotechnology and biotechnology, AI, big data, and those involved in IR 4.0, which are increasingly complex. This helps stakeholders to learn from one other and improves collaboration among many stakeholders as a result. This knowledge enables them to accomplish common goals and decisions and determines the necessary courses for future technical advancements. Because the significant difficulties are attributed to several social sectors (civil society, commercial sector, and government), the solution to these big challenges necessitates the active engagement of many stakeholders. It is the goal of stakeholder engagement to better understand the various viewpoints and interests of stakeholders and to actively shape the future direction of research and development. It is also widely accepted that stakeholder engagement is a vital way for considering, assessing, and determining the aims and outcomes of innovation [75].

The concept of "collective stewardship" lies at the heart of responsible innovation [70]. Economic and non-economic stakeholders would be actively involved in order to achieve cognitive and moral legitimacy, as well as ethical and social acceptability, in accordance with the framework's guiding principles. These stakeholders have been divided into four helices as per the quadruple helix framework. 1) Academia 2) Government 3) Industry 4) Society [76]. The quadruple helix framework was used to develop these helices/stakeholders, however since the RI viewpoint of stakeholders differs slightly from the quadruple helix perspective, we will examine the RI perspective of stakeholders. Public and private entities work together in the quadruple helix to transform various inputs into beneficial outputs for themselves and others, according to this research. In a RI setting, the focus is on the mechanisms of partnership, which includes the players participating (public and private), the pooled resources, the operations, and the outcomes of the processes themselves.

Firms have to interact with a diverse set of stakeholders, including suppliers, consumers, workers, governments, universities, and non-governmental organizations.

It is an open-ended discussion on who counts as a legitimate stakeholder and why, and there are several theoretical viewpoints on stakeholder engagement, including normative, descriptive, and instrumental approaches. Stakeholder engagement in responsible innovation has a normative perspective on stakeholder engagement. As per the normative view, stakeholders have an inherent value and valid interest in the systems and good of the business, and the organization must take these concerns into account. Stakeholder engagement can be described as "practices that an organization undertakes to involve stakeholders in meaningful organizational activities. "Stakeholder engagement" involves the exchange of knowledge and cooperation between stakeholders. This affects knowledge flows in all ways, including all knowledge from stakeholders to the firms and knowledge from the firms to the stakeholders. One way to facilitate knowledge exchange and two-way conversion is through dialog [41]. Stakeholder dialog offers an understanding of stakeholders' interests, strengthens shared awareness, and allows win-win scenarios to be generated. Sharing knowledge and expertise is also a means of building trust between stakeholders since it's a trust-based partnership and trust-building practices such as coordination and collaboration are pre-requisite.

According to the literature on responsible innovation (RI), it's critical to involve people from all walks of life, not only those with a vested financial interest in the outcome. For example, Brand and Blok [22] take a critical look at the tensions between openness and efficiency in manufacturing and find that participation alone is not adequate. Stakeholder engagement and management is a relatively new area of research in RI, and thus, there is no empirical evidence on how to do it.

4.2.1 Ground rules for responsible innovation relationships

The ground rules refer to the four fundamental rules outlined outside the stakeholder boxes inside the bigger circle in rectangular shapes (See **Figure 1**). These rules form the basis of the relationship between RI dimensions and stakeholders throughout the RI process. These are 1) Trust, 2) Co-responsibility, 3) Transparency, and 4) Interaction [41].

Several essential concerns have been identified in the literature that needs to be addressed when stakeholders are involved in responsible innovation challenges. When a stakeholder's collaboration with a rival is feared because of the risk of leaking secret knowledge and expertise information or because of power imbalances, there is a need to address these concerns [41, 77]. For these reasons, the aforementioned ground rules have been given as game rules. These guidelines would force the organization to take a number of critical procedures to avert a potentially disastrous outcome. As an example, "Trust" drives the company to open culture, equal interests of stakeholders and representatives, acceptance of disputes, alignment of partners' expectations, experience and identity as well as the presentation of accurate and reliable information. "Interaction" leads to discourse and relationship-building, formal and informal socialization methods, commitment, and the choosing of aligned partners. Developing an open culture, sharing important information and expertise, being trustworthy, implementing semi-formal protection techniques, intellectual property management, and taking advantage of first-mover advantages are all examples of "Transparency." To sum up, as all participants were democratically included throughout the whole innovation process, "Co-responsibility" leads to joint accountability for all initiatives.

To summarize, openness to facts and knowledge is crucial for analyzing the social ethical, and environmental implications of innovation processes from the perspective of many stakeholders. Stakeholders may utilize this knowledge and skills to better understand innovation pathways' priorities and goals. Through contact with many stakeholders, RIs are able to respond to the needs and concerns of society as a whole. In essence, RI can be trusted. As a result of their reciprocal response, stakeholders are responsible for this innovation route.

5. Implications of responsible innovation for artificial intelligence

Due to the complexities of artificial intelligence technology, as well as their future social and ethical consequences, a strategy that is capable of learning, incorporating external voices, incorporating reflection, and bringing together diverse stakeholder groups is needed. RI takes this approach. Big data and artificial intelligence research and development have the potential to provide tremendous social and economic benefits. However, such research and innovation will also result in a slew of unfavorable outcomes. This is a well-known fact by researchers, funders, politicians, and the general public. What is required is a more comprehensive understanding of the strengths of evolving technological innovations, the potential consequences, how relevant stakeholders see them, and the appropriate responses. The responsible innovation framework may help us resolve this issue by involving various stakeholders for collective stewardship and sustainability of the world.

Computer and engineering societies, governmental regulations, university experts, civil societies, and ethical organizations jointly can formulate some rules and regulations regarding sharing, storing, transparency, adhering to the privacy laws, regulations and technical standards, and so on. Governments of various countries have to play a vital role in defining such regulations. Responsible firms do adopt responsible innovation frameworks deliberately for gaining societal desirability and ethical acceptability. They formulate their internal control mechanism for sharing, storing, and publicizing of user's data themselves through the consent of relevant stakeholders. They do not like to have scandals like The Facebook–Cambridge Analytical data scandal, and then they have to apologize for their actions since such actions are never liked by their users, which they performed for earning money only. Responsible firms build artificially intelligent machines in a controlled environment and under a controlled mechanism through relevant stakeholders' consent. RI framework binds these firms to seek input from its stakeholders at each step of product development to share collective stewardship and responsibility. Since it's not about money now, therefore; these firms do not play with the safety and security of their customers as well as the peace of the world.

In general, the media also needs to play its role as a societal and community at large stakeholder. Awareness should be spread regarding the efficacy and drawbacks of such technological innovations. It should be conveyed to all the stakeholders that they should have in mind from the start that AI systems lead to world peace; however, they have to take steps to recognize and resolve threats, such as damage to users' lives, bodies, or property caused by actuators or other devices; and ensure their safety and security. Consider such risks over the lifespan of AI systems, and verify them where appropriate and feasible; conduct extensive testing in real-world environments to ensure they are fit for use and meet product specifications; collaborate closely with all stakeholders to maintain and develop the applications' efficiency, protection,

DOI: http://dx.doi.org/10.5772/intechopen.107372

usability, and security. It should be mandatory for all AI machines that, upon improper functioning, such as working against humans, the AI machine should have a self-destruction mechanism.

6. Conclusion and future research

The purpose of highlighting the fears and concerns associated with artificially intelligent robots is to help the world prepare, plan, allocate resources, strategy, execute, and regulate the future negative repercussions of such a profound transformation affecting everyone's life. The authors have convinced that artificial intelligence technology has the potential to bring enormous benefits, such as ease, flexibility, and accuracy, as well as improvement and advancement in the daily lives of humans. However, the research expresses grave concern about the human race's sustainability and views unregulated, uncontrolled, and irresponsible technological innovations as a significant danger. Thus, not only should we be mindful of the undesired results, but we should also take significant and coordinated steps to combat the threats.

The study proposes to develop a dedicated and holistic strategy covering all aspects of industrial revolution 4.0, particularly the much-heralded technologies of big data and artificial intelligence. This should be done in consultation with various non-economic and economic stakeholders through the deliberation of all such issues and technological innovations. The developed strategy should not be oriented around industrial interests but rather around the sustainability, well-being, and welfare of the entire society. Organizations may use RI dimensions as governance mechanisms and guiding principles, assisting them in achieving social desirability, ethical acceptability, and a sustainable competitive advantage. However, a legal framework is required to assure the strategy's implementation, and personal autonomy should take precedence in developed communities. Most importantly, businesses should be held accountable for their products. It must be assured that artificially intelligent supermachines have a contingency mechanism in place; for example, they should self-destruct if they go out of control. Thus, there are a number of challenges that can be overcome with hard work and the implementation of technological solutions, norms and values, rules and processes, and a legal framework.

Finally, this research is theoretical in nature that suggests a framework for responsible innovation. Other studies may undertake empirical research on the suggested framework or another framework to demonstrate the influence of responsible innovation on businesses that are developing artificially intelligent robots.

Author details

Khalid Rasheed Memon* and Say Keat Ooi
Graduate School of Business, Universiti Sains Malaysia, Penang, Malaysia

*Address all correspondence to: khalidilm@hotmail.com

References

[1] de Sousa Jabbour ABL, Jabbour CJC, Foropon C, Godinho Filho M. When titans meet–can industry 4.0 revolutionize the environmentally-sustainable manufacturing wave? The role of critical success factors. Technological Forecasting and Social Change. 2018;**132**:18-25

[2] Zhong RY, Xu X, Klotz E, Newman ST. Intelligent manufacturing in the context of industry 4.0: A review. Engineering. 2017;**3**(5):616-630

[3] Bartodziej CJ. The Concept Industry 4.0 an Empirical Analysis of Technologies and Applications in Production Logistics. Best Masters. Wiesbaden Gmb H: Springer Fachmedien; 2017. DOI: 10.1007/978-3-658-16502-4_1

[4] Memon KR, Ooi SK. The dark side of industrial revolution 4.0-implications and suggestions. Academy of Entrepreneurship Journal. 2021;**27**(S2):1-18

[5] Piccarozzi M, Aquilani B, Gatti C. Industry 4.0 in management studies. A Systematic Literature Review. Sustainability. 2018;**10**:3821. DOI: 10.3390/su10103821

[6] Ekudden E. Five technology trends augmenting the connected society. Ericsson Technology Review. 2018. p. 2-12

[7] Winfield AFT, Jirotka M. Ethical governance is essential to building trust in robotics and artificial intelligence systems. Philosophical Transactions of the Royal Society A. 2018;**376**:20180085. DOI: 10.1098/rsta.2018.0085

[8] Wang L, Wang G. Big data in cyber-physical systems, digital manufacturing and industry 4.0. Journal of Engineering and Manufacturing. 2016;**4**:1-8. DOI: 10.5815/ijem.2016.04.01

[9] Jazdi N. Cyber physical systems in the context of industry 4.0. In: 2014 IEEE International Conference on Automation, Quality and Testing, Robotics. IEEE; 2014. pp. 1-4 Available from: https://DOI.org/10.1109/AQTR.2014.6857843

[10] Müller JM, Kiel D, Voigt KI. What drives the implementation of industry 4.0? The role of opportunities and challenges in the context of sustainability. Sustainability. 2018a;**10**(1):247

[11] Wang P. On defining artificial intelligence. Journal of Artificial General Intelligence. 2019;**10**(2):1-37

[12] Helbing D. Societal, economic, ethical and legal challenges of the digital revolution: From big data to deep learning, artificial intelligence, and manipulative technologies. In: Towards Digital Enlightenment. Cham: Springer; 2019. pp. 47-72

[13] Monett D, Lewis CW. Getting clarity by defining artificial intelligence—A survey. In: 3rd Conference on "Philosophy and Theory of Artificial Intelligence". Cham: Springer; 2017. pp. 212-214

[14] Russell SJ, Norvig P, Davis E. Upper Saddle River. Artificial Intelligence: A Modern Approach. 3rd ed. NJ: Prentice Hall; 2009

[15] Perez JA, Deligianni F, Ravi D, Yang G-Z. Artificial intelligence and robotics. ArXiv Preprint ArXiv. 2018;**1803**(10813):1

[16] Helbing D, Frey BS, Gigerenzer G, Hafen E, Hagner M, Hofstetter Y, et al. Will democracy survive big data and artificial intelligence? In: Towards Digital Enlightenment. Cham: Springer; 2019. pp. 73-98

[17] Müller JM, Buliga O, Voigt KI. Fortune favors the prepared: How SMEs approach business model innovations in industry 4.0. Technological Forecasting and Social Change. 2018b;**132**:2-17

[18] Cath C, Wachter S, Mittelstadt B, Taddeo M, Floridi L. Artificial intelligence and the 'good society': The US, EU, and UK approach. Science and Engineering Ethics. 2018;**24**(2):505-528

[19] Gordan M, Chao OZ, Sabbagh-Yazdi SR, Wee LK, Ghaedi K, Ismail Z. From cognitive bias toward advanced computational intelligence for smart infrastructure monitoring. Frontiers in Psychology. 2022;**13**:846610-884661

[20] Buhmann A, Fieseler C. Towards a deliberative framework for responsible innovation in artificial intelligence. Technology in Society. 2021;**64**:101475

[21] Dreyer M, Chefneux L, Goldberg A, von Heimburg J, Patrignani N, Schofield M, et al. Responsible innovation: A complementary view from industry with proposals for bridging different perspectives. Sustainability. 2017;**9**:1719. DOI: 10.3390/su9101719

[22] Brand T, Blok V. Responsible innovation in business: A critical reflection on deliberative engagement as a central governance mechanism. Journal of Responsible Innovation. 2019;**6**(1):4-24

[23] Burget M, Bardone E, Pedaste M. Definitions and conceptual dimensions of responsible research and innovation: A literature review. Science and Engineering Ethics. 2017;**23**(1):1-19

[24] Chatfield K, Borsella E, Mantovani E, Porcari A, Stahl B. An investigation into risk perception in the ICT industry as a core component of responsible research and innovation. Sustainability. 2017;**9**(8):1424

[25] Russell SJ, Norvig P. Artificial intelligence: a modern approach. Malaysia: Pearson Education Limited; 2016

[26] Legg S, Hutter M. A collection of definitions of intelligence. Frontiers in Artificial Intelligence and Applications. 2007;**157**:17

[27] Gottfredson LS. Mainstream science on intelligence: An editorial with 52 signatories, history, and bibliography. Intelligence U. 1997;**I**:13-23

[28] McCarthy J. From here to human-level AI. Artificial Intelligence. 2007;**171**(18):1174-1182

[29] Copeland BJ. Artificial Intelligence. In: Encyclopaedia Britannica. 2019. https://www.britannica.com/technology/artificial-intelligence [Accessed: August 26, 2019]

[30] WooldridgeM, Jennings NR. Intelligent agents: Theory and practice. The Knowledge Engineering Review. 1995;**10**(2):115-152

[31] Turing AM. Computing Machinery and Intelligence. In Parsing the Turing Test. Dordrecht: Springer; 2009. pp. 23-65

[32] Fogel DB. Evolutionary Computation: Toward a New Philosophy of Machine Intelligence. NewYork: John Wiley and Sons; 2006

[33] Sapre K. Impact of Artificial Intelligence on Society. Mahratta. 2019. p. 45-49

[34] Dombrowski U, Wagner T. Mental strain as field of action in the 4th industrial revolution. Procedia Cirp. 2014;**17**:100-105

[35] Horváth D, Szabó RZ. Driving forces and barriers of industry 4.0: Do multinational and small and medium-sized companies have equal opportunities? Technological Forecasting and Social Change. 2019;**146**:119-132

[36] Frey CB, Osborne MA. The future of employment: How susceptible are jobs to computerization? Technological Forecasting and Social Change. 2017;**114**:254-280. DOI: 10.1016/j.techfore.2016.08.019

[37] Kiel D, Müller JM, Arnold C, Voigt KI. Sustainable industrial value creation: Benefits and challenges of industry 4.0. International Journal of Innovation Management. 2017;**21**(08):1740015

[38] Lasi H, Fettke P, Kemper HG, Feld T, Hoffmann M. Industry 4.0. Business and Information Systems Engineering. 2014;**6**(4):239-242

[39] Kiel D. What do we know about "Industry 4.0" so far? In: Proceedings of the International Association for Management of Technology Conference, 2017, no. Vol 26, pp. 1-22

[40] Schroeder D. RI–a drain on company resources or a competitive advantage? In: Responsible Innovation. Dordrecht: Springer; 2020. pp. 51-69

[41] Blok V, Hoffmans L, Wubben EFM. Stakeholder engagement for responsible innovation in the private sector: Critical issues and management practices. Journal on Chain and Network Science. 2015;**15**(2):147-164

[42] Scherer AG, Voegtlin C. Corporate governance for responsible innovation: Approaches to corporate governance and their implications for sustainable development. Academy of Management Perspectives. 2020;**34**(2):182-208

[43] Lubberink R, Blok V, Van Ophem J, Omta O. Lessons for responsible innovation in the business context: A systematic literature review of responsible, social and sustainable innovation practices. Sustainability. 2017;**9**(5):721

[44] Rip A, Misa TJ, Schot J, editors. Managing Technology in Society. London: Pinter Publishers; 1995

[45] Stirling A. Opening up or closing down? Analysis, participation and power in the social appraisal of technology. Science and citizens: Globalization and the challenge of engagement. 2005;**2**:218

[46] Wilsdon J, Wynne B, Stilgoe J. The Public Value of Science: Or How to Ensure that Science Really Matters. London: Demos; 2005

[47] Barben D, Fisher E, Selin C, Guston DH. Anticipatory governance of nanotechnology: foresight, engagement, and integration. In: Edward OA, Hackett J, Lynch M, Wajcman J, editors. The Handbook of Science and Technology Studies. 3rd ed. Cambridge, MA: MIT Press; 2008. pp. 979-1000

[48] Karinen R, Guston DH. Toward anticipatory governance: Te experience with nanotechnology. In: Governing future technologies. Dordrecht: Springer; 2019. pp. 217-232

[49] Guston DH, Sarewitz D. Real-time technology assessment. Technology in Society. 2002;**24**(1-2):93-109

[50] Schot J, Rip A. The past and future of constructive technology assessment. Technological Forecasting and Social Change. 1997;**54**(2-3):251-268

[51] Fisher E, Mahajan RL, Mitcham C. Midstream modulation of technology: Governance from within. Bulletin of Science, Technology and Society. 2006;**26**(6):485-496

[52] Schuurbiers D. What happens in the lab: Applying midstream modulation to enhance critical reflection in the laboratory. Science and Engineering Ethics. 2011;**17**(4):769-788

[53] Von Hippel E. Democratizing innovation: The evolving phenomenon of user innovation. Journal für Betriebswirtschaft. 2005;**55**(1):63-78

[54] Chesborough H. Open Innovation Harvard Business School Press. Boston MA, 2003;**44**(3):35-41

[55] Ambrosini V, Bowman C. What are dynamic capabilities, and are they a useful construct in strategic management? International Journal of Management Reviews. 2009;**11**(1):29-49

[56] Hitt MA, Ireland RD, Camp SM, Sexton DL. Strategic entrepreneurship: Entrepreneurial strategies for wealth creation. Strategic Management Journal. 2001;**22**(6/7):479-491

[57] Kor Y, Mesko A. Dynamic managerial capabilities: Configuration and orchestration of top executives' capabilities and the firm's dominant logic. Strategic Management Journal. 2013;**34**(2):233-244

[58] Surroca J, Tribo JA, Waddock S. Corporate responsibility and financial performance: The role of intangible resources. Strategic Management Journal. 2010;**31**(5):463-490

[59] Galbreath J, Galvin P. Firm factors, industry structure and performance variation: New empirical evidence to a classic debate. Journal of Business Research. 2008;**61**(2):109-117

[60] Leonidou LC, Christodoulides P, Kyrgidou LP, Palihawadana D. Internal drivers and performance consequences of small firm green business strategy: The moderating role of external forces. Journal of Business Ethics. 2017;**140**:585-606. DOI: 10.1007/s10551-015-2670-9

[61] Kamasak R. The contribution of tangible and intangible resources and capabilities to a firm's profitability and market performance. European Journal of Management and Business Economics. 2017;**26**(2):252-275

[62] Stahl, BC, Obach M. Yaghmaei E. Ikonen V, Chatfield K, Brem A. The responsible research and innovation (RRI) maturity model: Linking theory and practice. Sustainability, 2017;**9**:1036. DOI: 10.3390/su9061036

[63] Lees N, Lees I. Competitive advantage through responsible innovation in the New Zealand sheep dairy industry. International Food and Agribusiness Management Review. 2018;**21**(4):505-524

[64] Salam MA. Analyzing manu-facturing strategies and industry 4.0 supplier performance relationships from a resource-based perspective. Benchmarking, Vol. ahead-of-print No. aheadof-print, Benchmarking: An International Journal. 2019. DOI: 10.1108/BIJ-12-2018-0428

[65] Scholten VE, Van der Duin PA. Responsible innovation among academic spin-offs: How responsible practices

help developing absorptive capacity. Journal on Chain and Network Science. 2015;**15**(2):165-179

[66] Memon KR, Ooi SK. Rediscovering responsible innovation: A road-map towards corporate sustainability. International Journal of Sustainable Strategic Management. Vol. ahead-of-print No. aheadof-print 2022 in press

[67] Lubberink R, Blok V, van Ophem J, Omta O. Responsible innovation by social entrepreneurs: An exploratory study of values integration in innovations. Journal of Responsible Innovation. 2019;**6**(2):179-210

[68] Ribeiro BE, Smith RDJ, Millar K. A mobilising concept? Unpacking academic representations of responsible research and innovation. Science and Engineering Ethics. 2017;**23**(1):81-103

[69] Stahl BC. Responsible research and innovation: The role of privacy in an emerging framework. Science and Public Policy. 2013;**40**(6):708-716. DOI: 10.1093/scipol/sct067

[70] Stilgoe J, Owen R, Macnaghten P. Developing a framework for responsible innovation. Research Policy. 2013;**42**:1568-1580. DOI: 10.1016/j.respol.2013.05.008

[71] Gwizdała J, Śledzik K. Responsible research and innovation in the context of university technology transfer. Folia Oeconomica, Acta UniversitasLodzensis. 2017;**2**(328). DOI: 10.18778/0208-6018.328.04

[72] Ooi SK, Amran A, Yeap JA. Defining and measuring strategic CSR: A formative construct. Global Business and Management Research. 2017;**9**:250-265

[73] Ooi SK, Ooi CA, Memon KR. The role of CSR oriented organizational culture in eco-innovation practices. World Review of Entrepreneurship, Management and Sustainable Development. 2020;**16**(5):538-556

[74] Blok V, Lubberink R, van den Belt H, Ritzer S, et al. Challenging the ideal of transparency as a process and as an output variable of responsible innovation: The case of "The Circle". In Responsible Research and Innovation Routledge. 2019 pp. 225-244

[75] Blok V. Look who's talking: Responsible innovation, the paradox of dialogue, and the voice of the other in communication and negotiation processes. Journal of Responsible Innovation. 2014;**1**(2):171-190

[76] Carayannis EG, Campbell DF. 'Mode 3'and'Quadruple Helix': Toward a 21st-century fractal innovation ecosystem. International Journal of Technology Management. 2009;**46**(3-4):201-234

[77] van de Poel I, Asveld L, Flipse S, Klaassen P, Kwee Z, Maia M, et al. Learning to do responsible innovation in industry: Six lessons. Journal of Responsible Innovation. 2020;**7**(3): 697-707